WARRIOR KING

WARRIOR KING

THE TRIUMPH AND BETRAYAL OF AN AMERICAN COMMANDER IN IRAQ

t. Col. (Ret.) NATHAN SASSAMAN

WITH JOE LAYDEN

ST. MARTIN'S PRESS ≈ NEW YORK

www.stmartins.com

Design by Sarah Maya Gubkin

Library of Congress Cataloging-in-Publication Data

Sassaman, Nathan.
     Warrior king : the triumph and betrayal of an American commander in Iraq / Nathan Sassaman with Joe Layden.
         p.   cm.

     ISBN 978-0-312-56396-7

     1. Iraq War, 2003—Personal narratives, American.   2. Sassaman, Nathan.
3. Soldiers—United States—Biography.   4. Iraq War, 2003—Regimental
histories—United States.   5. United States. Army—History—21st century.
I. Layden, Joseph, 1959–   II. Title.
DS79.76.S28   2008
956.7044'34092—dc22
   [B]   2008010604

First Edition: June 2008

P1

**"Greater love has no one than this,
that he lay down his life for his friends."**
John 15:13

There is no greater honor than commanding American men and women in combat in foreign lands and there is no greater sense of failure than to lose those soldiers under your command.

17 November and 2 January are dates that are forever burned into my "hard drive" memory. Not a day goes by that I don't think of Staff Sergeant Dale Panchot and Captain Eric Paliwoda. To me, they will always be young, full of life, vibrant leaders of army soldiers in Iraq. They paid the ultimate price; made the supreme sacrifice for a cause far greater than themselves.

I dedicate this book to

Staff Sergeant Dale Panchot, B Company, 1-8 Infantry, KIA 17 November 2003, Albu Hishma, Iraq

Captain Eric Paliwoda, D Company, 1-8 Infantry, KIA 2 January 2004, Balad, Iraq

I sincerely apologize for not being able to bring them back to America.

ACKNOWLEDGMENTS

I knew within two months of my command in Iraq that I wanted to tell my story, mostly for my family and friends, and then several months later, for the American people and future military and civilian leaders. I quickly surmised that I was living in a surreal world over there, like something out of a movie, and I was the movie star. Iraq was the best and worst year of my life and the story needs to be told.

This work began in late March 2004 as I sketched a rough, fifteen-chapter outline at Camp Arifjan, Kuwait, awaiting the Freedom Bird home. Along the way, I received a lot of encouragement and I would like to acknowledge with sincere gratitude the invaluable help.

To Ivan Kronenfeld for tracking me down in Colorado and insisting I write my story. Ivan is a great fan of West Point and was very helpful in the start of this book.

To Frank Weimann, my literary agent, who was the first to tell me that "you write well for an Army Officer," but that I was going to need help to get this published. Frank calls them like he sees them—my kind of guy.

To Joe Layden, my cowriter and good friend, who spent

countless hours poring over my chapters, intently listening to my anguish while reliving painful moments as well as to my satisfaction with more pleasant memories, and then transcribing and transforming this work into a book that the American people can read. I really appreciated Joe's passion for my story and his thoughtful and diligent work to see it through all the way. I enjoyed my talks with Joe and count him a good friend I can talk to anytime.

To Lloyd Rich, Denver publishing attorney, thanks for reading through the book agreement and keeping me straight.

To Robert Gwinner III, Darron Wright, Todd Brown, Matt Cunningham, Frank Blake II, and Darren Amick, thanks for putting up with the late-night phone calls to make sure I had it all together. These officers represent some of the finest fighting men this country has ever seen. I am indebted to them on many different levels. Fighting Eagles!

To Brigadier General (Ret.) John Brown, thanks for taking the time to read through this work and provide instruction and comment. I enjoyed our talks and time together.

To Marc Resnick, my St. Martin's Press editor, thanks for taking a chance on me. I appreciate your confidence and trust in this project.

To my mother-in-law, Dorothy Trygg, for giving the book drafts a great proofread and offering appropriate wisdom.

To my Mom and Dad, Marcus and Nancy Sassaman, your love, prayers, and help throughout this entire season of my life have been unbelievably helpful. Dad, thanks for the late-night calls, countless reads of the drafts, and endless encouragement. That which does not kill me only makes me stronger.

To Marilyn, Nathan, and Nicole, my beautiful wife and children, you guys are the best and I know you have had to put up with some tough moments as I worked on this book. I just wanted you guys to have something that told my side. Marilyn, thanks for all you do, you go above and beyond for our family.

To the officers and soldiers of 1-8 Infantry who lived the dream with me in Iraq, you are the best that America can give and you gave your best. It is still my hope that the next generation of Iraqis will be free as a result of your efforts. Thanks for giving this old man the memories of a lifetime. For me, there will never be a greater honor than to have served with you in combat. Fighting Eagles! Strike Fear!

WARRIOR KING

PROLOGUE

MARCH 13, 2004
TIKRIT, IRAQ
Fourth Infantry Division Command Post,
Forward Operating Base Ironhorse

And there we were.

Fighting Eagle 6 and Attack 6 at the position of modified parade rest inside the vast outer chamber of one of Saddam Hussein's sprawling marble palaces, on a hot, breezy afternoon in central Iraq.

Owing to its history as both a monument to Saddam's ego and a playground for the dictator and his minions, this particular location was known as the Water Palace—majestically constructed on the banks of the Tigris River, with swimming pools in several of the buildings on the compound. Saddam's palaces were undeniably breathtaking in both scope and beauty. Each building boasted unique handiwork in the walls and on the marble floors; the arches of the entryways were inlaid with gold in exquisite, intricate designs. Then there were the gigantic ceilings, stretching skyward, twenty-five, thirty, sometimes forty feet above the palace floor. Saddam clearly had no reservations when it came to spending his country's money on himself, and one could not help but be both oddly impressed and overtly repulsed by the arrogance (or madness) required to fuel such selfishness. If a skeptic required proof that Saddam was siphoning off money from the United Nations and other sources—money intended for the Iraqi citizens—he needed to look no further than one of Saddam's palaces. The waste was staggering, the greed nothing short of sickening. I had spent most of the previous year in Iraq, serving as commander of the Fourth Infantry Division's 1-8 Infantry Battalion, and while there were many things about my experience that had left me confused and disenchanted, this much I knew for certain: the money Saddam burned on just one of these palaces could easily have provided food, shelter, and clothing for a large village of his people. For years to come.

Such thoughts and observations often filled me with sadness, and they stay with me now, even as the years melt away and the anger and hurt subside. When I look back on my time in Iraq, I feel a sense of pride at what we accomplished (sometimes against almost insurmountable odds), and at the professionalism and courage we brought to our jobs. I also feel sad—for any number of different reasons. I'm sad for the men and women who have lost their lives over there, for the soldiers who have been wounded, and for the families whose lives have been destroyed back home. I'm sad for the marriages that have been broken under the stress of separation. I'm sad for the Iraqi people and for the children who became casualties of war. I'm also sad for the American military, to which I gave twenty years of my life, primarily because I think we made serious mistakes in Iraq—strategic and philosophical mistakes at the highest levels of military and political command, the effects of which trickled down inevitably and tragically to the battlefield, resulting in casualties and the failure to accomplish a mission and complete what should have been an overwhelming victory. I discovered too late that we were not really a nation at war in Iraq; too often, in fact, we weren't even an army at war. We were a handful of battalions at war, led by an even smaller group of officers (and I include myself here) silly and naive enough to think that winning was a legitimate option . . . or that it mattered in the least.

The important thing, as it turned out, was not winning or losing, but simply putting the best face possible on something that is, by definition, unpleasant: war. There were countless days when it seemed as though I had tumbled down the rabbit hole, and not merely because of the inherent lunacy and inhumanity of combat. What I found most bothersome and frustrating were the days when there seemed to be no coherent objective, when all that really mattered was whether we were winning the propaganda war (and by the way—we lost that one, too). Whether we were delivering money to a local hospital or clinic, or handing out soccer balls to wide-eyed Iraqi schoolchildren—as long as we looked generous and efficient on a daytime patrol, it meant that all was right with the world. Looking good was tantamount to doing good. But that was all very much surface stuff—winning hearts and minds, and that sort of thing; it had little or nothing to do with the root of the mission, or at least the mission as I saw it. The real mission was this: *secure and stabilize the region.* Almost comical in its simplicity and abstraction, this directive, as we soon discovered, actually involved a great deal of complicated, messy, and dangerous work. It involved the risking of our own lives and the taking of others. It involved the primal and bloody toil of combat, an experience that forever changes and scars anyone who has been through it.

I don't think there are a lot of battlefield veterans, even at the highest ranks of the military, who are bloodthirsty. Anyone who has been to combat and seen American soldiers die, and who has gotten blood on his hands while trying to save his own men . . . well, let's just say it gives you a different perspective. The best general officers and government leaders are those who have "seen the elephant," for this profoundly moving experience leads them to become advocates for exhausting every diplomatic and economic tool available before putting young American men and women into ghastly situations where many will have the chance to be maimed or wounded . . . or, worse, killed. I can say with a degree of assuredness that when you go to one of those Veterans Day ceremonies, and you see those guys—sixty, seventy, eighty years old . . . men who fought in World War II, Korea, Vietnam— wearing their beanies or berets with the number of their unit on the brim . . . you know what they are? Those men are nineteen-year-old kids with broken hearts. I know this because, in some ways, I will always be a forty-year-old battalion commander with a broken heart.

Soldiers are expected to be robots. We're expected to not feel anything. Everybody looks at the military and thinks we're all the same; but we're not. We're individuals in those desert camouflage uniforms, and we all have different feelings. I can assure you that every single person who has been outside the wire, in the fight, is wounded deeply inside his heart; a combat veteran will always be whatever his age was at the time he served in conflict. If he was nineteen hitting the beach at Normandy . . . if he was twenty-three fighting on Christmas Hill in Korea . . . if he was a thirty-three-year-old company commander in the Ia Drang Valley in Vietnam . . . or if he was a forty-year-old battalion commander in Iraq's Salah Ah Din Province . . . he will always be that broken-hearted soldier, locked at that stage, for the rest of his life. For in answering their country's call, right or wrong, these soldiers not only earned their citizenship, but gave everything they had to offer—heart, soul, mind, and body. They fought for themselves and their buddies, and even for the citizens of a foreign land, and along the way they saw things they shouldn't have seen, and did things people should not have to do. There is so much of combat that is contrary to all that we are taught as human beings and so much of war that is horrible and tragic. I believe it is necessary sometimes, but that doesn't diminish the fallout. War is a terrible thing, the depth of its ugliness is understood only by those who have been through it. And in every war there are casualties.

Captain Matthew Cunningham (Attack 6), my Alpha Company commander, and I had been waiting at the Water Palace since 1500 hours (3:00 P.M.), having made the forty-five-minute trip by UH-60 Black Hawk helicopter from Logistics Support Area (LSA) Anaconda earlier that afternoon with our brigade commander, Colonel Frederick Rudesheim. There were a lot of things that scared me in Iraq, and flying in a helicopter into Tikrit ranked right up there at the top of the list. More than one United States helicopter had been shot down in and around Tikrit. The young pilots routinely managed some wild and acrobatic flying in and out of this place to avoid enemy heat-seeking antiaircraft missiles. One moment I would be looking at the blue sky and the next I would be staring straight down at the city. The most terrifying and nauseating roller-coaster rides had nothing on these helicopter trips into Tikrit.

So it was just the three of us in the huge anteroom waiting on the commanding general of the Fourth Infantry Division, Ironhorse 6, Major General Raymond Odierno. The brigade commander, as it turned out, had gotten the times wrong. The general would not be arriving until 1700 hours (5:00 P.M.) to begin legal proceedings against both Matt and me. Neither of us was in much of a talking mood, so with two hours to kill, I had plenty of time to replay in my head all of the factors—the bizarre string of incidents and decisions—that had led to this moment.

I couldn't help but think that it was ironic on many levels. First, I had just completed the transfer of authority (TOA) of my battalion's area, a 750-square-kilometer "garden spot" of the Sunni Triangle that would now be "managed" by Lieutenant Colonel Dave Hubner and the Steel Tigers of First Battalion, Seventy-seventh Armor Regiment out of Germany. In fact, we had executed the TOA just a few hours earlier. After completing nearly nine months of leading the men and women of the Fighting Eagles of First Battalion, Eighth Infantry against a growing, organized insurgency, my reward was apparently going to be a General Officer Article 15 nonjudicial punishment proceeding. From serving as the division's main effort on four major operations (the most of any battalion in the division while we were in Iraq); to capturing or killing over 1,100 insurgents (nearly 60 percent of the entire brigade's total; the other five battalions captured or killed a total of 800 insurgents); to executing the Sunni Triangle's first city council elections in Balad, Iraq, on October 17, 2003; to relieving First Battalion, Sixty-sixth Armor Regiment when it was getting hammered in Samarra, I had given my best effort in support of the most complicated and untenable U.S. military operation in the past three decades. That's not to mention the assassination attempts on my life, dozens of attacks that I was involved in, or the countless raids, ambushes, and cordon-and-search missions executed alongside my soldiers.

After all of this, the definitive act of my time in Iraq would be a general officer administrative hearing—effectively a career-ending legal action, which I could view only as some sort of odd and arbitrary punishment for trying to win a war that by now had become unwinnable. It was so classic . . . and so like the army.

I found it almost amusing that the final chapter of my life in the military would take place in Tikrit, Saddam's hometown. The reason we had gone to war, as I understood it, was to oust his regime, capture Saddam and fifty-five of his closest advisers, and liberate a persecuted, tortured, powerless majority of people. Forget for a moment the nonsense about weapons of mass destruction (trust me—I've been all over Iraq; there weren't any). On many levels we had been successful. We had liberated the Kurds and Shias from a tyrannical, unfair regime; we had captured Saddam hiding out in a rat hole; 1-8 Infantry had dominated the Salah Ah Din Province battlefield against countless insurgent and criminal cell organizations; we had stood up to a confident, proud, and arrogant enemy in Samarra that had made virtual cowards out of 1-66 Armor; and we had done the division's "dirty work" on more than one occasion. Now, in one of Saddam's palace complexes, in his hometown, my career was going to come to an ignominious end.

Tikrit, located approximately 160 kilometers northwest of Baghdad, and home to about one hundred thousand people, had played a substantial role during Saddam's reign of terror. Saddam recruited many of his closest allies and leaders of his large national bureaucracy from the al-Tikriti clan. This was in keeping with Middle Eastern tradition, and reflected the Arab mind-set (something Westerners routinely fail to grasp) in matters related to conflict: I will argue with my brother . . . but if threatened by another family, I will stand by my brother's side. And so on: my brothers and I against my cousin; my cousins and I against the next family; our families against the next tribe; our tribes against the village; our villages against the province; our provinces against the national government; our country against yours. The violence and the struggle for power just never seemed to abate, and for an outsider it was difficult to identify the ever-shifting alliances. Further, Tikrit had been adorned with many great official buildings, schools, and some of the best infrastructure in all of Iraq, courtesy of Saddam and the world's UN dollars.

Now, when reference is made to one of Saddam's palaces, it actually is a series of palaces or huge marble mansions spread out over acres of land. In this case, the palaces were set high on the ridgeline overlooking the Tigris River. It really was an awesome sight, and thus provided a rather dramatic backdrop for what turned out to be the defining moment of my army career. Though it was the beginning of the end in the army, this legal action represented a refreshing beginning, as well as a new perspective on the preciousness of life that so many people in America take for granted. I would not trade any of that painful experience in Iraq for the newfound appreciation I have for everyday life. For life is not about the number of breaths we take, but rather about the moments that take our breath away.

As an officer in today's army, you get only one General Officer Article 15 in your career. It is a nonjudicial action that punishes the soldier for an offense that normally does not qualify for a general or special court-martial. The U.S. Army's Uniform Code of Military Justice is a strict system predicated on the presumption that the accused is guilty until proven innocent—in other words, precisely the opposite of the civilian judicial system. As a veteran of a dozen or more courts-martial as a panel member, and having listened closely and repeatedly to my senior leaders over the course of the previous eighteen years, I knew that most officers within the military's judicial system operated on the belief that if a case reached the court-martial level, then somebody, somewhere, must have done something wrong; and that person deserved to be punished. Suffice it to say, in this case I had not followed strict army policy—but then, there were many times in Iraq when I veered from policy, and even disobeyed direct orders, for in my heart I knew that by following such orders I would be placing my soldiers at risk. In this particular case I had decided that the right thing to do was to place my loyalty with the men who had trusted me with their lives in combat, rather than align myself with senior leaders—men whom I believed to be flawed—and that only happens once in a lieutenant colonel's life. Such a decision has serious and irrevocable consequences.

A lot of things run through your mind when you have two hours to wait. The ultimate irony in this entire action was that the battalion commander of arguably the finest fighting battalion in the division was about to take one for Big Army because he had decided to do what was right in view of the circumstances, as opposed to blindly making his men walk the gangplank. The army desperately wanted to project its image as a fair and just organization that was fighting a fair fight, when in fact there was nothing fair about the war in Iraq. Indeed, American soldiers were being killed and wounded at an alarming rate so that the army could fight "fair." Well, life is unfair in many ways, and war is no exception.

My dilemma was doubly ironic because anyone who knew me as a boy or teenager knew that I rarely got into any trouble. The son of a Free Methodist minister, I was a classic firstborn, always trying to please my parents, do the right thing, and live an honorable life. In high school, I never smoked, drank, or did drugs— period. Selected for West Point, I graduated in 1985, making the dean's list once and earning honorable mention Associated Press All-America honors at quarterback for the Army football team. In fact, I think that at West Point I earned a total of just sixteen demerits and eight room tours (ridiculously low figures) over a four-year period. To say that I was not rebellious would be an understatement. I was just the all-American kind of kid, and I was happy to be that way. For me to be awaiting an Article 15 proceeding seemed thoroughly incongruous. I had tried to do the right thing in Samarra and the rest of the Salah Ah Din Province, not just for my soldiers, but for the Iraqi people we had come to liberate, and for the future of Iraq.

Freedom is not free. I knew that before I went to Iraq, of course, but I see it today with newfound clarity. Freedom comes only with selfless service and incredible sacrifice. I know who I am: a West Point graduate, a member of the Long Gray Line, a person who strongly believes in General MacArthur's "Duty, Honor, Country" address to the United States Corps of Cadets, and a retired Army officer whose last military job was serving proudly as the commander of the First Battalion, Eighth Infantry Regiment in the Salah Ah Din Province based out of Balad city proper, Iraq. There were 802 men and women under my command; 800 of those soldiers returned home. I say that not to boast, but rather to express the profound sorrow and regret I feel at having failed two of them. Many others, of course, were seriously injured. Such is the price of doing battle in the heart of the Sunni Triangle—a place where evil resides, fear is the norm, and hope is the goal. A place where strategic and objective policies set forth by the Coalition Provisional Authority (CPA) and senior U.S. military commanders frequently clashed with what was reality for tactical commanders on the ground, and set off negative chain reactions that were virtually impossible to foresee. A place where there did exist a Sunni-Shia Muslim fault line, as Balad, a predominantly Shia town of one hundred thousand people, was surrounded by three smaller Sunni villages and a countryside with roughly the same number of people. A place where as the sun set over the Tigris River, you could hear the voices of children playing, and you would think for a moment that you had stumbled upon one of the most naturally beautiful places on earth—until the tranquillity was shattered by the rhythmic sound of heavy-machine-gun fire, or the concussive blast of a rocket-propelled grenade (RPG), improvised explosive device (IED), or mortar shell, all bringing death and destruction to American forces and Iraqi noncombatants alike.

For a while this was my home, and this was my war. Then, standing in the Water Palace, alongside my friend and fellow soldier, I could scarcely believe it was ending this way. Some time later a reporter for the *New York Times* would say that I was "the right warrior for the wrong war." I suppose there is some truth to that, although the compliment, if you can call it that, provokes no great comfort or pride. I was, it seemed, a man out of time . . . in more ways than one.

Matt went first. As he walked away, my heart beat faster, in part because I worried for him, and in part because now I was alone. There were times in Iraq when I worried more about dying of a heart attack than from a chunk of shrapnel or a sniper's bullet. Explosions would go off at all hours of the day or night, and sometimes the shock and reverberation would leave you stunned and breathless. I felt almost like that now, wondering how it had come to this, and what would happen next.

I used to preach to my soldiers—they were kids, really, so many of them—that what truly defines a man is not what he accomplishes when life is good—anyone can ride the crest of a wave—but rather how far he rises after he falls. I believed that, too, with all my heart. I'd just never really had an opportunity to practice what I preached.

Until now.

CHAPTER 1

I was a soldier made, not born.

While the tradition of military service is deeply rooted in some families, it was little more than white noise in my early life. Four of my uncles on my mother's side and one uncle on my father's side of the family had served in the army: one in World War II, one in Korea, two in peacetime, and one in Vietnam. Their war stories were offered only grudgingly, and I have no recollection of sitting at their feet, taking in with wide-eyed innocence everything they said. It was just something they had done once, a long time ago, and was no more or less important or interesting than the jobs they held now or the families they raised. It would be many years later, when I entered West Point, before I began to understand the depth of commitment that runs through some families, and how many of my classmates were third- and fourth-generation cadets. There was a time, when I worked in the West Point admissions office, that I received a call from a gentleman by the name of Westmoreland. I don't think it was *the* General West-moreland, but it was definitely one of his relatives—a brother or a son, perhaps—and he wasted little time in letting me know that his daughter was applying to West Point, and that the Westmore-land line at the Academy could be traced back, unbroken, to 1827. So the message was clear: Just go ahead and get her in, because this is where she belongs. The Ivies, I learned, had nothing on West Point when it came to tradition and legacy.

If our household lacked any overt connection to the military, however, it did not want for structure and guidance. My parents both grew up in Pennsylvania and met as students at Roberts Wesleyan, a small Christian college located near Rochester, New York. My dad, Marcus Bailey Sassaman, attended Western Evan-gelical Seminary in Portland, Oregon, and eventually he and my mother, Nancy Jean Sassaman, settled in the Northwest and began raising a family. My father was a Free Methodist minister and his vocation was the family business, so to speak. Mom and Dad sub-scribed wholeheartedly to the precepts of Samuel and Susanna Wesley in matters both personal and theological, so ours was a conservative upbringing, to say the least. There is a line of scrip-ture that says, in essence, *If a pastor can't control his own home, then he has no business being in charge of a church and a congregation.* My par-ents were young and I was the firstborn, and as a result I suffered the consequences of their taking that advice rather literally. They did not spare the rod, and I can recall taking it in the shorts quite a bit early on. I can also remember as early as first grade, sitting in the front row of my father's church, and trying desperately to re-main still as a statue for the duration of the entire service. No small task for a six-year-old, especially one as energetic as I was, but I understood what would happen if I succumbed to the urge to twitch or even itch. Mom was at the piano, Dad was in the pul-pit, and the entire church was watching. If I caused them any embarrassment, someone would take me out afterward and administer a little parental discipline—usually a shoe or a belt across the backside.

There was less of this as time went on, a natural loosening of the leash as more children came into the home (I was the oldest of three children) and my parents grew more comfortable with their social and professional standing. I know they probably look back on this period with some regret, maybe even a little bit of horror, but I'd be dishonest if I said mine was an unequivocally happy childhood. It wasn't a sad childhood, either. My mother and father were very affectionate toward each other and very kind and generous toward others, but when it came to their children, there was some fear and intimidation involved, coupled with compassion and love. So there were some conflicting dynamics and emotions in our household. I guess you could say it was a childhood of . . . expectations. There was, from my earliest memory, a drive to succeed, and I think it was initially focused on the classroom and in music, and then it just carried over into athletics.

Both of my parents were musical. Dad sang in the choir in high school and college, and later at his church, but my mother was the gifted musician in the family. By the time she completed a twenty-plus-year career as a music teacher in the Beaverton, Oregon, School District, she had become something of a legend for the passion and professionalism she brought to the staging of elementary-school musicals and choir concerts. My brothers and I all became reasonably accomplished musicians, thanks to our parents' influence. I had to take piano lessons for four or five years until I brokered a deal with my mother in seventh grade. By this time I had also begun studying the slide trombone, and my parents agreed to let me stop playing piano—as long as I promised to remain committed to the trombone throughout my high school years. Having grown tired of watching my friends playing baseball on summer days while I sat inside practicing the piano, I jumped at this offer. In the end I wound up forming a brass trio with my younger brothers, Jonathan (who played trumpet) and David (French horn).

It was in the musical arena that I first learned to deal with pressure. In some ways playing in the Army-Navy football game, even on national television, is a walk in the park when compared to playing a trombone solo at a state musical competition when your mother is a music legend in the state and you're being judged by three of her peers. Slide trombone did not come naturally to me, either—I had to work really hard at that, and there were high expectations in my family to achieve as a musician. By the time I was able to go into sports, which was a more natural fit for me, I had already gone through a crucible of fire with the trombone. Through music I learned the value of discipline and mastery, skills that proved useful in just about any competitive endeavor.

Not that my parents were particularly interested in sports. In fourth grade, on a whim, I entered a football skills contest known as the Punt, Pass & Kick competition, and finished first in my age group at my elementary school. The following week I won the citywide competition, which allowed me to qualify for the regional level. I'm pretty sure this surprised my parents (it surprised me, as well), who no doubt had never considered the possibility that one of their children might have any athletic ability, since it wasn't of any great concern or interest to them. In fact, I wasn't permitted to compete in the regionals—my father had planned a family vacation and wasn't about to delay the trip so that I could kick a football. At the time, my parents considered music and academics far more important than sports, so they went through an education process with their children as we began to excel on the playing field; they started to see that sports, and the natural attention that came with success in the athletic arena, might have some benefit after all.

My first lessons in competitiveness, interestingly enough, were taught by my father. Although Dad had run cross-country and track, and played soccer and basketball in high school, sports seemed to play no role in his life by this time; as far as I could tell, he was a nonathlete. Yet, there was quite a bit of the Great Santini in my father, an unwillingness to appear weak or fragile in even the most benign of situations. Thus did a simple game of backyard basketball become something akin to March Madness. The very first time I shot baskets with Dad it turned into a war. I was ten years old at the time, and absolutely enthralled with the game of basketball. We had just moved to a new parsonage, and I had been begging almost daily for a hoop of my own. It had been this way for a few years. Once I discovered balls, nothing else (including music) held my interest. I never played with toys, trucks, or cars. (I never even played "war" with my friends.) I was always about balls. If you gave me a ball I could disappear for hours on end. Baseball came first, in second grade, followed a couple years later by basketball and football. My father eventually put a basket up in the driveway, probably just because he was tired of listening to me whine. I stayed out there for hours on end; Dad even put up a spotlight, and soon I was dribbling tirelessly through the drizzle and fog of the northwestern nights. One day, tired of playing alone or with one of my brothers, I tried to entice my father to join me in the driveway. I had no motive, no objective, aside from wanting to show my dad what I had learned since he had erected the basket. Basically, I just thought it would be neat to shoot some hoops with my father.

He had something else in mind.

"Let's play a game."

Even better, I thought.

Dad laid out the rules: two points per basket, fifty-point game. Winner's outs, of course.

All right! This should be fun!

The final score was 50–2; it would have been 50–3, but we didn't have a three-point shot in 1973. My only basket resulted not from a concession or moment of generosity on the part of the old man, but rather from a stroke of luck—a hook shot from twenty-five feet that sailed over my father's head and through the basket. We must have played hundreds of games over the next five or six years, and Dad never relented. Every time we picked up the basketball and walked outside together, it was with one objective in mind: to win the game. We never just shot baskets, never played a lighthearted game of H-O-R-S-E or P-I-G or Around the World. It was always a game, always a battle, the two of us bumping and throwing elbows and doing our best to dominate the other in the driveway. He never went easy on me, never let me win to boost my ego. Over time, of course, the inevitable happened: I got bigger, stronger, and better, and my father got older, slower, and less dominant. I still recall the day we played in the backyard of our home in Portland. I was sixteen or seventeen years old. We were almost the same height by then, and I was perhaps a little wider across the shoulders, a bit thicker in the chest. I had discovered that I could move my father around, put him on my hip and muscle the ball to the basket. I beat him for the first time that day, and I do not recall him taking the loss well. That was the last time we ever played one-on-one basketball.

In high school, as I became more obsessed with football, my father expressed his competitive nature in other ways. Even though he had never played a down of football, Dad was the kind of guy who felt compelled to share his views on the sport in general, and my performance in particular. After a Friday-night game, I'd typically go out for pizza with my teammates or my girlfriend;

sometimes I wouldn't get home until well after midnight, but my father would always be awake, waiting for me to return, not so much because he worried that I might have gotten into trouble (as I said, bad behavior wasn't an option), but so that we could review the evening's competition. It happened without fail. Dad would be sitting in the living room with the light on, reading the Bible, and after an exchange of pleasantries, he would invite me to sit down beside him; there, together, we would analyze the game, breaking it down play by play. He would offer compliments on what I had done right, and suggestions on how to improve in areas where I had been less than stellar. Whether he was trying to help me realize my potential or simply projecting his ambition onto me, I don't really know. Maybe a little of both. I only know that he'd be sitting there, program in hand, with a description of each play scribbled in the margins. I used to joke that I never had to worry about film sessions in high school, because by the time Monday afternoon rolled around, I'd already spent hours reviewing plays with my father.

It's different around my house today. I remember when my son, Nathan, was in third grade, and I took him to basketball practice after I'd been away for some time on a deployment. Nathan just sat there bouncing the basketball, kind of dreamily, while the coach was talking, and the coach responded by ordering Nathan to run a few laps—punishment for interrupting and not paying attention. When we came home that evening I said nothing to Nathan, but I told my wife, "In twenty years of playing organized sports, I never had to run laps because of not paying attention. I ate it up, hook, line, and sinker." She just smiled and shrugged, and I knew what she meant: my son was not like me. At first I was mortified, and then I got over it. I think he enjoys the social part of the game more than anything else. He's going to be a good athlete, he's going to contribute, and it's my hope that he becomes the go-to guy. That's okay. I've tried to be very careful about giving advice to my kids or micromanaging their childhood. I've lost more backyard basketball games than I've won. I've never questioned any of their coaches. All I do is thank coaches for spending time with my son or daughter. Again, I think that's just a by-product of my upbringing. My father was neither an athlete nor a soldier; I was both. Yet, in some ways, particularly when it comes to family and children, I am gentler than he ever was.

Challenging as it might have been, the tough love we received at home had its advantages. I had no chance to go to hell when I was growing up. None whatsoever. From the earliest age I was engulfed by the church and all it represented. There was no alcohol, no smoking, no drugs. There was, instead, devotion and prayer and meditation; there were Bible lessons. None of this seemed odd to me, for it was my only frame of reference, and as a result I was among the most naive teenagers you'd ever want to meet. Here's an example of the ways things worked in our family. When I was thirteen years old, and it came time for Dad to have the age-old father-son talk with me—you know, the one about the birds and the bees—the exchange of wisdom occurred not in the comfort of our home, but at my father's office. The time was scheduled into Dad's day—my mother even called to make an appointment. I arrived at his office early, shuffled in nervously, and sat patiently and silently as my father walked through the dusty pages of a Christian book on human sexuality and emerging manhood.

And that was that.

There were no questions afterward. He checked the block. We had the appointment. The forty-five-minute meeting ended and we never talked about it again. Dad closed the book, gave me a pat on the back, and went back to work, figuring I was good to go. This was fine with me, since I was extraordinarily uncomfortable for the duration of the meeting and wanted nothing more than to get out of there as quickly as possible. High school, for me, was one surprise after another, as the realities of adolescence came slowly into focus. I can recall even as late as my senior year, while visiting colleges as a football recruit, an acute awareness that for all my success as a student and athlete, I was incredibly immature and inexperienced.

"Mom . . . Dad," I'd say when I returned from these visits. "You guys have sheltered me so much. Do you have any idea what's going on out there?"

They did, of course, and their attempts to protect and shield their children, while perhaps a bit extreme, no doubt sprang from someplace genuine. In many ways my parents were (and are) an amazing couple. They have totally dedicated their lives to God and to their work (and to their family). I learned from my father not only competitiveness, but compassion. It would be unfair to suggest that my father was a total monster; he wasn't. He was an intimidating and domineering presence around the house, but he was also the type of man who would, quite literally, give you the shirt off his back.

For a long time I just thought my father had a lot of friends, because every Saturday when we lived at the parsonage, my mom would rise with the sun and create elaborate breakfasts, with eggs and bacon and pancakes, and giant bowls of fruit. Dad and his buddies, generally a quiet, disheveled lot whose names I never knew, would usually eat out on the patio, rather than at the kitchen table with the rest of our family. It wasn't until many years later that I realized who these men really were. They weren't friends of my father's—they were men he had found at the city mission or the Salvation Army. Dad would drive down there every Saturday morning and pick them up, take them home, feed them breakfast, and help them find work. For all his flaws, Dad was a very sensitive and kindhearted man to those less fortunate than he. He had a great sense of empathy for others (even if he sometimes had difficulty sharing those feelings with his own children). I know for certain that some of those traits were passed on to me, because of the way I felt about the people in Iraq and their situation. In the midst of so much brutality and hatred, while trying to protect my soldiers and bring everyone home alive, there were times when I wanted nothing more than to hold a small Iraqi child and tell him that everything would be all right. Even if I knew that it wasn't true. I know I have my father to thank for that.

West Point presented itself as an option during my senior year at Aloha High School in Beaverton, Oregon. Football had been the defining experience of my adolescence. If I wasn't practicing, I was in the weight room or out on the track running. Playing Division I college ball had become a serious goal of mine, but I was a five-foot-ten, 170-pound quarterback, so the odds were not in my favor. I got a brief look (but no offer) from Stanford; a couple other Pac-10 schools extended opportunities to walk on (although they strongly suggested a switch to the defensive side of the field). Moreover, there were serious economic considerations. I was recruited by Princeton, but when the financial numbers came out, there was just no way it was going to work for us. Princeton was generous with its financial aid, but almost anything short of a full scholarship was going to be insufficient.

Although I was not a kid who had ever expressed any interest in a career in the military, the service academies offered a legitimate and attractive alternative to what I had been hearing from other college recruiters. I was intrigued by the possibility of leaving the Pacific Northwest, and I liked the notion of graduating from college without a penny of debt. There was, obviously, the little matter of a five-year commitment to consider, but that seemed at the time like a small price to pay. The U.S. Military Academy and the U.S. Air Force Academy offered appointments; in the end, I chose West Point, primarily on the strength of a subtle but powerful recruiting visit in January 1981.

During the air force recruiting visit, I spent most of my time off campus, hanging out with other football players, observing and testing a lifestyle not markedly dissimilar from that of any other college athlete. The most notable aspect of my visit involved a close encounter with a flight simulator, a dizzying, disorienting contraption that left me slightly nauseated and sweat-soaked. I'd never been the kind of guy who lay on the hood of his car and watched airplanes take off overhead at the local airport, but I was something of a traditionalist in my views: it made sense to me that if you were going to serve in the air force, you might as well be a pilot; clearly, though, that wasn't in my makeup. If the flight simulator told me anything, it was that I was better suited to land duty.

The West Point visit was different. We spent considerable time in the classroom, mess hall, and dorms. We rose early to attend church services. I requested and received an hour-long meeting with the chaplain. Nothing seemed to be hidden at West Point, and there was only a modest amount of emphasis on football. The sales pitch, such as it was, could be distilled to this simple sentiment: *This is what we're all about. If you're up for the challenge, great. If not, that's all right, too. Maybe this isn't the place for you.* I decided pretty quickly that it was the place for me. Not that I really understood what I was getting myself into. I found the academy attractive not because of any fascination with the military (I had never been the type of kid who played "war" or built forts in the backyard; I had never learned to hunt, never owned so much as a BB gun), but rather for a combination of practical reasons. West Point offered a first-rate education without demanding a penny in return. It held the promise of access to a different stratum of society, one where important decisions were made and power was brokered. On some level I was intrigued by the idea that I would be challenged—physically, emotionally, socially. Really, though, I went there for one reason: to play football. It was as simple as that.

I arrived in July of 1981, and I don't think I stopped sweating until Christmas. I can remember standing out at formation in the first week of Plebe Summer (also known as Beast Barracks) as one of the upper-class cadets in charge of my platoon stood in front of me, screaming, "New Cadet Sassaman, I order you to stop sweating!" I could not. My entire uniform was drenched. This was an unfortunate quirk of physiology (I do sweat more than the average person), combined with an acclimatization process that hadn't quite taken root. I'd grown up in the Pacific Northwest, where summers were mild and humidity was rarely an issue. To me, the northeastern summer was as stifling as a sauna. Add to this recipe an exhausting, pressure-packed schedule—one that included a ceaseless barrage of insults and a daily to-do list that could not possibly be completed—and you have one seriously soaked cadet.

Indoctrination at West Point began the moment I bid farewell to my father and walked through the front gates. For a tough old minister, my father was surprisingly nervous and emotional. I later discovered, tucked within the pages of my Bible, a collection of handwritten notes—quotations from scripture, mostly, but personal messages as well. He was not the type to share these thoughts face-to-face, but he did take the time to commit them to paper and place them strategically, in the hope that they would provide strength and wisdom during difficult times. And I'd be less than truthful if I said I didn't have some of those. On my very first day, while reciting a list of factoids and trivia and personal information (something required of all plebes) to one of the upper-class cadets (known traditionally as the Man in the Red Sash) in charge of my dorm, I copped a bit of an attitude. All plebes know that this sort of testing is part of their introduction to West Point; they know that shortly after their arrival, they will be ordered to report to the Man in the Red Sash, who, after testing their mettle, will give them their roommate assignment, their dorm number, instructions on setting up their room, and various other bits of information. So there is ample opportunity to prepare. I had the recitation down perfectly, ripped it right off without making a single mistake; unfortunately, as I finished, I couldn't resist smiling just slightly, not so much out of arrogance or cockiness, but from relief at having passed the first test. The Man in the Red Sash was not amused. "Wipe that smirk off your face!" he screamed. Then I was ordered to exit the room, go to the end of the line, and perform the duty all over again. There were some cadets, crippled by nervousness, who spent hours with the Man in the Red Sash, and I don't doubt that some of them became part of the roughly 30 percent of the class of 1985 that ultimately washed out of West Point. That is not an unusual rate of failure at the Academy. Indeed, it's typical. Most of those who choose to withdraw from school do so in the first year.

The first day was a blur—immersion therapy, you might say. They cut our hair, fed us, ran us from one station to another as we frantically tried to keep pace and soak up all the information being thrown at us. In the afternoon we took part in a reception parade, marching in ragged formation (we hadn't yet learned the intricacies of proper marching) down to Eisenhower Hall for an orientation lecture as our parents stood off to the side, craning their necks for one last look at their children. My father, like most other fathers, was desperately searching for me, rising on his toes and scanning the line of cadets for some sign of familiarity—but none was forthcoming. We were as one, each wearing gray pants and white shirt, with a cap pulled snugly over a newly shaved head. I was indistinguishable from the cadet to my left or the cadet to my right, and there was no way that I was going to wave to my father to let him know where I was—not with so many upper-class cadets all around. I glanced once more to the side, saw him walking through the crowd, struggling for a final glimpse. Then we were gone. It would be Thanksgiving break before we saw each other again.

I was not, in the beginning at least, a model cadet. In the first month I received several performance reports that made specific note of my "lack of military bearing." This was a way of suggesting that I was not taking my duties seriously, and I don't deny that the reports had some merit. I was at West Point for two reasons: (1) to play football, and (2) to get an education. I was not particularly fastidious about how my bunk looked, and frankly wasn't interested in cleaning my room or shining my shoes. In time I would come to understand the importance and value of these things, and I did eventually embrace the extra duties expected of plebes; but it did not come naturally to me. I had to work at it. As a result, the first official counseling report I received from my squad leader offered the following opinion: "New Cadet Sassaman has no military bearing whatsoever, and will never make a presentable army officer." I believe that sentence ended with an exclamation point. It was followed by a second, even harsher assessment: "I doubt he'll make it through the first semester at West Point."

Whether the cadet who authored this evaluation believed it was true or was merely trying to get my attention—firing a warning shot across the bow, as it were—I don't know. Regardless of the intent, it worked. From that day on I became a more committed and serious cadet, one who tried hard to balance the demands of athletics, academics, and military leadership. Really, though, there was no other option. There was no way I could go home, no way I could quit. The decision had been made and announced to the press, which naturally provoked a good deal of small-town hoopla. For reasons related to pride, economics, and family pressure, there was absolutely no chance I was going to fail. I signed up, and never looked back or questioned the decision. I was just somewhat clueless about the things expected of me. That's why cadets who had been to prep school or cadets with West Point lineage were so far ahead of middle-class kids such as me. For some cadets, the learning curve is rather steep, and I was one of those cadets.

Football was my salvation. It kept me sane and focused, and, difficult as it was, provided a welcome respite from the drilling and studying that devoured so much of a cadet's time. I made the varsity travel team as a freshman, which was a bonus because the football team left campus every Friday evening. When playing at home we'd stay at a hotel in nearby Newburgh, so that we could bond and prepare without any distractions. Of course, we'd fly all over the country for road games. In many ways I was like a kid in a candy store. I didn't get a lot of playing time as a freshman, but I did suit up for every game, and on several occasions I found my way onto the field. Pittsburgh, a national power at the time, beat us 48–0 in the second to last game of the season, but my primary recollection from that day is the thrill of warming up alongside Pitt's

Dan Marino, who would become one of the most successful quarterbacks in NFL history. A minor brush with greatness, perhaps, but it meant a lot to me. Football made the West Point experience tolerable. I didn't mind the off-season workouts or the daily sessions in the weight room. Football was familiar, comfortable.

In contrast, I found daily life as a West Point plebe to be enormously stressful. The academy courts and attracts type A personalities—overachievers driven to lead and succeed. I certainly fell into that category, and I quickly discovered that if most cadets shared a common trait, it was an almost pathological fear of failure. Washing out was not an option; yet, the statistics did not lie. A significant portion of our class would not graduate. I was determined to avoid being a casualty, and that determination allowed me to survive the first year—but there were consequences. When my parents drove me to the airport at the end of Christmas break, I found myself so racked with anxiety over returning to the academy that I had to duck into a restroom and vomit before boarding the plane. This, unfortunately, was the beginning of a rather disturbing pattern that persisted throughout most of my college career. Every time I left campus for more than a few days, I would become physically ill at the prospect of returning. It didn't matter if I was visiting my parents in Oregon or an aunt and uncle in Pennsylvania. Each vacation ended with an unsettling and perhaps cathartic trip to the bathroom. It wasn't until sometime in my senior year that I developed an ability to handle the tension in other ways.

In all candor, I was neither a gifted student nor a gifted athlete. Whatever I achieved came at a significant cost. I was a worker. Whenever my name appears in the media, it typically is accompanied by the descriptive phrases "West Point," "football star," and "dean's list student." Well, I made the dean's list exactly once—in the spring semester of my junior year. A minimum grade point average of 3.0 was required for inclusion on the dean's list; I made it by the narrowest of margins (exactly 3.0), and I worked my butt off to make it happen.

I majored in international relations, but the core curriculum at West Point is so demanding and broad-based that a sizable portion of any cadet's time is devoted to classes outside his or her area of interest. I took numerous science-based courses: electrical engineering, systems engineering, and thermodynamics. I probably received a minor in engineering, whether I wanted it or not. In general, what I remember most about the academic end of West Point was spending vast blocks of time on classes that did not interest me, and that I found enormously difficult.

Perseverance, I discovered, was the key to survival at West Point (and, indeed, in the army); much of what I learned was absorbed on the football field. Between my sophomore and junior years we experienced a major coaching change, with Ed Cavanaugh's departure from West Point, and the arrival of a man named Jim Young. Coach Young came to Army from Purdue University, where he had instituted a sophisticated, pro-style passing offense. Mark Herrmann and Scott Campbell had excelled as quarterbacks in Coach Young's system, but I knew that his coming to West Point would not be a good thing for me. I was not a drop-back passer; I was an option quarterback, a bit on the smallish side, but with decent speed, field vision, and toughness. Predictably, I was moved to defense shortly after Coach Young's arrival. I played safety throughout spring practice sessions, and after a while I began to question whether I wanted to remain part of the program. I was really down on myself, debating not only whether I should continue playing football, but whether I wanted to stay at the academy. Cadets are permitted to opt out at any point in the first two years of their education without incurring any sort of penalty; anyone who leaves West Point after that point, however, owes the military a term of service. Football had been largely responsible for making my academy experience tolerable, and now, suddenly, football wasn't a lot of fun, either. We had a new coach and I was out of the picture. At best, it appeared that I would be a second-string defensive back.

Coach Young was an impressive motivator. His motto—and it could be found plastered on the locker room walls and in the weight room and just about anywhere he traveled—was this: "Those who stay will be champions." I think Coach Young actually borrowed that phrase from Bo Schembechler, for whom he once toiled as a defensive coordinator. Regardless, Coach Young made it his own. Frankly, I found it a bit hard to swallow in the beginning, as I moved from the glamour of quarterback to the faceless work of defensive back, with barely a nod from the coaching staff. Deep down, I understood that football was not the key to my future. I was too small to play professionally; in all likelihood my athletic career would end the moment I graduated, so common sense dictated a bit of introspection, and the posing of some hard questions. What did I want out of life? What did I expect? From this period of crisis came a moment of clarity, during which I decided that I would finish my education at West Point, and that I would leave just as I had entered: as a member of the football team. Why? Because I had made a commitment, and for some reason it seemed important to fulfill that commitment. Maybe it was nothing more complicated than the fact that I couldn't stomach the notion of being branded a "quitter."

As fate (or good fortune) would have it, Jim Young's pro-style offense, intelligent and ambitious though it might have been, proved incompatible with the talent available in the West Point locker room at that time. I spent most of my junior season on the sideline, watching Army suffer through a 2-9 season that ended, embarrassingly, with a 42–13 rout at the hands of Navy, at the

Rose Bowl in Pasadena. Coach Young, though, was nothing if not practical. He looked around, assessed the talent at his disposal, and did something few coaches are willing to do: he changed. By the spring of 1984 Army had instituted a wishbone attack and I was back on the offensive side of the ball; in fact, I was at the top of the depth chart at quarterback, a reversal of fortune attributable primarily to the fact that I was the only person qualified for the job. My high school team had run a veer offense, which is similar to the wishbone, and that experience, coupled with my status as an upperclassman, suddenly proved a tremendous asset.

Jim Young was one of the most intense people I'd ever been around. He was totally committed to winning, and for that reason, more than any other, we formed a strong connection. As much as I respected him, I also feared him—and I wasn't alone. Everyone feared Coach Young—even the men on his coaching staff. I can still recall the day that one of our offensive coaches failed to respond quickly enough when summoned by Coach Young. We were in the middle of a passing drill when the assistant realized what had happened, and he heard Coach Young screaming his name. The drill came to a dead stop as the beleaguered assistant, his face ashen, sprinted down the field, unconcerned with anything other than the tongue-lashing he was about to receive. I'd never seen a grown man act that way before, and it had a profound and lasting effect on me. Our entire team had tremendous respect for Jim Young because he was committed to winning, and he was going to do whatever he thought was right to get Army football turned around. In part, that effect came out of his intensity, and an absolute, palpable fear of having to endure being dressed down by that man.

I've always said that I learned as much about leadership and winning during my time at Michie Stadium, playing football, as I did while training with the other cadets in more traditional military exercises. Working with Coach Young confirmed a few things I'd already experienced and suspected to be universal truths. I learned that fear, respect, and intensity were intertwined, maybe even inseparable. Here's a story that illustrates my point, at least as it relates to the concept of fear as a motivational tool. In my senior year, in the fall of 1984, we traveled to Knoxville for a game against the University of Tennessee Volunteers. First of all, we had no business playing Tennessee; they were a big-time football power from the Southeastern Conference, a legitimate Top 20 program; we were somewhere near the bottom of the bottom 20. I don't know who scheduled that game, but he must have had a sadistic bent. Regardless, there we were, on the field in Knoxville, in ninety-plus-degree heat and wilting in the late-summer humidity, holding our own against a team that was favored to beat us by four touchdowns. The Tennessee crowd of more than ninety-five thousand fans was wild—I've never seen so many orange leisure suits in my life—but we were holding our own. This was only the second game of the season (we had easily beaten Colgate in our opener), but already it was quite a departure from the previous year. Late in the game, with Tennessee trying to run out the clock while nursing a 24–17 lead, I found myself sitting on the bench, attempting to cool down by applying wet towels to my head and neck. The game appeared to be over by this point, and none of us felt particularly disheartened by the way things had gone. We had traveled half a country away and acquitted ourselves admirably against one of the best teams in college football, in front of one of the sport's largest and most fanatical crowds, in a storied stadium. The next thing I knew, we had stopped Tennessee cold and the Volunteers were lining up to punt. We'd have one more shot on offense. As I stood up, wobbling slightly from the heat, I caught Coach Young's eye. Now, I'm sure he would never remember this, but the look he cast seemed to say, *It's on you, buddy*. All I could think at that moment was how much I did not want to let him down; I feared Coach Young far more than I feared anybody on the Tennessee defense, because I knew I'd have to answer to him sooner than I'd have to answer to anybody else. So we went out on the field and got it going. I scored with a minute to go, we tied it up, and that was that. There were no overtimes back then, so we left Knoxville with a tie against a Top 20 team, which, considering where we'd been just a few months earlier, was tantamount to victory. What stands out for me isn't the crowd or the tying touchdown or anything like that. It's the memory of fearing my coach, and fearing failure. That, more than anything else, became the driving force in my football career.

Coach Young had vowed to make champions of those who remained at West Point, and he made good on that promise. The turnaround he engineered was nothing less than astonishing—from 2-9 in 1983 to 8-3-1 in 1984. From a humbling loss to our archrival one year, to beating both Navy and Air Force the next year and winning the Commander in Chief's Trophy outright for only the third time in West Point history. We finished the season ranked twenty-second in the nation, and in Army's first major postseason appearance, we beat Michigan State, 10–6, in the inaugural Cherry Bowl, at the Silverdome in Pontiac, Michigan. This was rarefied air, and the climb had confirmed for me everything that life was supposed to be like. I had rushed for more than 1,000 yards and been selected as corecipient of the Exemplary Player Award by *Football Roundup* magazine; I shared the award with Boston College's Doug Flutie, the 1984 Heisman Trophy winner, who would spend the better part of the next two decades in the NFL.

Sometimes I'm still at a loss to explain this transformation, but I do believe much of it had to do with Coach Young, and my desire to please him and to avoid his wrath. As I would discover many years later in Iraq, where the stakes were exponentially higher, fear can be a powerful motivational force. It may not be optimal, but at times it's more than adequate.

Not until after I returned from Christmas break in my senior year did I really start thinking about life without football . . . and life after West Point. It wasn't unusual for football players who had known success to stay on as graduate assistant coaches for a year, but I chose not to do that. Instead, I decided that I would embark on a serious career as an army officer immediately after graduation, and the first step in that journey was to figure out—a bit late, admittedly—what West Point was all about, and what it had to offer. I had been drifting along for more than three years, surviving classwork that did not interest me while devoting the majority of my energy and ambition to the football field. That was over now. It was time to embrace a different kind of life—an army life—and to ascertain exactly where and how I'd fit in. To that end, one of the first things I did was volunteer for the Sandhurst Military Skills Competition, which is a competition involving marksmanship, road marching, technical expertise, and a variety of other events. At the time it was a big deal; today it's even bigger. My team actually performed reasonably well. I was probably the weakest of the four of us when it came to the technical skills, but we finished sixth out of seventy-two teams in the entire corps.

It was only in my final semester that I tried to develop a macro point of view. Don't get me wrong—I'd always been very patriotic, and I was all about fighting and winning; I felt honored and privileged to attend West Point. But some guys ate it up in a way that bordered on the fanatical. From the moment they set foot on campus, they were trying to plan every inch of their military careers. Over time I've come to realize that this isn't necessarily the best approach. Some of the most enthusiastic and confident cadets—guys who brazenly tried to game the system—ended up leaving the army after fulfilling their five-year commitments. Conversely, a lot of guys who were just trying to work through the process are still at it, more than twenty years down the road. That's a general observation, of course. As in any line of work, there are some people who just figure it out—through a series of shrewd political career moves, and with an innate sense of knowing which boxes to check, they ascend to the highest levels—but those officers aren't necessarily doing the right thing for the soldiers they command. (That much I know through first-hand experience.) I probably fell somewhere in the middle. I felt good about what I was doing, but didn't fully understand what the army was all about.

I don't doubt that the academy, today, does a much better job of training its officers and letting them know what to expect, but it still can't replicate the actual conditions of working in the army, and there's no way West Point comes close to replicating the conditions of combat. When I returned to the academy many years later, after serving in Iraq, I told a group of cadets, "We might as well be on Mars right now." I understand how tempting it is to sit in a sterile classroom or theater setting and second-guess actions and decisions that are being made thousands of miles away by soldiers enduring unbelievable conditions: with no rest, lacking food, and subject to terrible pressures. West Point can't replicate such conditions, and neither can the army, despite its best intentions, replicate them during training. It's just not possible. What West Point does quite well is help cadets (and future officers) learn how to make good decisions. Most of these decisions are fairly mundane and related to time management, but they're important nonetheless, for if you make good decisions, you're going to reap the rewards; conversely, if you make poor decisions, you'll suffer the consequences.

The army expects its young officers to be able to make good, sometimes difficult, decisions. Consider the platoon sergeant who has eighteen years in the army and has been to Iraq three times. Sure, he can run a superior physical-training program and he can probably handle a morale and welfare inspection with greater precision than a newly commissioned officer; he probably understands all the duties and responsibilities required of his soldiers during an ambush. The West Point cadet, however, has had more values-based decision-making training than that platoon sergeant. So when the platoon sergeant decides that it's okay to take an Iraqi detainee behind the shed and beat the living daylights out of him with a brick? Well, this is where West Point training becomes crucial. It is the duty of the young lieutenant to tell the platoon sergeant he's wrong, to point out, in no uncertain terms, "That's not going to happen."

This takes tremendous strength and personal courage—to overrule an experienced platoon sergeant, a man who might be ten to fifteen years older than you are, with vastly more real-world army experience. Add to this mix the hostility and darkening of the soul that come with war and you have a job that can seem overwhelming, but it is the job. As I told the cadets on that visit, "If you can't even tell a friend in your own company to shine his shoes or tuck his shirt in or make sure that his room is clean—if you can't make a simple correction on your own buddy—then you can forget about even trying to tell a platoon sergeant who's been to war three times that it's not okay to beat up an insurgent detainee in custody.

"*To tie an insurgent up, put flex cuffs on him, blindfold him, and bash his head in?* Guess what? It's not okay. And you're not going to be able to man up and say that if you don't start making those calls right now. Those guys are tough guys; they've been to war, and they've seen things you can't imagine. West Point has trained you to make moral decisions, to determine, in the heat of battle, what's right and wrong. But guess what? It's not going to be a black-and-white world over there, and you may move over to the dark side, and you have to be sure that whatever decision you make . . . you're able to live with the consequences that come with that decision."

West Point, unfortunately, fails to deal adequately with the inherently ambiguous nature of warfare: Do we walk to the edge of the cliff and look over? Do we try to stay as far back as we can? And if we stay back, do we win? And where does winning fit into all of this? Former secretary of defense Donald Rumsfeld must accept a significant share of the responsibility for what went wrong in Iraq. He totally ignored the cultural and human endeavors of combat by suggesting that we could win the war with cell phones and F-16 rockets and a handful of Special Forces troops riding camels and donkeys through the desert. The arrogance of that assessment is staggering, and it cost us a lot of American lives.

Not that I understood any of this when I left West Point, carrying only an abstract notion of what it meant to be an officer . . . a soldier. But I was eager to explore the territory. I graduated on May 22, 1985. Senator John Tower delivered the commencement address, and I was among a group of fifty cadets given the honor of walking on stage and shaking the senator's hand. (Forty-eight of these cadets had earned their place on stage through academic accomplishment; I was one of two cadets honored for their athletic accomplishments.) At the end of ceremony, when the other cadets, in time-honored tradition, heaved their caps high into the air, I gave mine a gentle toss, so that it floated right back into my hands. I did this not for myself, but for my father, who had expressed an interest in keeping the hat . . . for sentimental reasons. I think now he regrets that request. I remember a few years back he said, "Boy, I wish I'd let Nate throw that thing as far as he could—like everyone else." That's what you're supposed to do—just chuck it. A lot of cadets would stuff a dollar bill inside, or a five-dollar bill (it might be a twenty-dollar bill today), and then little kids in the audience would sprint from the side to pick up the cap and run home with a souvenir. Nevertheless, Dad asked me if he could have it, and I was the dutiful son. . . . That's okay, though. I think it meant a lot to him. The truth is, it didn't mean much to me.

I've come to believe that all good servant-leaders are kind of like that. There's a humbleness about their experiences. I don't wear my West Point class ring; I don't wear my ring from the Cherry Bowl. I wear my wedding ring, and that's it. I would prefer that people not even know that I'm from West Point, not because I lack pride in the achievement, but simply because I do not want it to define me. I felt that way even on graduation day. For some people, graduating from West Point is the crowning achievement of their lives; from the moment they toss that cap into the air, it's a downhill slide. For me it was just another milestone. Frankly, I could not wait to put West Point in my rearview mirror; I was ready to move on.

CHAPTER 2

SEPTEMBER 11, 2001
CAMP DOHA, KUWAIT

The news arrived around six o'clock in the evening, as the sun was setting and the temperature had fallen to a balmy 112 degrees. I was a brigade operations officer on temporary assignment in the Middle East—specifically, at Camp Doha, Kuwait. Throughout the more than ten years that had passed since Operation Desert Storm, the United States had maintained a significant military presence in the region, rotating thousand-man battalions through Camp Doha at roughly six-month intervals. This was one of several trips I'd made to the area, where my job was to help facilitate planning and preparation for the next wave of soldiers, whose purpose was to serve as a stabilizing and deterring force in the event that Iraqi troops were tempted to spill over the border into Kuwait.

Our compound was located about a mile from the camp proper, and sometimes, at the end of the day, I'd drive to Doha so I could go for a jog around a makeshift packed-dirt track. On the ride over I'd heard a vague report over Armed Forces Radio about some sort of accident in the metropolitan New York area—something about an airplane skidding off a runway in New Jersey. The details were sketchy, as they often are when you're halfway around the world. Then, while getting out of the car, I'd heard another report: the plane had crashed, and not merely overshot the runway. I didn't think much of it, of course; how often do you hear about plane crashes or other tragedies and simply shake your head and go on with your life? This one seemed no different. So I got out of the car and started to run. A typical evening's jog was between four and six miles. The heat could be brutal, but it was a cathartic experience, a good way to relieve stress at the end of the workday. After about thirty minutes, though, another vehicle approached the track, and when one of my captains exited from the driver's side, I knew something was wrong.

"Sir, you need to get back to the compound right away," he said. "Something has happened back in the States."

"Yeah, I heard. A plane crash, right?"

He shook his head. "No, it's much more serious than that."

"Are you sure?"

"Yes, sir. We have to go right now; they're going to shut this base down and you're going to be stuck here if we don't leave."

We returned to the compound in tandem; by the time we arrived it was nearly seven o'clock, local time. Kuwait is eight hours ahead of the eastern time zone in the United States, meaning it was shortly after eleven o'clock in the morning in New York. The initial wave of information was nearly overwhelming: There had been terrorist attacks on the Pentagon in Washington and the World Trade Center in Manhattan. The Twin Towers had collapsed and thousands of innocent people were presumed dead. One of the first things I did was call home and let my wife,

Marilyn, know that I was all right, and that in all likelihood we'd be hunkering down for a while. Within minutes after I'd completed that call, all telephone lines were disconnected and the compound was closed, and we ended up sequestered for the next four days; we weren't even allowed to visit the main camp. Security was extraordinarily tight—unlike anything I'd ever experienced.

On the other side of the planet, my country was under attack. I was a career military officer whose life, ostensibly, was devoted to serving and protecting a country now under siege. Yet, I felt oddly disconnected. I know now that for the better part of a week, maybe a month, the attacks of 9/11 dominated every waking moment in the United States. But those of us stationed in the Middle East, ironically enough, did not really share in the immersion, nor in the collective grief that followed. This is not to say we failed to grasp the horror, or that we lacked empathy. We were just so far away. I've thought about this a few times recently—how I was in another world when the attacks took place, and how those very attacks ultimately led to my returning to the Middle East, and a life-changing tour of duty. At the time, however, there was a distance, emotional and physical, that made the enormity of 9/11 difficult to comprehend. My wife shared some news via e-mail, and after a few days phone service was restored; slowly, the details began to seep in. There were benefit concerts, stories of incredible sadness and courage at Ground Zero. Every time Marilyn and I spoke, it seemed she had a dozen stories about the aftermath of 9/11. Still, I had no palpable sense of what it all meant. From Kuwait I went directly to Fort Hood, Texas, for an intense six-week training exercise. It was late October by the time I got home and resumed some semblance of a normal life—except there was no such thing as "normal" anymore. Not for most of the United States, and certainly not for anyone in the military. Everything had changed.

Like most members of my generation, I had spent the vast majority of my military career as a peacetime servant, although I worked hard to prepare for the possibility of combat. I enjoyed the physical demands of Ranger School and the exhilaration of live-fire training exercises. As a young infantry company executive officer on deployment in Honduras in the late 1980s, I felt that the work I was doing was worthwhile. Essentially we were there to conduct counterinsurgency missions in response to the Nicaraguan death squads that were coming across the border and terrorizing poor villages and taking young Honduran men and boys and conscripting them into their insurgent forces. The skirmishes were relatively minor compared to what we experienced in Iraq, but for a young officer with a hard and long competitive streak, it was a mission of profound influence. I felt like I was contributing something to society. There was a teamlike atmosphere to the army at this level, and it seemed as though I was learning something new every day. There was a simplicity and immediacy to life, with no hidden agenda. I was young, single, healthy. I was living a soldier's life, and it didn't seem to be a bad life at all. Granted, I'd never be rich, but that didn't bother me in the least. (Indeed, as I approached the five-year mark and the end of my initial military obligation, I considered entering the private sector; it took only a few interviews, and a close look at the cubicle life, to realize that I was completely unsuited to the suffocation of the nine-to-five world; and that remains true to this day.)

When the United States invaded Panama in December of 1989, my unit was in Panama, and I was awaiting my next assignment in the States. I remember feeling nothing so much as disappointment when I heard the news of Operation Just Cause, as the Panamanian invasion was formally known. If it had happened seven months earlier, the vagaries of scheduling and troop rotation might have led to my active involvement in the mission.

I could have been there . . . missed it by that much!

The "near miss" touches something in all army officers. You spend your life working, training, leading. Inevitably there's a desire to do what you've been trained to do: fight. And to do it *live,* so to speak. Now, in retrospect, I'm not so sure that's a good thing, but I do believe it's unavoidable. The army is such a testosterone-driven organization that virtually everyone, at some point, feels a primal tug. You see soldiers who fought in Vietnam proudly displaying their combat infantryman's badge on their uniforms, and your eyes widen in envy and awe. You hear a couple of war stories about what it's like to see the elephant, about how it feels to pull the trigger, knowing another human being is in your sights, and you wonder . . .

Will I measure up?

I don't know if everyone asks that question, but it certainly ran through my mind: How will I perform when my country calls on me? Will I be able to answer the call and meet the expectation that earlier generations of men have established? The awful truth, of course, is that war is horrible and to be avoided at all costs; yet, if you're a soldier, how do you measure your worth other than by going through it? War changes everyone who experiences it. For some, the changes are on the outside—amputations and other disfigurements. For others, the scars are within. Obviously, some soldiers are also killed, a consequence that alters forever the lives of loved ones left behind. So there is a strong, almost inexplicable dichotomy involved in the soldier's outlook. It is precisely the knowledge that war is terrible that makes it so compelling, and that contributes to the chasm that separates those who have experienced combat from those who have not.

There was a long period in U.S. history (from roughly the end of the Vietnam War in 1975 until the Iraq invasion in 2003) during which it wasn't uncommon for a soldier to serve twenty or twenty-five years without fighting. When an opportunity to fight presented itself, the response was startling. I was a young captain serving at Fort Lewis, Washington, during the Gulf War, and I can vividly recall a sense of yearning at the possibility that we might be summoned. General Norman Schwarzkopf had served in the Third Brigade, Ninth Infantry Division, and that was the unit I was in at the time. The story was that Schwarzkopf had called for just the Third Brigade, Ninth Infantry Division, but the division commander, Major General Chuck Armstrong, resisted splitting the division. So no units over company size from the Ninth ID went to Desert Storm. It's worth noting, however, that a few individual replacement officers made it there. I remember seeing majors and colonels with twenty-five years of experience climbing over each other for an opportunity to serve in Desert Storm, jumping on any available airplane to Kuwait—just so they could put on their right shoulder a patch that signifies combat experience. The truth is, some of these men had no desire to see combat; rather, they were careerists making the most of an opportunity. A lot of career army officers believe that a combat patch will lead inevitably to a promotion, and they're often correct. For the vast majority of soldiers, however, the motivation lies elsewhere. After twenty-five years in the army, they're willing to leave their families and rush off to war because *that's what they're supposed to do.* To the average civilian, I suppose, that seems a bit insane. To a soldier, however, it makes perfect sense.

With the passing of Operation Desert Storm, I settled into the rhythm of a more traditional army life, which is to say, a life of constant movement—of packing and unpacking. Marilyn and I had known each other since middle school, although we did not start dating until I was a cadet at West Point. We waited a few years to marry, so that I could focus on the demands of being a young army officer, but by 1994 we were part of a busy household that also included two beautiful small children, a boy named Nathan and a girl named Nicole. As they do for most young parents, the pages of the calendar fell away in a blur. I received a master's degree in public administration from the University of Washington in 1995; for the next three years we led an idyllic existence at West Point, where I worked as an admissions office representative for the western portion of the United States. I refer to West Point as Camelot, which makes some people laugh, but it really is a special place—and it's so much more pleasant and less stressful the second time around. There were days when I would just stop on my way to work and stare at the architecture, as if I'd never seen it before. As a cadet who was merely trying to survive the undergraduate experience, I had walked past these buildings a thousand times or more, but the beauty had escaped me. Now there was time to take it all in. There was a sense of perspective and history. The job itself was challenging and time-consuming, but highly rewarding and enjoyable. I covered the eleven states west of the Rocky Mountains, visiting schools, meeting with students and counselors, giving presentations at academic fairs. West Point was a terrific place to raise a family—for a former Army football player, it doesn't get much better than being able to toss a Nerf football around with your five-year-old son on the very field where you once played—and Marilyn loved taking daytrips to New York. By the last year of my three-year appointment, however, I was growing restless.

As I climbed through the ranks I tried to focus on the things that I considered important and fulfilling. I stressed physical conditioning and camaraderie, and to that end I'd organize company flag football games that were more like tackle football—minus the pads. I divided the teams along the following lines: officers and noncommissioned officers on one side, everyone else on the other side. The way I saw it, the army was asking enlisted men to work hard, and maybe to risk their lives, for meager compensation. Most of them viewed military service as one of the few viable career options available to them; there was not a lot of joy in their lives. So this was just an opportunity to have some fun, and maybe take out some frustration on the officers. We all played according to one simple rule: What happens on the field stays on the field. Occasionally a little blood was spilled. Sometimes there were fights, but there was a method to the madness: to make the enlisted men feel as though they were on top, if only for an hour or two. It was almost like going to the movies, where you escape from everything for a while. At the end of those games we'd go back into formation and run to our area, and Joe Soldier would go back to being Joe Soldier. Albeit for a short period of time, I got a chance to strip away the leadership and watch the dynamics, and see whether informal leaders would emerge in these kinds of settings.

It all goes back to General MacArthur, who, when he was superintendent at West Point, instituted a policy of mandatory athletic involvement for all cadets. It was MacArthur who said, "Upon the fields of friendly strife are sown the seeds that upon other fields on other days will bear the fruits of victory." I believed in that philosophy then, and I believe in it now. You have to build competitiveness and the will to win in the youngest of soldiers. Sometimes we would do exercises and I'd withdraw the squad leader or sergeant and say, "You're dead . . . you're out," just to see how the squad would react and recover in his absence. This is not an uncommon tactic in the army, where training two levels down is considered strategically prudent. Ideally, if someone is killed in combat, there should be someone at least two levels below that person in rank who is capable of stepping in and taking over. Not everyone adheres to this philosophy, of course, but I was all about empowerment. I think that's the mark of a great unit: when a leader is wounded and the unit can still accomplish its mission in the absence of that leader. In Iraq this formula was often distilled to the simplest of directives: "In the absence of all guidance, please shoot your weapon and kill the enemy." That may sound obvious, but I found that young soldiers under fire frequently become paralyzed with fear, and they look to their leaders for guidance and motivation. I was far more concerned with building toughness in the company, and with encouraging each of my soldiers to be prepared to lead in some capacity.

In all candor, however, it never occurred to me that I would be in a position to command a battalion in a time of war; there are so few people who ever get that opportunity, and I was far down the list in terms of seniority. However, a strange thing happened. After Desert Storm, I was roughly number 120 on the company command queue. Suddenly, though, people started leaving. Officers who had missed out on the Panama invasion and Desert Storm reasonably figured that their time had come and gone—they had missed the fight for their generation, and there would be no more opportunities, so they resigned. As a result, almost overnight, I jumped more than seventy spots on the command queue, and from a four-year wait to a two-year wait. At the very least, it now appeared that I would eventually have an opportunity to command a battalion; and in the wake of 9/11, the possibility that I might lead a combat battalion became increasingly legitimate.

On my next trip to Kuwait, in January of 2002, the mood of the U.S. military was far more sober, its presence in the Middle East dramatically escalated. Our brigade alone was in the process of deploying 25 percent of its total force. When I had departed Kuwait the previous September, Camp Doha was a quiet and relatively peaceful base manned by approximately one thousand U.S. troops. When I returned, just four months later, the place was bursting at the seams. More than six thousand officers and noncommissioned officers were now living at Camp Doha, having been sent from Central Command in Atlanta. These were senior and midlevel planners, as well as support soldiers. It was on this trip that I became somewhat privy to the war plan that obviously had already been put in place. I attended a series of briefings in January, during which there appeared to be some confusion about whether this was to be an offensive or defensive plan, and how either plan would be executed, particularly with regard to coordination between the various branches of the armed services. What struck me, however, was the notion that we were no longer talking merely about how to protect Kuwait's borders in the event that Iraq invaded; considerable time was also devoted to the possibility that a preemptive strike into Iraq might be launched.

In either event, the plan was neither specific nor synchronized. This caused me some concern, since I would be one of the officers on the ground, leading his men into combat. Operation

Desert Shield had remained in place since the end of the Gulf War, and in that time had been subjected to few modifications. Now, more than a decade later, it seemed like we were just dusting off the old war plan and seeing if any of it made sense. There was more than a little confusion in the plan as far as where Kuwaiti forces were supposed to go and where U.S. troops were supposed to go; in short, there was no overarching plan for the defense of Kuwait. Typically, in the previous decade, a tour of duty in Kuwait involved a great deal of boredom, punctuated by the occasional trip to the firing range; I'm not sure battle plans were ever executed in any serious way. A degree of complacency had seeped in, and now, with six thousand people actively discussing the possibility of not merely defending Kuwait with greater gusto, but attacking Iraq, an understandable sense of anxiety swept over the compound.

I'd be lying if I said I was anything less than shocked by this development. Like most people, I presumed we would build some international consensus before employing any sort of military action, much like we had during Desert Storm—but I knew right away things were different. A decade earlier the United States had been part of a coalition of more than two dozen military forces. This time we were clearly alone. I didn't see a German, an Englishman, or an Aussie—just six thousand American officers, all working feverishly on something of obvious importance.

It was around this time that I called my wife and told her that our lives were about to get even more complicated than they'd been in the past. "I think we're going into Iraq and we are going to do it unilaterally, and by God, it's not a matter of *if* we're going to do it, it's a matter of *when*."

Marilyn found this hard to believe; no surprise, really. I was a seventeen-year Army veteran, and I found it hard to comprehend. Not only was it almost inconceivable that we would invade Iraq unilaterally, it was hard to imagine that we were even prepared for such an invasion. From an intelligence standpoint, we didn't know much about Iraq; like North Korea, it was something of a black hole. Moreover, at this point, there had been absolutely no public discourse about Iraq as a potential military target or a threat to U.S. interests. As far as the American public was concerned, we were busy chasing the Taliban and Osama bin Laden through Afghanistan, and that was sufficient. Clearly, though, our military and political leaders had something else in mind. I don't know whether it was President Bush or Secretary Rumsfeld who initially suggested putting this plan in motion, but I do know that when six thousand American officers and noncoms show up in Kuwait, just ninety days after the deadliest terrorist attack on U.S. soil, they have something more ambitious in mind than a planning exercise. It just doesn't work that way. Not since Desert Storm had so many American soldiers been stationed in Kuwait. To my eyes, at least, it was clear that we were going to war. I also suspect rather strongly that the issue had been on the table for quite some time, perhaps long before 9/11.

This, of course, begs the obvious question: Why?

On numerous occasions I had taken briefings with senior officers who said, in effect, "There's only one reason we have a battalion of soldiers rotating through Kuwait every six months, and that's for a three-letter word: O-I-L." That may have been true in Kuwait, but I'm not so sure about Iraq. I spent a lot of time in Iraq, and oil never seemed that abundant or accessible. As the possibility of an invasion of Iraq became increasingly real, another reason was postulated: the presence of chemical weapons, or other weapons of mass destruction, and the likelihood that Saddam Hussein would not hesitate to use them. Again, I'm not buying that excuse. Maybe we found some old mustard gas in Iraq, but there were no hard-core chemical or nuclear weapons anywhere in that country.

I don't think there ever were. I think the Bush administration used the issue of weapons of mass destruction as a legitimizing argument—in other words, for public relations purposes.

So . . . why invade? Well, crazy as it sounds, I think the president really wanted to try to build a Western democracy within a Muslim country in the Middle East. The administration's big mistake was in attempting to create such an elaborate smoke screen, rather than acknowledging the real reasons behind this invasion. I was naive at the time. I didn't really understand why the president felt such a need to build a case for the American people. Why not just be honest? Why not just say, *You know what? 9/11 was really bad. We know there are terrorists in Afghanistan and we think Saddam has been helping finance their operations or letting them train in his country; he's giving them help. And we're just not going to tolerate that. So as part of our war on terror, we're going to begin with Iraq and Afghanistan.* I still think it's brilliant that Bush took the fighting out of the United States and gave the American people a chance to breathe a collective sigh of relief. There is, however, no question that it was intellectually dishonest, and an insult to the intelligence of most Americans. It's like when an officer stands in front of a group of soldiers and uses false motivation; they look at him like he's an idiot.

So it was with the Bush administration. They pushed so hard to make the case against Iraq that in the end, the case became unbelievable. Do I think the president wanted to finish off Saddam? Perhaps. Do I think there was some nobility in ousting a murderous dictator and attempting to give the Iraqi people control over their own destiny? Absolutely. But those weren't sufficient reasons to hastily invade Iraq. Not without first attempting to build a consensus and exhausting every available diplomatic and economic tool at our disposal. The argument that Iraq needed to be "liberated" falls apart for any number of reasons, the most obvious being that there are countless nations whose citizens face even greater oppression and bleakness. We chose Iraq for a simple reason: because we could do it. North Korea is arguably more deserving of our scorn, as is Iran, but both present far greater challenges and the likelihood of greater casualties. My personal feeling was that in the aftermath of 9/11, it was appropriate for the United States military to take some sort of action. Our small-scale invasion of Afghanistan, using primarily Special Forces units, made the most sense, and indeed seemed quite reasonable. Iraq was a different matter entirely. It involved the mobilization of the entire American military, and I think sometimes there is a tendency to forget just what that involves. You see, the army is such an enormous machine that once you've committed it to action, it's gone. It is a giant, overpowering ship that is extraordinarily difficult to turn around; you can't just hit the brakes.

———

Imagine returning from a twelve-month unaccompanied overseas tour of duty working every day for a four-star general in Seoul, South Korea, knowing that you have four short weeks to spend with your family, draw equipment, and receive final instructions from stateside army senior leaders before leaving your loved ones for another year—a year that will find you commanding a United States Army infantry battalion in the heart of the Sunni Triangle in Iraq; a year that will test all your experience as a military leader, challenge your lifelong personal value system, and ultimately bring you the greatest joys of your life, and the absolute worst feelings of despair and hopelessness that humanity can offer.

That was my situation in the spring of 2003. After returning from Kuwait in early 2002, I was sent on an assignment as the deputy of the Commander in Chief's Initiative Group in Seoul, South Korea, working under General Leon LaPorte, one of the

Army's highest-ranking general officers (although my direct supervisor was General LaPorte's special assistant, Brigadier General John Shortal, an expert on Korean affairs who at the time was the only active army officer to hold a Ph.D. in military history). I was a brand-new lieutenant colonel and had reluctantly opted for another year separated from my family for two reasons: (1) it offered the shortest route to battalion commander; (2) the other option, a longer assignment in Germany, would have necessitated relocating my family, which, given the fact that we now had school-age children, seemed less appealing than it might have a few years earlier.

Two weeks after I arrived, Brigadier General Shortal went on a much-needed vacation, leaving me to serve as a temporary special assistant in his absence. The special assistant typically rides next to the four-star general in a bulletproof BMW, accompanies the four-star on all aircraft trips, and generally does whatever the four-star asks him to do. The assistant take notes, tracks down information, provides answers to a thousand different questions each day. It's a different sort of job, and one I wouldn't have wanted to do for any great length of time. For anyone with aspirations of reaching the rank of general officer, however, it represents a significant career opportunity, a chance to see how "Big Army" works. In short, it's a job where you're being groomed for bigger (and supposedly better) things. General LaPorte had hundreds of officers working for him, mostly in personnel, intelligence operations, logistics, and civil affairs. At the top of this complex pyramid were six to eight officers (myself included) who served as the four-star's eyes and ears. The first two weeks were completely disorienting—I couldn't take my eyes off the four stars on General LaPorte's shoulder, and was so nervous that I spoke hardly at all. Over the course of a year, however, I grew more comfortable. It would be a stretch to suggest that we became friends or that General LaPorte took me under his wing, but he certainly knew who I was and was aware of my abilities. Because of my early exposure to the four-star, General Shortal felt comfortable asking me to stand in for him on those occasions when he needed to catch up on work and couldn't spend a weekend flying all over the Korean Peninsula.

Among the many lessons I learned during that tour of duty, perhaps the most valuable was this: If you want to become a general officer, you'd better be a shrewd politician. General LaPorte exercised caution in everything he did; rarely did he go off script. Preparation and rehearsal were hallmarks of General LaPorte, as they are of any four-star general. Sitting in on one of my first video conferences to the Pentagon with General LaPorte, I watched Secretary Rumsfeld stop him cold in the opening minutes of a presentation. Three slides into the briefing, Rumsfeld abruptly halted the briefing and said, "You're showing me nothing new. I was the secretary of defense in 1975, and this is the same old stuff. If you guys can't come up with something more creative than that, I will find somebody who can."

This admonishment was directed not only at my boss, a four-star general in charge of all forces on the Korean Peninsula, but at a four-star admiral as well. From that point on, whenever we'd fly to Washington for briefings with Secretary Rumsfeld, we'd arrive three or four days early, so that General LaPorte could spend time building a consensus among key civilian leaders at the Pentagon. We knew three or four people who were close to Rumsfeld, so my boss would work with these guys to get a feel for where the secretary stood on certain key issues. As information became available, General LaPorte would ask me and other members of his staff to tweak and fine tune our proposals and presentations. This would continue right up until the moment we walked into Rumsfeld's office. The goal, I discovered, was not so much to present opinions and knowledge based on our own experience, but to anticipate what the secretary wanted, and give him that information. It was an invaluable lesson in politics, diplomacy, and careerism, and it made me question whether I was cut out for that sort of life. My boss was an extraordinarily accomplished army officer in his late fifties. Yet, the very prospect of being dressed down by Secretary Rumsfeld left him shaken and sweaty, like a schoolboy going to the principal's office.

Those trips to the Pentagon represented an awakening of sorts; I came to understand that civilians in the government held the power. Never was this more evident than when I watched General Shortal, a fifty-two-year-old, one-star general, briefing one of Rumsfeld's special assistants. He was a kid, really, at least twenty years younger than General Shortal, with an Ivy League diploma on the wall of a large, lavishly furnished office. His only military experience had been a couple years in the National Guard, but in this setting, protocol dictated that General Shortal address him as "sir." Thank goodness I never served at the Pentagon, but I always got the distinct feeling that if you didn't know we were working for civilian bosses, you definitely knew it when you left there. That place was all about the civilian department heads and the civilian secretary of defense. Those guys ran the show, and I do believe that was part of the problem in Iraq, starting with Rumsfeld's insistence that a brief campaign of "shock and awe" would be sufficient to control the country. As we all discovered, boots on the ground—and lots of them—were necessary to do this job right. I'm not sure Rumsfeld ever really understood that or bought into it. It was not a sexy enough solution for him.

Sometimes it's the people who have no firsthand experience with combat who make the worst decisions. Madeleine Albright was that way as well—all fired up to use American forces wherever and whenever she wanted. Power, however, must be utilized carefully and thoughtfully. It's like holding a dove. You want to hold it tight enough to keep it in your hands, but not so tight that you crush it. The military is a tool that needs to be very carefully considered before you unleash it. There are inherent challenges in leading eighteen-year-old kids with no more than high school educations into combat. They do not necessarily understand the importance of diplomacy; they have not been trained to win hearts and minds. They have been trained to fight and win. Period. In my estimation, about 80 percent of Iraqi citizens can be classified as traditional Muslims; 20 percent are extremists or fundamentalists. It was a constant struggle to get our kids to understand that whenever we damaged or destroyed a home while conducting a search, we were encouraging that traditional family to move into the extremist category. It's so difficult and complex. You're asking young soldiers to exercise the power of the American military to wrest control of a situation, then immediately to back off and exercise restraint and maturity and compassion. This would often happen on the same day on which some of their fellow soldiers had been killed or maimed. It was, from the very beginning, an enormously difficult task, one that became increasingly complicated as time wore on, and U.S. forces became viewed less as liberators and more as occupiers.

Midway through my tour of duty in Korea I was informed that my next assignment would be at Fort Carson, Colorado Springs, Colorado (where my wife and children were still living), as commander of the First Battalion, Eighth Infantry Regiment. By January 2003, however, it was apparent that we were going to war, and that my battalion would be deployed to the Middle East. Any excitement I might have felt about this opportunity was tempered by the realization that I would be separated from my family for at least another six months, more likely a full year. The pain of the absence, at least on the home front, would be exacerbated by the specter of war, and the very real possibility that I would be seriously hurt in the line of duty. I called Marilyn right away, of course, and she was predictably nonplussed. She hadn't signed up for two full years of separation and single motherhood. We had agreed that my deployment to Korea was necessary if I was to chase the goal of becoming a battalion commander. Battalion command is all-consuming. It's 24-7, and if you're going to accept the job, you need the complete and total support of your family. So I had placed the decision in Marilyn's hands.

"You've been around battalion commanders. You know what that life is like," I said. "I need to know you're okay with it."

She was, in large part, because she couldn't imagine living with me when we were both in our fifties, wondering what might have been. So I accepted the assignment in Korea with the understanding that in one year's time, I'd be back in the United States, leading a battalion, and our family would be reunited. Instead I found myself on the phone, saying to my wife, "Marilyn, the good news is you get to stay in the house for another year; the bad news is I'll be home for four weeks and then gone for an indefinite period of time."

Let's put it this way: it was not a pleasant conversation. Tears were abundant, as were anger and disappointment. For some couples it could have been a deal breaker, but we decided to try to work through it as best we could.

In March I attended a precommand course at Fort Leavenworth, after which I returned to Korea for the final month of my assignment. In early May I took Marilyn and the kids on a trip to Palm Springs. This turned out to be the best family vacation we ever had, probably because I made a concerted effort to be the nicest, most accommodating father and husband I could possibly be. I'd wake early and make breakfast for the family; I'd cook dinner on the grill in the evening. In between, we took long hikes in the San Jacinto Mountains or just relaxed by the pool. My heart was filled with sorrow the entire week, aching at the prospect of leaving them behind again—leaving a wife I barely knew anymore and two children who could hardly remember what their father looked like after so many deployments all over the world. From a professional standpoint, leading a combat battalion was a terrific opportunity, but from a personal standpoint, it was brutal.

I stayed up late with the kids every night that week, telling stories and holding them close until they fell asleep. It was, in many ways, an idyllic week, and I'm sure Marilyn would say, hands down, it was the best vacation ever. I'm not a laid-back guy by nature, but on this trip I let nothing get in the way. I didn't get upset about lost luggage, clogged highways, poor service, or bad weather. I just wanted the kids to remember their dad in a positive way. If the worst thing happened, and I failed to return from Iraq, at least the final image of their father, one they would carry through life, would be a happy one. We didn't watch the news—didn't even notice that while we were in Palm Springs, the initial phase of the conflict came to an end. U.S. forces had moved into Iraq in March and swiftly overwhelmed any military opposition. Baghdad had fallen in early April, and on May 1, while I was on vacation in Palm Springs, President Bush had stood ceremoniously on the aircraft carrier USS *Abraham Lincoln* off San Diego, in front of a banner declaring MISSION ACCOMPLISHED, and delivered a speech in which he proudly announced that "major combat operations in Iraq have ended."

In hindsight, of course, this was a rather spectacularly ill-informed display of hubris. A few months later, for example, I stood on the tarmac of Samarra East Airfield in Iraq, conducting an interview with CBS News anchor Dan Rather on the eve of a final manhunt for Saddam Hussein. We were all joking around—Rather has a pretty good sense of humor—and all of a sudden the lights went on and he shifted into reporter mode and began to ask a serious question, opening with the words, "Colonel Sassaman, you know the president of the United States has declared all ground warfare complete as of May 1—"

Like the smart aleck that I can sometimes be, I interrupted. "Did we win?"

"What do you mean?"

"Well, if we won, I want to know why I'm still here and why I'm getting ready to go on an air assault mission in this godforsaken land to try to track down Saddam tonight."

Cut!

Eventually we reshot the interview, and I behaved more appropriately. The truth is, President Bush's declaration was terribly misguided, although I think it was completely in line with what Secretary Rumsfeld had been saying. That's why it's hard for me to fault the president. He probably said something like, *We want to win this thing, Don, so go ahead and win it.* They just fed him sound bites. I don't have a real problem with that, either. I don't want the president personally ordering bombing raids, the way Lyndon Johnson did in Vietnam. I applaud Bush for allowing the military leaders to try to pull this thing off, but what he said on May 1 was a mistake, and obviously, the longer the war went on, the worse that statement looked.

There was a small window for success in April, May, or June. After that, I never believed that a swift and bloodless end was possible in Iraq, and the danger associated with commanding the 1-8 Infantry was never far from my thoughts. My concern was not just about my own health and well-being, but with the awesome responsibility associated with leading eight hundred soldiers into combat. This naturally was unspoken during the last days before my deployment, but it hung in the air nonetheless. The short weeks leading up to my departure were a blur of paperwork and preparation—immunizations, the updating of a will, making sure all affairs were in order, as they say. On May 31, the eve of my departure, Marilyn and I took the kids to a local Baskin-Robbins, and we sat together on a curb outside the shop, eating ice cream in silence, holding each other and trying not to cry. I'll be honest—some men like deployments; they welcome time away from their wives and their families—not me. I dreaded leaving home. Never had the sadness felt so palpable as it did that night. I understood that the cause was noble and that this was my destiny. I was an army officer. For any army officer it was an awesome privilege to lead a battalion in a time of war, but I was also scared. I didn't know a single person in the unit I was about to command. I had no idea what waited for me on the other side of the world.

I was a forty-year-old husband and father of two, eating ice cream with my kids at a Baskin-Robbins in Colorado. Was there anything more American than that? Yet, within ten days I'd be crouching nervously in a Black Hawk helicopter—the command control bird—sweat pouring off my chin, with gunfire crackling over the radio, as U.S. forces kicked off Operation Peninsula Strike, wondering . . . *How in the hell did I get here?*

CHAPTER 3

"So, where you headed?"

"Iraq."

That stopped the conversation cold, which was fine by me, since I was miserable and wanted nothing but a little quiet and privacy on the first leg of my journey. I'd risen before dawn and put on a pair of khaki pants and a polo shirt, and I remember looking in the mirror before I left the house and thinking I'd probably never wear either item again. Everything I wore that day, in fact, would likely be burned or tossed out the moment I reached Iraq. From that moment on, I would dress like a soldier.

The trip began with a 5:30 A.M. commuter flight to Denver, followed by a fourteen-hour United Airlines flight from Denver to Frankfurt, and, finally, an eight-hour flight from Frankfurt to Kuwait City, where I arrived around ten o'clock on the night of June 2, 2003. Cryptic messages had been swapped in the preceding days and weeks, leaving me with no real sense of how I would link up with the Fourth Infantry Division. I had been told that someone would meet me at the airport in Kuwait City, but the details were sketchy. All I knew for sure was that I was scheduled to take command of 1-8 Infantry on June 17, somewhere in Iraq's Salah Ah Din Province. How I would get there was anyone's guess.

I'd been to Kuwait City on several occasions in the past, but I remained struck by how it seemed to have enthusiastically embraced Western culture. The smell of fresh coffee wafted up from a Starbucks as I rode an escalator to the airport's main lobby. There was a Pizza Hut, too, and a Burger King. After wandering around for about a half hour, I found a soldier wearing a Fourth ID patch and asked him for a ride to Camp Victory, the sprawling U.S. base that served as a launching pad for all forces entering Iraq. For three days I stayed at Camp Victory, completing more paperwork, reading to pass time, and waiting for the next phase of my journey. Life was pretty good at Camp Victory, with its massive and well-stocked mess tent, air-conditioning, and flat-screen plasma TVs, although I wasn't there long enough to enjoy it, and not exactly in a relaxing mood anyway. At one point I ran into some British troops who were on their way back home after a three-month tour in southern Iraq, and their outlook was decidedly optimistic: *Good to have you chaps here, but the war is over, just mop-up duty now for you mates.*

Eventually it became evident that there was no coherent plan to get me or anyone else north to find our units. We simply reported to the base and waited in a holding tent until there were enough soldiers to merit sending a flight in the general direction of where we were going. Four days passed before I boarded a C-130 flight heading north to Balad Air Base (formerly one of Saddam's huge air bases), which later became Logistics Support Area (LSA) Anaconda. My ultimate destination was Kirkuk, which is north of Tikrit. I didn't mind fending for myself, but I was a bit taken aback by the lack of planning that seemed to have gone into even the most basic of details. By any reasonable definition, I was assuming a fairly important job: battalion commander. Yet here I was, basically thumbing my way north to find my unit. It just seemed . . . odd.

Then again, everything about my experience in Iraq was odd, including the one-hour plane ride from Kuwait City to Balad. As we descended and began our approach to the airfield, with perhaps two dozen soldiers (most of whom were more than a decade younger than I) and a large load of equipment aboard, I heard something outside the plane—*ping-ping-ping*—a sound like hail slapping the roof of a car.

We looked at each other, our faces betraying a collective bemusement: *What was that?*

Then we began to smile nervously as the reality sank in: bullets hitting the side of the plane. *So much for the war being over. Unless that's our guys taking target practice, and missing badly, somebody out there is shooting at us.*

We exited through a large back door, the heat and exhaust slapping our faces and leaving us breathless; it reminded me of the first time I'd landed in Central America—the smell of burning petroleum and the suffocating heat. The terminal—if you could call it that—was nothing more than a concrete shack at the side of the runway. Inside, manning the counter—running the entire airport, really—were two air force sergeants. Behind them, on a wall, was a chalkboard with the names of various cities and/or airfields scrawled in capital letters: BAGHDAD . . . TIKRIT NORTH . . . TIKRIT SOUTH . . . KUWAIT CITY. Listed next to each of these locations was the type of aircraft scheduled to carry passengers to their destination. Below that was, essentially, a sign-up sheet: the names of every passenger looking for a ride to that particular city.

Not long after I arrived at the terminal I ran into a young female specialist who had just flown in from Baghdad after learning that her father had passed away. She was trying to arrange transportation back to the United States so that she could attend his funeral the next day. I couldn't help but feel sorry for her—there was no chance that she was going to get there in time; in fact, given the sorry and confused state of this airfield, I couldn't imagine her getting out of Iraq by the end of the day, and I couldn't help but wonder why everything seemed so disorganized and haphazard. There were people sprawled out on the terminal floor; there was no food or water. I slept on a pallet right outside the building. Fortunately, there was no gunfire during the night, surprising, really, since more than a few people had said that there was some occasional fire in and around Balad Air Base, and after what had happened during our C-130's approach, I didn't doubt them. Later, however, as I got a better feel for the topography, I figured out that the small-arms fire had probably come from a handful of lightly armed insurgents hiding in some heavy vegetation not far from the base. I still don't know what rocket scientist chose this particular site for a U.S. airfield, since it wasn't exactly the safest of locations.

Balad Air Base was not out in the open desert; rather, it was snug against the Tigris River, the banks of which were shielded by triple-canopy jungle. My unit ended up being responsible for Balad Air Base—which ultimately became a sprawling five-square-mile U.S. base—and one of the problems we encountered was that the insurgents figured out that the location worked to their benefit. They could effectively put fire into the base, knowing full well that we could not retaliate without either crossing the Tigris or having direct and immediate access to another unit already located on the other side of the river. Tactically speaking, it was simply an unsound place to put the largest supply base for the U.S. Army in Iraq. It wasn't like Danang, in Vietnam, where the army wisely cut down entire forests, creating open space for miles beyond the runway. Here, at Balad, the vegetation rimmed the runway. It was foolish, and it was dangerous.

I had only a vague sense of this at the time. For the most part, the base was quiet. There was a MASH hospital and an air-field, but not much else. By the time I left the country, a year later, this base had been transformed into a showcase, with fast-food joints, bowling alleys, an officers club, paved roads, and sidewalks. It was completely over the top. In early June of 2003, however, it was stark and lifeless. There were no patrols and no weapons. I didn't even have a pistol to protect myself, the impli-cation being, I guess, that protection wasn't necessary. The war, after all, was over.

The following day I hopped a flight on a Chinook helicopter to Tikrit North, where Fourth Infantry Division's support area was located. There I found someone wearing a Fourth ID patch, so I knew I was getting close. I got on the radio, called brigade head-quarters, gave them my location, and asked for advice.

"Should be a couple Black Hawks flying out of there soon," they said. "Try to catch one of them."

So I dragged my stuff outside, walked about a mile down the road, and found two Black Hawk helicopters sitting idly, pilots at the ready.

"You guys going to Kirkuk?"

One of the pilots nodded. I tossed my gear into the back and climbed aboard. On the choppy forty-five-minute ride to Kirkuk, the adrenaline started pumping. We were north of Baghdad— seriously in-country—and I wondered what the next few hours and days would hold.

One of the first people I met in Kirkuk was Colonel Frederick Rudesheim, the brigade commander. Things were fine between us in the early days. Fred, as far I could tell, took his role very seriously: he wanted to train everyone and impart wisdom to his young officers. Fred was supposed to be my mentor, which was a little awkward, since he was only about four years older than I, but then, that's a common problem in the army. Most of my company commanders were in their late twenties, so there was a chasm of experience issues between us, and it made sense for them to act as students. It's a little different when you're talking about a lieutenant colonel and a full colonel, a battalion commander and a brigade commander. At this point, however, I was eager to soak up as much information as possible, so I embraced the opportunity to take what was supposed to be a weeklong "right-seat ride" with Colonel Rudesheim, during which I would basically shadow his every move. At the end of the week I would have a pretty good feel for brigade operations, his standards and his command philosophy, and theoretically be prepared to assume control of 1–8 Infantry.

From what I could discern, the brigade had been moving north at an incredibly rapid pace since the middle of April, rarely staying in one place for more than a few days or a week. They'd blown through one airfield after another—each time they'd set up a perimeter, secured the area, and then moved on. Unfortunately, as we later discovered, as soon as U.S. forces left, the locals would come in and loot the bases, taking, among other things, tons of weapons and ammunition. Generally speaking, these forward battalions were living off the land, with no real area of operation and no clear objective or mission. By the time I showed up they had moved as far north as Kirkuk and were beginning to loop back around to the south. The division had decided to establish headquarters in Tikrit. The First Brigade, commanded by

Colonel Jim Hickey (whose units later had the distinction of finding and capturing Saddam), would be responsible for the northern part of the division's area of operation (AO); Colonel Dave Hoag and the Second Brigade would cover Baquba and the surrounding area, located farther south and east of the Tigris; Colonel Rudesheim and Third Brigade would be in the middle, closer to Balad. The division's AO was shaped like an L, with Tikrit at the top of the L, Balad at the bottom, and Baquba at the lower right. Later, when people would talk about the Sunni Triangle, the center of so much violence in Iraq, they would be talking about an area in which Balad proper was basically the dead center. This was where 1-8 Infantry eventually set up its headquarters.

Riding with Colonel Rudesheim was an interesting, if somewhat disconcerting experience. I got the feeling pretty quickly that we approached our jobs differently. I was into fitness and training and preparation; I liked the idea of being a soldier, and I wanted my units to be physically and mentally prepared to fight. I tried not to sweat the small stuff. Fred, in contrast, seemed fussy to the point of obsession. He liked to ride around and stop soldiers whose uniforms weren't exactly right. Admittedly, some of it made sense—your helmet should always be strapped tightly in a combat zone—but some of it just seemed like a waste of time and energy. I would later come to realize that this was just the type of person Fred was; in my opinion, he was better suited to peacetime leadership.

My right-seat ride with Fred ended up being cut short, thanks to an impending mission known as Operation Peninsula Strike. I was dropped off at Samarra East Airfield, located just north of Balad Air Base, on July 11, five days before I was scheduled to take command, and began a long meeting with Lieutenant Colonel Phil Battaglia, the outgoing battalion commander of the 1-8 Infantry. I'd met Phil briefly when I first arrived, but hadn't realized until now just how tired he seemed. Phil was clearly ready to leave Iraq. He'd been in command of the 1-8 Infantry for two and a half years, which was an anomaly attributable to the war; a typical battalion command spans two years, but Phil, like many others, was locked in when we invaded Iraq. The job had obviously taken its toll. His eyes were hollow, his shoulders slumped, and he spoke with the cadence of a man long deprived of sleep. I had received mixed reports on Phil—some people claimed that he had done a competent job as battalion commander; others disputed that assessment. I was not yet in a position to judge, and surmised only that he appeared to be extremely exhausted.

The sun was setting on Phil's command, and I don't think he was overly concerned with making much of an impact anymore, but I do know that he was generous in sharing his experience and knowledge with me. It's not always like that during a change of command. Some officers are so territorial that they won't even speak with the person who will be taking their place. Not Phil. He held nothing back—the good, the bad, and the ugly—and there was a lot of ugly. He knew there were problems in the unit, in terms of personnel and logistics, and wanted me to be aware of them. Beyond that, Phil invited me to attend meetings with some of the officers, and would even solicit my opinion in these settings. Finally, a couple days before the official change of command, Phil encouraged me to start making decisions and giving orders on my own, with him serving as backup. This may seem perfectly reasonable and logical, since I'd be taking over, and the decisions I would make might have a profound impact on the lives of the soldiers in 1-8 Infantry. You'd be surprised how rare it is for an outgoing commander to be so benevolent toward his replacement. Whether this grew out of a generosity of spirit on Phil's part, or was simply a by-product of his exhaustion, I don't know, but I do know it helped make my job easier.

Not that it was, in any way, an easy job.

Operation Peninsula Strike was a massive effort conducted by more than one thousand U.S. troops over a period of roughly one week in the middle of June. Encompassing a series of raids centered around Ad Duluwiyah, a sleepy Sunni village on the banks of the Tigris where many of the higher-ranking officials in Saddam's government had vacation homes, Operation Peninsula Strike was at once a mighty display of American military force and a classic example of poor execution and intelligence. The idea was to cast a wide net and capture hundreds of targets using joint military forces. (This was a commonly employed technique in the early stages of the war, and one that would rapidly give way to specific raids on specific targets based on multiple, specific intelligence hits.) In the end we detained and interrogated nearly four hundred Iraqis, but all but a dozen or so were quickly released. In this group were several hard-core Saddam Fedayeen planners, financiers, and tactical leaders, along with a couple of two-star generals. The methods employed, from the very beginning, however, were crude.

The 2nd Battalion, 503rd Infantry Division, based in Vicenza, Italy, led the assault. Unfortunately, the mission began horribly, with a nontactical vehicle—in this case, a white Toyota truck—spearheading the attack into the peninsula area. This was a catastrophic mistake, inasmuch as a military police (MP) battalion had previously infiltrated the area and set up checkpoints along key avenues of approach. Orders had been given to fire at any nontactical vehicles approaching any of the checkpoints. Apparently, however, this had not been sufficiently communicated to the 503rd, so when the white truck came barreling down the road at one o'clock in the morning, the MPs opened fire. Thus did Operation Peninsula Strike begin with four U.S. soldiers being wounded—in a couple cases, seriously wounded—by friendly fire. I was up in the command control helicopter when this went down, the news crackling over the radio that lead units from the 503rd had been attacked. I remember thinking, *Either they've got us all figured out, or we just shot our own guys.* Frankly, I didn't know which was worse. I only knew that my first live action was quickly becoming a soup sandwich, which is another way of saying . . . FUBAR . . . SNAFU.

By the time I took command, on June 17, Operation Peninsula Strike was in its waning stages. Detainees were held at Samarra East Airfield, and the first time I saw them, sitting cross-legged on the tarmac, hands bound behind their backs with flex cuffs, white robes drenched with sweat in the 120-degree heat, I was somewhat dismayed.

"Is this the way we treat detainees?" I asked Colonel Rudesheim.

Fred nodded, then responded, soberly, "It's an intelligence unit running the operation; I'm sure they know what they're doing."

I was still naive, still the minister's son prone to empathy even in the darkest of circumstances (this would not always be the case, I must admit). I looked at these guys, some of them significantly overweight, and was legitimately concerned for their health. We had them sitting on a blistering hot tarmac for hours, with no food or water. To me it just seemed a bit inhumane. To be fair, I don't believe cruelty was the objective. Rather, the mission simply hadn't been thoroughly planned; no one had given due consideration to the aftermath: what do you do with four hundred detainees? Intelligence officers were trying to determine their names, and then check to see if the names matched with any of the targets on our Most Wanted list. A sophomoric approach, of course, since there was no assurance that any of the detainees would provide an accurate name.

At one point during Operation Peninsula Strike, I noticed a cloaked figure walking among the American soldiers, assisting in the interrogation process. When I inquired as to his background, I was told, "That's the guy who set this whole thing up for us."

"Why the mask and the hood?" I asked.

"Because he doesn't want any of his Iraqi buddies to see him; he's the one who ratted everybody out. If they find out, he's a dead man."

So, in the end, the relative success or failure of Operation Peninsula Strike—a weeklong mission utilizing a massive combination of air force and army assets—came down to the reliability of information supplied by a single Iraqi citizen. Not long afterward, I would find out, this was not a happy man; he was, in fact, quite disgruntled with a number of things that had happened to him over the years in Ad Duluwiyah. This was his opportunity for payback, so he started pointing out people he didn't like, for whatever reason. Compared to the way we would conduct strikes in later months—never hitting a target unless we had solid intelligence from multiple specific sources and were absolutely certain the target was active—this was amateur hour.

I took command of the 1-8 Infantry on June 17, 2003, on a blistering hot day at Samarra East Airfield just outside of Ad Duluwiyah. I briefed the Fourth Infantry Division commander, Major General Raymond Odierno, and was told, "You have three weeks before you go south of the Tigris River and assume your new area of operations." As a brand-new battalion commander with a new battalion executive officer, five new company commanders who had changed out or were scheduled to change out in the next two weeks, and no operations officer as of yet, I knew we had little time to get to know one another and begin military and reconstruction operations in Iraq.

My first impressions of Ad Duluwiyah were sobering: hundreds of young Iraqi men lined the village streets as we patrolled. This was a direct result of Ambassador L. Paul Bremer III and the Coalition Provisional Authority's decision to disband the Iraqi army (easily one of the top three major policy blunders of the war). In Ad Duluwiyah, a Sunni town, not a single one of these men was waving or trying to be friendly. This, as it turned out, was just the beginning of the Iraqi insurgency. U.S. forces probably had a window of opportunity to seize the initiative in the reconstruction of Iraq between the time that we began the invasion in March of 2003 to the end of June. That period represented a time when (mostly) clueless Army Civil Affairs officers traveled all over the country delivering amazing promises to the Iraqi people about how their lives were going to change overnight, thanks to the United States providing great and unending piles of money for reconstruction. However, when the Iraqis realized there was no real plan for rebuilding or reconstruction—no clear-eyed formula for anything that happened after the initial "shock and awe"—and how glacial was the process of acquiring and implementing aid, then how incredibly insignificant the early aid turned out to be, the populace began to turn on the American forces. By July 1, the insurgency had capitalized on the first of many American unfulfilled promises. Using influential imams and local leaders highlighting America's lack of will and commitment, the insurgency waged an impressively successful information operations campaign, turning the common, traditional Iraqi families against the American units. Almost overnight the attacks on U.S. forces began and an insurgency was born, paving the way for a guerrilla war that continues to this day.

The other thing we all noticed at our base camp at Samarra

East Airfield was the incessant gunfire south of the Tigris River. The Sunni-Shia Muslim fault line ran right through Balad and Azziz-Balad (a suburb north of the city), and as a result we often were witness to red tracers arcing high into the night sky; we'd listen to the nightly AK-47 and RPK-74 machine-gun automatic fire south of the river, fully realizing that we would be in the thick of this fight—probably sooner rather than later. The combination of seeing large groups of young Iraqi males wandering the streets during the daylight hours, and then fireworks south of the Tigris in the evening, had at least one positive effect: it helped everyone in the outfit become more focused and alert. We ramped up our live-fire training on the base and tried to stay sharp with daily mechanized and foot patrols in and around Ad Duluwiyah. I referred to these three short weeks as the preparation phase. It was only the prelude before we entered what would come to be known as the 100 Days of Hell.

Although still somewhat disoriented and concerned about what appeared to be a distinct lack of anything resembling a master plan for Operation Iraqi Freedom, I was, in those early days at least, a tireless and enthusiastic battalion commander committed to achieving the admittedly nebulous objectives put forth. Our stated mission was simply this: *to provide security and stability for our area of operations, and to eliminate all violence.* It was left largely up to the individual battalion commanders to figure out precisely how to realize these goals. I considered "security and stability" to be virtually indistinguishable from "no violence." Without security and stability, there would be violence. That much seemed obvious. Beyond this, we were expected to aid in the reconstruction of Iraq, either through the construction (or reconstruction) of clinics, schools, hospitals, and government buildings, or by sowing the seeds of small, democratic economies at a grassroots level.

The pace at which all of this was supposed to occur was rather alarming—the soldier's mantra, after all, was "Home before Christmas"—and a great many people, myself included, believed that we'd be out of Iraq sometime in the fall. In retrospect, this was a painfully ill-informed assessment of the job, but it did not feel that way at the time. When I met with General Odierno on June 17, for my first official briefing as commander of 1-8 Infantry, I could not have been more enthusiastic or ambitious. While I had become increasingly flexible and secure in terms of leadership style (as a young officer I was fairly rigid; now I had no qualms about asking for advice and delegating authority), I remained a type A personality who had never believed it was necessary or productive to slowly ease into a new position. I figured there was no need to spend two weeks walking around deciding what looked right and what didn't look right. It's pretty simple, really: if the guy before you was doing something stupid, and now you're in charge and you keep doing it, then you're responsible and you're stupid for letting it continue that way. So while I didn't say much during my right-seat ride with Colonel Rudesheim and Lieutenant Colonel Battaglia, in my head I compiled a checklist of things that would be changed the moment I became battalion commander. That started with the battalion tactical operations center (TOC), which had been employing a half dozen soldiers working four-hour shifts.

The TOC was the battalion's nerve center, with most important information passing through its ranks. Short, constantly changing shifts resulted in disruptions in the flow of information. In the real Army, TOC shifts typically span twelve hours, with an hour of overlapping transition time, so the second shift has been adequately briefed by the first shift, and vice versa. So when I assumed command, I said, "Okay, we're going to pretend we're in the real army now. We'll have two shifts, twelve hours each." Then I turned to my sergeant major and said, "You're the man, dude, so go ahead and make that happen." Living conditions for the troops were, frankly, appalling. We set up the TOC and other administrative offices in a series of abandoned ammunition bunkers, with no fans or air-conditioning. The heat was stultifying, with relief coming only in the evening hours, and the two liters of water rationed to each soldier was completely inadequate for maintaining hydration. Food, such as it was, came in the form of field rations (also known as an MRE, or meal, ready to eat). So right off the bat I went on a campaign to secure more water, ice for coolers (so that the water would be drinkable), and one hot and healthy meal per day. One of the bunkers was turned into a mess hall, and the first air conditioner we procured went into that bunker, so that guys could eat in relative comfort, and take a break from the heat and stress of their work. Mail was an issue as well, as was personal hygiene. So I made sure that mail calls became more frequent, and I authorized permission to build makeshift shower units. The goal was to boost morale as much as anything else. On the first night of my command, I addressed all of the officers; over the course of the next two days I addressed the noncommissioned officers and the enlisted men. Each time, I spoke from the heart about my background and my philosophy about our mission. I had laid all of this out in advance and given it the name Eagle Vision, the foundation of which was the Eagle 7:

1. **Always do the right thing.**
2. **Respect others. Treat others with respect—everyone matters.**
3. **Build teams through shared physical and mental pain and suffering.**

4. Be all you can be—give 110 percent.

5. Find a way and make it happen.

6. Never let a fat guy pass you.

7. Have fun—make your tour memorable.

Additionally, I tried to personalize my introduction by talking about my uncle, who had served in Vietnam, and whose lasting memory of the experience seemed to be the camaraderie as much as the carnage. He used to talk about returning to the fire bases after a day of patrolling, and then grilling steaks and drinking beers with his buddies. While this wasn't exactly what I had in mind, I did see the value of giving the soldiers a break when they weren't on duty.

"We want our guys to be able to fight outside the wire, but when they come inside, they have to feel comfortable taking off their helmets," I said. "They need cool water and a comfortable place to sleep."

Each address was emotional and from the gut. I reminded them that there were only about a half million soldiers representing the United States, and of that number, approximately one hundred thousand would be serving in Iraq. "That's a small percentage of Americans fighting for what we think is right. So you're part of a select group; you're really earning your citizenship."

The message was one of hope, honor, pride. I wanted them to believe there was something positive in the work they were doing, in part because I believed it, but also because they appeared to be a downtrodden, tired group of soldiers and officers—and they hadn't been in Iraq that long; they hadn't even fired their weapons yet. Still, they were beaten; clearly they did not feel good about what they were doing.

So I pulled out all the stops. I invoked the memory of World

War II, reminded them that 1-8 Infantry had been in Normandy on June 6, 1944, storming Utah Beach as part of the D-day invasion. "You're following in the footsteps of some real heroes who have fought in this regiment," I said. "This is something you'll remember forever . . . something you'll be able to share with your grandkids. You'll tell them about our noble efforts, and about how we looked after one another."

To be sure, there were some extraordinary men and women in this battalion. One of them was our senior medic, Wayne Slicton, a physician's assistant and army reservist, introduced to me on the day I took command. Wayne, I was told, had served as a major in the Gulf War. He had also fought in Vietnam as a young Special Forces medic. Wayne, it turned out, was fifty-five years old. He'd been all set to retire when the United States invaded Iraq, and he felt that if the country was going to war one more time, he had a responsibility to be there. I was one of the oldest guys in the battalion, but I was a kid compared to Wayne, who looked like somebody's grandfather. Keep in mind that serving as a medic is not exactly a safe and docile job. Medics, especially in guerrilla wars, end up in the thick of combat, right in the line of fire. That Wayne had decided to join the cause, with no provocation whatsoever, filled me with pride and awe.

As battalion commander I was authorized to award Army Achievement Medals. There was some confusion as to whether these were peacetime awards or combat awards; I couldn't have cared less. I had asked General Odierno during our briefing that day whether I was authorized to hand out Army Achievement Medals, and he had looked at me like I was from another planet. "Of course," he had said. So during my tour of duty I authorized approximately two thousand Army Achievement Medals because I was all about honoring performance. Wayne Slicton was the first to receive one of those awards. I made sure that everyone understood what a special role Wayne played, and how extraordinary it was that this man who had already fought in two wars was now back for another tour.

"I want everybody in this room to get a good look at this guy," I said. "We're going to take good care of Wayne because he's going to take good care of our soldiers."

That proved to be exactly right. Wayne was an astoundingly upbeat and generous officer, as well as a gifted medic. He saved lives over there not just because of what he did with his own hands (although there was that, too), but because he was so calm and reassuring, and so diligent in the training of young medics.

Every new officer who joined 1-8 Infantry was required to pass a series of tests before taking command of his platoon and going out on patrol with it. In addition to taking a right-seat ride with me, he had to demonstrate proficiency in physical training and weapons use. He had to pass a combat lifesaving course; he had to know how to call for a medevac and for artillery fire missions. He had to understand and believe in the Eagle Vision. In no way was this meant to stroke my own ego; it was merely to ensure that the officers were competent and confident before they went out to lead thirty-five young soldiers in combat. In some cases they never got out, because they couldn't do what I wanted them to do. This became the basis for running the entire battalion: demonstrated proficiency in skills that I considered crucial to protecting and leading soldiers in combat. In Vietnam there was something called the Golden Hour. We called it the Eagle 30. I told soldiers, "You signed on the dotted line, you took the oath, you're over here serving your country. If one of you is wounded, you need to know that as your battalion commander, I will make sure that we do everything possible to get you to a MASH hospital in thirty minutes or less. You deserve to know that; you deserve to know that we will stop everything we're doing to save your life and not let you die on the battlefield. We will get you to a hospital, and you should know that once there, the odds are 99.9 percent that you will live."

As much as I believed in order and discipline, I understood that in a time of war, territoriality and strict adherence to protocol can have deadly consequences. One of the first rules I laid out encouraged the crossing of boundaries. Specifically, I said that if an American unit came in contact with the enemy, anybody within range was free to travel to that point of contact and participate in the fight. My philosophy (and I still think it's sound) was to crush the ant with a sledgehammer. In my battalion there was no requirement to get on the radio and ask permission to join the fray. You were free to move. This applied to anyone, whether it was an American soldier or a contractor. Believe me—a chill goes down your spine when you're listening to the brigade net, and you hear that a sister battalion's vehicle has been hit by a rocket-propelled grenade or an improvised explosive device, and they're screaming on the net for help, and on the other end of the line is a specialist at the battalion TOC calmly asking for grid coordinates, while all hell is breaking loose at the scene of the attack. You hear the shouting and the crying and the explosions, and you realize you're listening to the sounds of another man dying . . . another soldier dying. It breaks your heart. I heard several of these exchanges, and each followed a familiar pattern. They began calmly, with an officer trying to remain focused and assured, asking for backup. Then the pleas would grow louder and more frantic as the TOC botched up the coordinates and the support teams scrambled to help. In the end everything would go calm again.

"Never mind," someone would report. "It's too late."

You'd realize that the wounded soldier had expired. Fifty

minutes had elapsed since the initial attack and call for help, and the unit was still alone. Now someone was dead. It was inexcusable, and my way of dealing with this monumental screwup was to bypass the procedure entirely, to tell my soldiers that if they heard of another unit in trouble, they were free to provide assistance. Things like that, for me, were nonnegotiable, and that's why later on, as things became more confusing and markedly more dangerous, I made some of the decisions I made. Early on I decided that 1-8 Infantry would never patrol with less than platoon-level combat power, and that we would never run from a fight; moreover, we would drop everything to save one of our own in a fight. When this precept was not followed, oftentimes patrols were attacked, soldiers were killed or wounded, and our own actions on the enemy were far less lethal. Sufficiently armed and trained in this way, we always had enough soldiers to secure the perimeter, tend to the wounded, and evacuate the friendly wounded. We'd also have enough combat power to return fire, and to close with and destroy the enemy (something many units neglected to do). What happened all too often was that an American unit would come under fire, stop, secure the perimeter, treat and evacuate their friendly wounded . . . and then leave. There would be no further action. This effectively permitted the enemy to retreat back into the jungle or urban area to fight another day.

It would take some time, however, before any of these measures could be employed in a practical way. Aside from the friendly-fire blunder of Operation Peninsula Strike, and the occasional motor vehicle accident, I neither saw nor heard of many casualties in those first few weeks. Sloppiness or, in same cases, outright stupidity contributed heavily to the ranks of the wounded in those days. Shortly before I assumed command, for example, there was a company commander named Sean McDermott who had inexplicably ordered his unit to destroy a deserted ammunitions bunker that was of no danger to anyone. A more prudent measure would have been to confiscate the ammo, but Captain McDermott chose to issue an order that was inherently dangerous; moreover, he opted to stand atop his Bradley as the bunker erupted, thereby not only gaining a better view of the fireworks, but also assuring that he would be a likely target in the event of some unforeseen circumstance, such as shrapnel flying back at the Bradley and hitting the captain in the shoulder. Which is precisely what happened. Captain McDermott sustained injuries sufficient to warrant evacuation to the United States, where he was not reprimanded for his foolishness and hubris, but rather awarded the Purple Heart. That is the sort of thing that makes a seasoned army officer want to laugh and cry. It is the army way to chug along and do things as it has always done them, regardless of circumstances, so an irresponsible officer is treated like a hero for shooting himself (and that's basically what happened), which detracts from the accomplishments and heroism displayed by every soldier who has been legitimately wounded in combat. That just makes me sick. Everyone knew about this incident; everyone knew how ridiculous and almost comical it was, yet the guy still received the Purple Heart.

That provides some insight into the twisted logic of warfare. While it's true that not everyone was eager to fight, it is also true that there was no shortage of people who would have done almost anything to get a Bronze Star, Purple Heart, or Combat Infantryman Badge (CIB). Short of dying, of course, although I knew some people, miswired in ways obvious and disconcerting, for whom even mortality wasn't much of an obstacle.

On the flip side were the soldiers who wanted no part of combat. They were kids, for the most part, young men and women (although females were just a tiny percentage of my battalion, I can say with assurance they all served with distinction) for whom the army provided a viable alternative to a lousy, low-paying job. Some had enlisted because they had nowhere else to go; others had joined the service as a way to help defray the cost of college; and then there were those who had been inspired by the events of 9/11 to fight for their country. Any and all of these seemed like legitimate reasons to me, and for the most part I viewed these young soldiers with admiration; I wanted to protect them and help them learn to protect themselves. Sometimes, though, it was an insurmountable task. I spent a fair amount of time one night talking with an eighteen-year-old kid from Alaska, asking him how he was adapting and if he had any concerns or questions I could answer. I sensed he was having some trouble, that he was scared and confused, and it turned out my worries were well founded. This kid, along with one other young soldier, ended up going absent without leave (AWOL) in spectacular—and spectacularly illegal and public—fashion. Early in the morning on the day the army chief of staff, General Peter Schoomaker, visited our unit, these two guys, armed with M16s, hijacked an Iraqi citizen and his privately owned vehicle, and ordered the man to drive them to Kuwait. An ill-advised scheme, as it happened, since they were stopped at 2:00 A.M. at one of our sister battalion's checkpoints on Highway 1. The laundry list of charges included, most prominently, desertion, and the two men were summarily court-martialed and sentenced to lengthy prison terms (eight and nine years, respectively) at the military prison in Leavenworth, Kansas.

I certainly didn't anticipate that he was capable of anything quite so dramatic. Like so many kids in the Army, he seemed to be a little scared, unsure of what to expect. We'd had little or no contact at this point; there was a sense that the war was over and that we were merely trying to maintain control and limit unrest until a new government was in place. In the interim, we would magically rebuild this broken third-world country and restore services to the citizenry, and then just sort of disappear. Comparatively speaking (and by that I mean in comparison to what would transpire in the ensuing months and years), it was not a bad time: nightly patrols and interesting missions were executed with little concern for contact. That said, it was hardly an experience that could be termed pleasant. It was incredibly hot and uncomfortable. The soldiers didn't have enough water, and the food was generally awful. For some reason, dog-faced infantrymen are used to it—or at least, they're expected to tolerate it without complaint. My whole philosophy was, *We don't have to work at sucking, because this place already sucks. Let's do our best to get morale up.* This meant trying to improve conditions on the base, and ensuring that safety was paramount in everyone's mind when executing a mission. I made it clear that if I found a soldier outside the wire failing to wear his helmet or load-bearing vest, I would immediately fire that soldier's platoon leader and platoon sergeant. On the spot. Nonnegotiable. In my battalion, you did not go outside the wire without taking the proper precautions; there was no way I wanted to write a letter back to Johnny's mother and father explaining that stupidity killed their son—that the reason he died was because he was hot and wanted to take his helmet off. Sorry, but that wasn't going to happen on my watch. Better to be uncomfortable than dead.

So the early days were all about instituting changes and meeting the soldiers, along with training staff and junior officers in the art of military decision making. I devised an initial training mission called Operation Eagle Strike, in which the objective was to seize a target in an abandoned area. I thought it made sense to practice this sort of thing before heading south of the Tigris River to do it for real, and I even invited Colonel Rudesheim to fly in and offer his assessment. Fred, in another lifetime, had worked at the National Training Center, so he knew how to grade performances in training situations. I was obsessed with improving my staff's performance, then getting the entire battalion to think the way we should be thinking before we ventured south, where the prospect of real combat was significantly greater.

Meanwhile, some of the 1-8 companies were still maintaining a presence in Ad Duluwiyah. They operated out of abandoned schools and community centers, and when I visited some of these places, I was struck by how unsafe they seemed, and how unfazed the troops appeared. Security was inadequate, guys didn't have the proper gear, and weapons were not held at the ready. It was disturbing, even frightening. My response was to jack some guys up immediately. "I know you may have missed my briefings because they were back at the base," I said, "but this is the way it's going to be from now on."

I treated those first few weeks in Iraq like a more intense version of training at home. We used live rounds. I encouraged everyone to understand that there was a purpose and seriousness to our work, and that despite the absence of anything resembling a cohesive enemy force, it was a dangerous job. Real fear, however, requires a spark, and it hadn't come yet. Each time I walked through the streets of Ad Duluwiyah, though, and saw the looks on the faces of the young Iraqi men, former soldiers with time on their hands, access to weapons, and no legal way to put money in their pockets or food on their tables, I grew uneasy. There were hundreds of them, just hanging out and looking for something to do with their anger and energy. Sometimes we'd stop and try to talk to them, but the conversations, even with the benefit of interpreters, were stilted and unpleasant. It was apparent that they were in some sort of holding pattern—testily waiting to see whether the Americans would make good on their elaborate promises. Soon enough, their patience would erode, and when that happened, Iraq would become a far less welcoming place for American soldiers, and Operation Iraqi Freedom would become a full-fledged guerrilla war.

Our inability to cope with the flood of young, unemployed, disgruntled Iraqi males was a central failure of Operation Iraqi Freedom. I wondered in the first weeks of my command why no one had anticipated the consequences of disbanding the Iraqi army. Surely there was some way that we could have utilized the talents and energy of these people. Maybe not all of them, but a portion, at least, could have been kept on the payroll to help secure the bases that were abandoned during the drive north. It all goes back to common sense, and the logic of Sun Tzu, whose classic treatise on battle and the warrior spirit includes the following sentiment (paraphrased and adapted for these purposes, of course): *An insurgent with a full stomach is a less defiant and angry insurgent.* If we could have just given some of these guys a few hot meals and some economic promise, I think it would have taken the fight out of them early on, and made our job far more manageable.

That didn't happen. So, nearly four years later, I would find myself at a coffee shop in Colorado Springs, browsing *USA Today* and shaking my head at a front-page story about the ongoing conflict in Iraq, and the devastating effects of IEDs on U.S. forces. The thrust of the story was this: most IEDs had been manufactured using material heisted from munitions bunkers throughout the country in the early, ill-defined stages of the war. This came as no shock to me. U.S. forces had plowed through Balad Air Base back in May and June of 2003, before driving north to Kirkuk and circling back around to hit Tikrit. By mid-June, around the time I arrived, the Fourth Infantry Division had returned to Balad. We would spend the next year fighting the local populace, particularly the young men who had once been soldiers in the Iraqi army, and who now were armed to the teeth with thousands of munitions rounds, RPGs, and mortars that Saddam had stockpiled at this particular base. The madness of it was overwhelming. More than three years after my departure from Iraq I was reading about some army munitions geek explaining the importance of destroying the munitions that provided source material for the insurgents. We knew within two months of the invasion that we had screwed up in a major way, because we had now returned to Balad Air Base and the weapons were gone! Why? Because, supposedly, we needed only 120,000 soldiers to win this thing. Actually, to hear some senior-level administrators explain it, we didn't need any soldiers . . . no boots on the ground. Bombs over Baghdad—*shock and awe!*—were sufficient.

We knew that colossal errors had been made, and on more than one occasion I turned to my fellow commanders and said, "This is going to take a long time." Tragically, though, it didn't need to be that way. We had control of these bases. We could have secured each and every one of them, and destroyed every available weapon. Because there was such an intensity to drive north and find Saddam, by the time we started cutting off regions and areas of operation, it was too late: the bases had been raided— bases that we had already cleared! Here I was, nearly four years later, reading a newspaper story about an insurgency fueled by unlimited munitions that we had once held in our grasp. The incompetence that led to this tragic development reached into the highest levels of the U.S. government, in the form of poor tactical decisions and a deliberately misleading public relations campaign. The message communicated to the American people was one of ceaseless optimism, that a sufficient number of troops were in place and that everyone would be home in short order.

On the ground, however, a far different picture was beginning to develop.

CHAPTER 4

There is only one tactical principle which is not subject to change. It is to use the means at hand to inflict the maximum amount of wound, death, and destruction on the enemy in the minimum amount of time.

—GENERAL GEORGE S. PATTON JR.

President Thomas Jefferson founded the United States Military Academy in 1802 for one specific purpose: "to train military officers to fight and win our nation's wars." We clearly lost that perspective in Vietnam, when it became the standard to merely *fight* our nation's wars; sadly enough, a similar philosophy prevails in Iraq today. The U.S. military is saddled with a generation of senior officers interested primarily in survival in Iraq, and who do not possess the intestinal fortitude that General Patton displayed in World War II: the willingness to use overwhelming force to absolutely crush the spirit of an opposing force. Instead, our senior commanders have gone out of their way to limit the ground commander's ability to prosecute this war, in direct contradiction to the way President Jefferson intended our officers to fight and win our nation's wars.

It is a sobering thing to watch your men expire in combat on a foreign battlefield because someone above you in the chain of command decided that you did not need your engineer commander as part of your force in the division's largest joint military operation in Samarra; it's equally sobering to have one of your men lose a foot to an IED because, again, your senior commander decided that driving down the middle of the road backed up traffic for the Iraqis—better, he had indicated, to drive on the side of the road, despite knowing full well that the safest and most prudent way to travel in Iraq was to stay far from the shoulder, where virtually all IEDs were located. Niceties too often were valued over common sense and safety. We clearly lost sight of our primary purpose—to destroy the enemy with overwhelming force at every opportunity—and somehow drifted toward a twisted policy that aimed to make the fight as fair as possible. To use a sports metaphor, it was almost as if, rather than trying to win, we were merely trying to avoid losing. There is a difference.

I believe this reflects the troubling fact that most senior military commanders are chiefly interested in their own careers, surviving their one year in a theater of combat operations, and returning stateside for that coveted one-star promotion. I cannot even begin to describe the sickening feeling that I have for those overweight, scared, lost, misguided field-grade officers who displayed stunning levels of cowardice in Iraq. From the brigade commanders who sent men on the most dangerous of patrols while never leaving the comfort of their air-conditioned offices on their extravagant bases, to the grossly overweight military police battalion commanders who routinely bragged about outrunning RPG ambushes instead of fighting and eliminating the enemy, the army clearly suffered from poor modeling and indecisive senior leadership on the battlefield. The scariest part is that the lack of genuinely inspiring leadership is more a result of the current military culture than random individual performance.

In *The Pleasure of His Company*, Paul B. Fay Jr., a close friend of President John F. Kennedy and a serving undersecretary of the navy during President Kennedy's term of service, described the president's fascination with the military promotion system. President Kennedy stated, "The demanding promotion course has its advantages and disadvantages. Certainly it rewards the industrious, bright, ambitious officer, but only so long as he conforms to the pattern of the Establishment. . . . If you express a position in opposition to that of your commanding officer, who might be very unimaginative, even though you are confident it is a much better approach to the problem at hand, you're playing with dynamite. Number one, it is unmilitary; and number two, by the nature of the promotion system senior officers will most likely be in a position to stick it into you for years to come. So what happens? You end up with hard-working, industrious men but notoriously lacking in original thought as compared to their counterparts in civilian life."

I could not have said it better than President Kennedy in 1961; worse, similarly unimaginative military commanders cost American lives on the Iraqi battlefield and never coherently attacked the problems of reconstruction.

For much of 2003, the 1-8 Infantry was winning the war in the Salah Ah Din Province. We had found success, along with heartbreak, through the deft use of a complex combination of political, civil, economic, and tactical maneuvers to help put the people of Balad on a solid footing as we prepared to redeploy. However, in doing so, I was following an agenda gleaned from countless experiences with the Iraqi people, while ignoring the hopeless policies forced upon me from headquarters. We consistently sought refreshing dialogue with those Iraqis interested in moving their region toward democracy while simultaneously confronting insurgents who tried to kill American soldiers or key Iraqi leaders and generally sought to disrupt progress in our area of operation.

I'll be perfectly candid: We knew early on that we could kill every insurgent in Iraq and still lose the war. For me, it was always about setting the conditions for a new way of life and government for the Iraqi people. Unfortunately, it's exceptionally difficult for an invading Western army to represent all that is good in democracy. Maintaining order without shedding blood is virtually impossible. So it was an interesting situation to be in, especially when you have spent an entire career training to inflict maximum punishment on the enemy. In this case, the enemy was anyone attacking American soldiers, firebombing joint Iraqi–American political meetings, or assassinating key Iraqi citizens simply because they had been working with Americans.

Critics have argued that the Fourth Infantry Division's heavy-handedness contributed to what went wrong in the war in Iraq, but that could not be further from the truth. For the record, several key combat battalions in the Fourth Infantry Division appeased both Sunni and Shia tribes or cities, only to be cut to pieces and run out of their bases with their tails between their legs. Other combat support battalions chose to run from the enemy in virtually every action the enemy initiated. For those Fourth Infantry Division combat battalions that chose to stand and fight, valor was rewarded. Invariably, those were the areas and cities where predictability reigned for the Iraqi people. The high level of security and stability in these areas set the conditions for some legitimate civil, economic, and political progress. These places represented freedom of movement, freedom of economic markets, freedom of speech, and a thorough understanding that American forces would tirelessly hunt down, kill, or capture those insurgent cell groups who sought to destabilize Iraqi communities and thwart American reconstruction efforts.

In the cities and communities where American units sought to appease and not fight the enemy, chaos and lawlessness reigned. The common, traditional Iraqis walked their neighborhood streets in fear; worse, absolutely no progress was made on the security, political, economic, and education fronts. Those critics who bash the aggressiveness of our American combat units in Iraq lack perspective, of course. They haven't fought enemy guerrillas from in and around Samarra's Golden Dome Mosque, or furiously worked to save a young sergeant first class fatally wounded in an enemy ambush. These critics certainly did not walk my path in the volatile, violent Salah Ah Din Province in 2003–4 and can only provide theoretical conjecture regarding their appeasement proposals.

The insurgent attacks began in July 2003 and were clearly brought on by the frustration of the young unemployed men of Iraq, along with the frustrations of the imams, sheiks, and government leaders who realized that the promises American commanders and senior civil affairs officers made to them about improving their conditions were not going to come about for many months, possibly even years. The insurgent attacks represented a complete failure by the Department of Defense and State Department to put together any type of mini Marshall Plan for Iraq. The disconnects between the Department of Defense, the State Department, and senior American ground commanders reflected a profound lack of any synchronized or coordinated civil affairs plan for rebuilding local communities, regions, provinces, and governments. It was readily apparent that American military commanders on the ground were left to their own devices in terms of figuring out how to secure and stabilize their areas of operation. Unfortunately, between army companies, battalions, squadrons, brigades, regiments, and even divisions, there was no coherent strategy or formula for providing this security and stability to Iraqi communities. Within the same brigades, the tactics, techniques, and procedures for prosecuting this war and setting the conditions for real progress were miles apart, and senior military commanders did not seem to mind these dichotomies. There was no synchronization of effort between American battalions and brigades. Each of us was fighting his own war . . . in his own way. I found it to be almost transparently obvious that the war in Iraq was not going to be quick, easy, and without casualties. If we, as a government, people, and Department of Defense, had been serious about winning, we could have accomplished what we were unable to do in Vietnam. We were never serious; we never wanted to win in the first place.

"You and your battalion are an anomaly," Colonel Rudesheim once said to me. "You are by far the most aggressive and effective military force that I have under my command. You're also the most aggressive in the reconstruction and rebuilding efforts of the Salah Ah Din Province." Then he paused and gave me a hard, fatherly look. "But you don't have to be that aggressive. We can just finish out our days here and go back home and resume our lives." I knew on that day, in October of 2003, that I was about to depart from being a member of the . . . whatever you want to call it . . . the *brotherhood* of senior officers. Because I could neither tolerate nor advocate a policy of benign neglect and passive nonintervention.

"I can't do that, sir. My entire life has been based on winning. I am not over here to tread water and return home and get promoted to full bird. I'm actually trying to win the damn war, and that's how I am wired."

Colonel Rudesheim smiled, nodded. I knew from that

conversation, and I'm sure he did as well, that we were on different paths.

"You know, Nate . . . if you never patrol, no one will ever get
hurt."

That was the end of the conversation—and he was right. If
we hadn't patrolled in Iraq, no one would have gotten hurt. Of
course, nothing would have been accomplished, either.

From July to October of 2003, my young staff and commanders
developed and refined a usable formula for success. This formula
was a result of four months of old-fashioned lessons learned on
the battlefield, not of anything taught in a classroom at West
Point. From inside the politics of the community center hallways
to the armed fights in the city streets and country orchards . . .
from the city marketplace and farmers' markets to the homes of
Iraqi families . . . we sought to find a realistic formula that any
combat arms or combat support battalion could use to win in
Iraq. Despite receiving no specific training or guidance from
higher headquarters other than to "secure and stabilize the region," we took it upon ourselves to win our little corner of the
fight with four simple steps that had to occur in this exact order:

1. Establish legitimate authority to secure and stabilize the
   province. No open defiance, under any conditions, of
   American authority was allowed.
2. Train the local Iraqi community police forces and Iraqi
   Security Forces through the use of joint U.S.-Iraqi patrols.
3. Form credible Iraqi institutions of security, politics,
   economics, law, education, religion, and speech.
4. Transfer security and institutions to the total control of
   the Iraqis.

On the macro level for the country, this amounted to giving the Iraqis a voice in their ultimate destiny. On the micro level, for those of us fighting the insurgency, it meant being actively engaged in helping the local governments and local security forces with their water, electricity, hospitals, business and farming practices, irrigation, canal development, and mosques and religious freedoms; and it meant setting up these local governments and indigenous security forces while actively defeating and negating local insurgent efforts. If the U.S. government and military had worked through and issued this formula prior to the invasion, complete with resources and plans to introduce governmental and nongovernmental organizations to organize and direct the rebuilding effort, we could have put Iraq on the road to recovery and diminished the insurgents' gains during the early stages of the war.

I refer to the period between the first week of July and mid-October 2003 as the 100 Days of Hell. I call it this not only because temperatures soared into the 130s in July (and then into the 140s during the first two weeks of August, before beginning a slow decline), and not because I seriously hurt my left ankle on a night mission and spent the better part of July hobbling around like an old man while simultaneously trying to ignore the heat rash all over my body. No, it was the 100 Days of Hell because we averaged three attacks on our battalion's forces every day. In fact, there were days when we had seven combat actions in a single twenty-four-hour period, with several occurring simultaneously throughout our 750-square-kilometer area of operation. On some days I felt as if we were cutting our teeth on the enemy and they were cutting theirs on us. For the most part, though, aside from Operation Black Flag, a battalion air assault mission into Albu Tallah to hunt for Saddam Hussein, and several isolated missions geared toward the capture of high-value targets, we had to react to many different kinds of enemy attacks at once. This was also the time we began to work in earnest on the reconstruction of the city of Balad, setting up the city council, improving the hospital and clinics, forming youth soccer leagues, opening markets, and trying to normalize the school day for both boys and girls. I can't stress strongly enough the affection and empathy many American soldiers felt for the Iraqi people, especially in the beginning. The common Iraqi dad just wants a good job to provide for his family, and the common Iraqi mother wants her children to go to school and receive decent health care. The kids just want to enjoy their birthday parties and act like . . . well . . . kids. I'm convinced of that. There were many times when I wanted nothing more than to hug the children and say, *You know what, guys, it's going to be all right.* But I couldn't do that. I mean, I could . . . but I just knew that it was never going to be all right. I could hug them all I wanted, but I knew deep down that it was never going to be the way it was before, because too much water had passed under the bridge.

I don't deny that there were contradictions within my soul, or that there were times when I edged toward the dark side. Such is life during wartime. At the core of my philosophy was a simple, inflexible doctrine: If you shot an American soldier, in my area of operation, I was going to do everything in my power (and there was, undeniably, quite a bit of that) to make sure that this was your final day on the face of the earth. That was the duality of our existence. There were many nights spent hunting, fighting, and killing fanatical insurgents, followed by a swift transition into daytime reconstruction efforts with peaceful Arab citizens. For we knew that no amount of military might would matter if we failed to stabilize the region and begin the formation of security, legal, political, religious, and educational institutions that are so vital to providing a people with a chance at life, liberty, and the pursuit of happiness. So, just as we planned our tactical offensive operations in minute detail, we also meticulously planned our reconstruction efforts, prioritizing military civil affairs projects to target the hospitals, schools, police stations, local power plants, sewer systems, and water facilities. It was a hectic time, when forces were committed to the fight at night and to the rebuilding efforts of the day. Finally, tired of continually reacting to enemy attacks and struggling with a local, ad hoc governing body, the Fighting Eagles of the 1-8 Infantry went on the offensive on all fronts—tactically, politically, and economically, establishing legitimate authority to secure and stabilize the region. We essentially focused our operations to fulfill step 1 of the Iraq formula:

1. ESTABLISH LEGITIMATE AUTHORITY TO SECURE AND STABILIZE THE PROVINCE.

War really is chaotic, unpredictable, and incomprehensible. It's that way for any number of tactical, philosophical, and emotional reasons, one of the most urgent and obvious of which is the presence of an enemy on all sides of your force, constantly reacting to your moves. Early on, I instituted a weekly evening patrol headed up by my battalion executive officer. We affectionately called it "the Village People" combat patrol because its makeup included an assortment of troops with a mission to gauge the local populace's friendliness toward American soldiers. Major Robert Gwinner, assisted by interpreters, led these patrols, which consisted of our civil affairs unit, psychological operations unit, scout platoon, and various elements of the 1-8 Infantry headquarters company (mostly soldiers who worked in the tactical operations center and rarely got outside the wire). Their mission was clear: to conduct mounted and dismounted combat patrols each week through different villages in an attempt to gauge the "American factor," as we called it. To that end, the patrols moved through areas and attempted to engage the populace in dialogue. In some areas, the patrols were met and treated like liberators; in others, children would throw rocks at our soldiers. In the worst cases, the patrols came under direct-fire attack from local enemy insurgent cells. The patrols were crucial from a strategic standpoint, providing a grassroots assessment of different areas and their feelings toward our presence, and helping us to focus our efforts on those places where resistance and violence seemed likely.

No open defiance was allowed under step 1 of our winning formula. Open defiance could show itself in many different forms. It could be passive, such as anti-American graffiti on school buildings or police stations that we had rebuilt; or it could be more flagrant—a group of preteen schoolboys giving us the finger as we drove by. In some cases it was downright lethal, in the form of attacks on American patrols in broad daylight. In any of these cases, the open defiance of our authority had to be addressed immediately. The guidance I issued was to respond to each measure of defiance with a commensurate measure of authority and force. For example, in the case of the graffiti, the instant it was spotted, the local police force had less than twenty-four hours to scrub it away. If boys flipped us off, it was appropriate to stop, detain the kids, and wait for the parents to show up, and then lecture them on the positives of our presence. In the case of rock throwing, we threw rocks back. When we were openly attacked, we responded with deadly force. I know it's ironic, but we garnered the respect of the local Arab populace through displays of raw power and violence. These were concepts the Iraqis understood at a fundamental level. It may be foreign to Western culture, but in Iraq, and some other Arab countries, there can be only one response to acts of defiance, and that is one of strength and power. Anything less is interpreted as weakness and vulnerability, characteristics we could not afford to display if we hoped to secure or stabilize the villages, cities, and provinces of Iraq.

The simple, somewhat barbaric truth is that we had to convince the Iraqi people that they should fear us more than they feared the insurgents who threatened to steal their money and conscript their sons into the insurgency. I was criticized for telling *The New York Times,* rather casually (and perhaps ill-advisedly), "With a heavy dose of fear and violence, and a lot of money for projects, I think we can convince these people that we are here to help them." If that sounds like a self-contradictory statement, well, that's only because you've never fought in Iraq. It was true when I said it, and it remains true to this day. Once the Iraqis "feared" (i.e., "respected," because in this culture and setting, the two terms were practically synonymous) U.S. troops more than their local insurgent cells, then we could successfully initiate economic, political, legal, and educational reforms. Like it or not, the first, necessary step toward winning in Iraq was to enforce authority ruthlessly and deal with any open acts of defiance with quick, forceful, commensurate responses. For once the Iraqi community understood that we could provide for their security against outside raiding parties, the stability facilitated a more open dialogue toward rebuilding efforts in their neighborhoods.

Unfortunately, there were plenty of villages—from Ishaki to Albu Hishma and all points in between—where Iraqi youth openly challenged our authority. These villages did not greet us warmly, were not grateful for the supplies we handed out, and were eager for us to leave their country as soon as possible. It is one thing to drive Iraqi forces out of Kuwait (Desert Storm); it is quite another thing to drive out insurgent cells from within their own country. My only satisfaction in these ungrateful places was in knowing that Major Gwinner's patrols blasted the Village People's "YMCA" over the psyops loudspeakers as they moved through the city streets and farm roads of the Salah Ah Din Province, thereby annoying the insurgents far and wide.

2. TRAIN THE LOCAL IRAQI COMMUNITY POLICE FORCES AND IRAQI SECURITY FORCES THROUGH THE USE OF JOINT U.S.-IRAQI PATROLS.

We pursued step 2 immediately after martial law had been established in those places where open defiance of American authority was the rule. In August 2003, we linked up American units with three separate Iraqi police forces (Ishaki, Balad, and Baldah). There was a critical need for the local populace to see joint Iraqi-American patrols in the cities and villages as a show of united will to improve overall security. This, however, was easier said than done. The Iraqi police forces were corrupt beyond belief. In the United States, when an American calls 911 and the police show up, there is a strong likelihood that the policemen who respond will be honest, competent, and disciplined; in short, they are usually professional law enforcement officers trained to do the right thing in accordance with the law. In Iraq, it was just the opposite. The vast majority of police officers were dishonest, incompetent, and undisciplined—which is why hardly anyone in Iraq ever sought their assistance. The Iraqi police during Saddam's reign carried out his directives of torture and death in their police stations. Iraqi law enforcement officers routinely extorted money, stole from locals, and allowed tribal and religious affiliations to color their actions.

Even with our supervision, the Iraqi police situation improved only modestly, and changes came in fits and starts. There were pockets of disciplined police forces, but they were few and far between. Initially, many of the police stations had hundreds or even thousands of Iraqis on the payrolls; yet, only about 10 percent of the force would actually show up for duty. Over several months, thanks in large part to the dedication of several American infantry platoons, some Iraqi police forces began to look like public service organizations; however, it remained a ceaseless struggle. If we had not had strong Iraqi leaders, such as Balad police chief Lieutenant Colonel Fadhil Hadir Abad, then we might never have made any progress. There were just too many Iraqi officers who did not believe in what we were trying to do, and simply would not come to work or would report to work and undermine our joint efforts. Over the course of a year, we ultimately replaced the entire police force, but the transformation came at a high cost. It was simply too vast a problem for us to train, educate, and motivate new Iraqi police officers while fighting an insurgency amid a simultaneous rebuilding effort. The Iraqi police problem will exist until at least the next generation because the majority of law enforcement officers are motivated by selfishness, greed, and fear rather than public service. Sadly, there are not enough men like Colonel Fadhil, and those who demonstrate his particular brand of courage and righteousness run the risk of assassination. Indeed, that was the fate that awaited Colonel Fadhil, who was killed in broad daylight less than a week after we left Balad in March of 2004. Nonetheless, by the end of August 2003, joint American-Iraqi patrols were ongoing and would remain in effect until we left the province in March 2004.

The first class of Iraqi Security Forces graduated in January 2004, and we quickly appointed Lieutenant Colonel Shaker Faris as its battalion commander. Lieutenant Colonel Shaker Faris had served in the Iraqi Army in the 1980s and was captured during the Iran-Iraq War as a young lieutenant. He was a prisoner of war in

Iran from 1985 to 2002. Upon his release, he had returned to Balad, married, and started a family. He and I were roughly the same age, but he looked years older. It was clear he had suffered for a long time. He was rail thin with a bushy mustache and was always impeccably dressed in a crisp camouflage military uniform. He constantly carried an ornate stick in his hand, and he reminded me of the German Colonel Klink from the old television show *Hogan's Heroes*: in charge, but not really sure of what to do next. Lieutenant Colonel Faris enjoyed his position, and as we built his five-hundred-man Iraqi Security Forces (ISF) battalion, we were careful to surround him with as many competent leaders as possible.

From the very beginning it was evident that we were going to get out of the ISF battalion exactly what we put into it. Two non-commissioned officers from the training command at Fort Knox were assigned to me for the express purpose of training the ISF soldiers over a six-week period culminating in graduation and an assignment to one of the three company locations (Ishaki, Balad, or Albu Hishma). There were plenty of characters who participated in this training, and none was more bizarre than Lieutenant Hamsa. Hamsa and I met on the hottest day of my life in mid-August 2003 in Albu Hishma. We had received intelligence tips that Hamsa and his brother had weapons buried in the orchard behind their house. Confronted with this revelation, Hamsa vehemently denied that he had any weapons in his fields, so I had the scout platoon pull out its metal detectors and start working through his orchard. It took less than five minutes before we hit our first weapons cache, and we continued to find caches spread out over several acres of fields. When all was said and done, we had uncovered over a hundred AK-47 rifles with ammunition, several mortar tubes and base plates, and countless mortar rounds—all immaculately wrapped in layers of cloth and plastic . . . just waiting to be used.

To say I was upset by this discovery would be an understatement. Hamsa had lied to me, and as several of our soldiers were digging up the caches, they began to suffer from dehydration. So I employed Hamsa and his brothers to help us dig out the rest of the weapons in the scorching afternoon heat. By the time we were finished, everyone was exhausted. Every part of my uniform, including my Kevlar helmet, was drenched in sweat. When we returned to the base and put Hamsa in temporary detention, he went completely berserk, reaching through the razor wire and trying to kick and claw at me; he vowed to kill me as soon as he was released. We sent Hamsa to the division detention center in Tikrit, where he stayed for nearly four months before being released.

During those four months, I routinely stopped by Hamsa's house to visit with his mother, who always politely, but emphatically, invited me to stay for tea. On the occasions I accepted her kind offer, she would serve tea and then persistently beg for help on behalf of her son. She was elderly and missed her son desperately; Hamsa was her youngest and the only son who still lived with her. Upon Hamsa's release from Tikrit, rather than seeking vengeance, he immediately sought me out to express gratitude for my visits with his mother; incredibly, he also requested permission to apply for officer training in the new Iraqi Security Forces! Time behind bars, combined with a mother's influence, apparently had prompted a dramatic change of attitude in Hamsa. He later successfully completed the officer training course and was appointed second-in-command of the Albu Hishma ISF company, at great risk to him and his family. In the ensuing months I continued to visit his house for tea and a chat with his mother. In the end, our ISF training program churned out adequately trained officers and soldiers, and Lieutenant Hamsa was easily one of the best officers in Lieutenant Colonel Shaker Faris's battalion.

While the Iraqi police force is a generation away from evolving into the sort of democratic organization that will garner the trust of its citizens, the ISF is much further along. Undeniably, though, it suffers from sectarian divisions. Both security institutions were continually bolstered by 1-8 Infantry soldiers, and toward the end of our tour we were routinely medevacing and treating ISF soldiers wounded on the battlefield just as if they were American soldiers. They were part of our force and we treated them as such. That respect went a considerable distance toward building the trust that was needed between Iraqi and American forces to jointly battle insurgent cells.

The irrefutable truth is this: It is extraordinarily difficult to instill the values of honesty, discipline, and public service into a culture that has known nothing but fear, intimidation, and tyranny for more than three decades. This is not a process that occurs overnight. However, once step 2 had been accomplished in a reasonable fashion, and our efforts had been publicly recognized by communities across the province, then the conditions were set to move forward with step 3.

3. FORM CREDIBLE IRAQI INSTITUTIONS OF SECURITY, POLITICS, ECONOMICS, LAW, EDUCATION, RELIGION, AND SPEECH.

This is where so many commanders (myself included) struggled to piece this fight together. We were given limited direction and guidance to erect police and fire stations, form political parties and help with local governance, energize free markets in a black-market world, rewrite court systems, reeducate teachers and their pupils, protect newfound religious freedoms, and finally allow public demonstrations. We were definitely in uncharted waters—many of us relied upon our high school civics and college economics classes to establish the institutions that we believed were fundamental to the reconstruction and democratization of Iraq. Though these issues were temporarily resolved at local levels, it could have been a slam dunk if we had more carefully and thoughtfully planned and resourced this part of the war. For me, as a battalion commander risking over eight hundred American lives for the sake of democracy and free markets, it was reprehensible that the president, secretary of defense, and Pentagon had neither a game plan nor resources allocated to accomplish this strategic part of the mission. There is no question that many of us believed in the conventional wisdom: "As Baghdad goes, so goes Iraq." It was understandable, then, that the Coalition Provisional Authority applied the majority of its time and resources to Baghdad. Unfortunately, these proved insufficient in the capital city and nonexistent outside Baghdad, a development that compounded the dire circumstances faced by American ground commanders shortly after Saddam relinquished his power.

Our battalion decided to pursue reconstruction of security institutions first, followed closely by improving the hospital, clinics, and local government. Schools, electrical power distribution, banks, and improved public markets were next. We followed this with roads, bridges, community recreation, and money for rebuilding mosques. The problems were endless, and we attacked them one by one while trying to do as much as we could simultaneously, and enlisting trusted Iraqi help when appropriate. I started to hold council meetings almost immediately with local leaders, and found that many promises had been made to these people even by June 2003; sadly, it was evident right away that there was no way we could deliver on them.

One of the first issues brought to my attention by the local Iraqi council leaders was an ambitious dual project incorporating paved roads and a city park. They wanted to build a park in the center of town, complete with fountains, grass fields, playground equipment, and a beautiful garden. The road project was far more comprehensive, including paving or repaving countless roads in the province. In each case, contract proposals were attached to the tune of more than $100,000. Both projects were out of the question—the park was just never going to happen (or at least not in this first year), and the road project was dubious at best. Eventually I was able to get air-conditioning for the city's community center, build a soccer field, and finance a youth soccer league, but that was as close as we would get to the concept of a municipal park. Roads were constructed and repaved, but only near the end of my tour and under strict contract supervision (road contracts were open to incredible abuse and, in some cases, provided financing for insurgents to arm and equip themselves with our own money—to fight us).

I guided the council toward security for its city, improved medical facilities, a water treatment plant, local elections, and schools for the children. In addition, though I have been chastised in some circles for embracing a policy of aggressive defense and for not retreating from the violence that is, by definition, a central part of warfare, I maintained a habit of visiting the local hospital in Balad at least once each week. The water was so unclean and adequate medical supplies were so scarce that the number one cause of infant death in the province was dysentery; in fact, this particular hospital averaged eleven infant deaths per week from complications related to dysentery. The weekly night visits to the Balad hospital were emotionally draining, but important for reasons related to both public relations and, on a more personal level, my own spirituality and humanity. I placed a great deal of importance on relating to the Iraqi people, understanding their needs and wants, and empathizing with the drastic turn of events that had thrust their lives into chaos. To see the mangled bodies of children trapped in violent cross fires, or the civilians with shrapnel in their legs, hands, and feet, or the wounded Iraqi contractor truck drivers who were routinely attacked and killed for "helping the Americans" bring supplies into the country for the Iraqi people, or simply to speak with the exhausted and overworked doctors and nurses who were dealing with unprecedented numbers of wounded, sick, and dying people, was enough to break the heart of even the most hardened soldier. This was war—cold, tragic, and unforgiving.

Though the Iraqi insurgents seemed to place little or no value on human life, we as Americans did, and I fought to show that compassion to a populace that only knew fear, power, and intimidation. I knew that as an invading and occupying American army officer, it was going to take more than shock and awe to convince these people that "Saddam was bad and America was good," and it was foolish to think otherwise.

We, as a nation (or at least as a military power), however, were never serious about step 3. If we had been serious about winning this war and taking care of Iraq, we would have put the resources in place to rapidly develop and rebuild this war-torn nation. We would have prepositioned American and British policemen, firemen, economic and political advisers, lawyers, teachers, administrators, and religious leaders to work alongside the Iraqis to help them move forward. It's just not acceptable in the twenty-first century to invade other nations on the premise of eliminating a dictator without first demonstrating a commitment to putting that nation back on its feet. It is hardly helpful to leave the important details (such as "rebuilding a nation") to officers trained in the profession of arms. If this is to be the case, then my recommendation is to appoint the invading army commanders as military governors and allow us to run the provinces until the bureaucrats and administrators are trained in the skills to properly run their local, provincial, and national governments, much as

General MacArthur did in Japan following the conclusion of World War II.

4. TRANSFER SECURITY AND INSTITUTIONS TO THE TOTAL CONTROL OF THE IRAQIS.

We never got there.

Oh, we tried . . . but we never got as close as we would have liked. Samarra was an abysmal failure, even with 1-8 Infantry providing a two-month blanket of security for a military police battalion to train hundreds of Iraqi policemen, an armor battalion attempting to set up an infant city council, and a division pouring over $7 million into civil projects to improve the city's hospitals, government buildings, and schools.

Balad came closer to achieving this goal. Iraqi police forces patrolled regularly by the time we departed. There was also an active judicial system trying court cases and working adequately with local police. The Balad hospital was understaffed, but benefited greatly from a million-dollar makeover that drastically improved its facilities. Power distribution had improved to all communities, and there seemed to be an economic vibrancy in the marketplace that was nonexistent at the beginning of our occupation. However, there also existed an undercurrent of fragility that ran through these institutions—it seemed that at any moment they could collapse without the support of a local American force, so we stayed intimately involved in many of these core institutions. In fact, upon our redeployment, several key institutions suffered tremendous setbacks because our replacement unit lacked awareness and understanding of the tenuous nature of some of the key provincial and city organizations. It seemed that the slightest step backward resulted in catastrophic consequences, including not only the assassination of Colonel Fadhil, but an unprecedented number of RPG and heavy-machine-gun attacks resulting in the deaths of dozens of Iraqi Security Forces soldiers in Balad.

Step 4 was (and still is) the most difficult part of this plan. As is the case with the withdrawal of troops from Iraq, it is the hardest step because it will send the country into a state of anarchy like nothing it has ever known. This is inevitable based on history and culture, and most especially the powerful sectarian divisions within Iraq. There are too many warring factions to conduct a smooth transition from American help to solely Iraqi-run institutions, which is why step 4 could take twenty-five years . . . or even longer. As I told my soldiers many times, "We're fighting this war for the next generation."

These are the four steps that we needed to follow in order to win the war. It should not have taken an American infantry battalion commander to figure this out while simultaneously fighting a ground war. There should have been a reconstruction plan somewhere in the Department of Defense or the State Department that outlined what we needed to do once Saddam was out of power. (I'm sure it existed and was just ignored somewhere along the line.) The toughest thing for me to accept is the monumental sacrifice made by so many U.S. (and British) soldiers. Significantly more American lives have been lost in Iraq than on September 11, 2001 (many thousands more who have been fortunate enough to survive have been horribly maimed or disfigured); promising military careers have ended; families have been shattered. With all of this comes the stark realization that maybe we just never wanted to win in the first place—and that is unforgivable. I can assure you that fighting for the sake of fighting, rather than fighting to win, is not taught at West Point, or at any other service academy. Not a day goes by that I don't question our tactics, and wonder why we didn't simply commit our full might to the cause, with hundreds of thousands of troops and every bit of muscle we could bring to bear. Not a day goes by that I don't repeat the formula to myself, so elegant in its simplicity: Destroy the insurgents with overwhelming force; govern the provinces; train the leaders, administrators, and bureaucrats; then hand the country back to the Iraqis. And then go home.

Not a day goes by that I don't reflect on this, and hardly a week goes by that I don't feel extreme sadness, just thinking about what could have been.

CHAPTER 5

Americans tend to be profligate and our armed forces are no exception. Amassing huge quantities of all kinds of supplies on the grounds that supply lines might be interrupted was an example of overly cautious logistic planning. Similarly, administrative support and base facilities were too comfortable for some American headquarters and personnel. This had bad psychological effects, [and] set a poor example for our own fighting soldiers. . . . A more Spartan existence would have been better for all.

—GENERAL BRUCE PALMER JR., DESCRIBING AMERICAN
OPERATIONAL PERFORMANCE IN VIETNAM IN
THE 25-YEAR WAR

JUNE 2003

It seemed like a good idea at the time.

In my second week as battalion commander, before we headed south of the Tigris to join the fighting, I issued a command that could have had catastrophic consequences. Already reeling from frustrating and disturbing encounters with the mayor and the director of the local hospital (a hard-edged woman who made it clear that she neither wanted nor needed any help from American forces, whom she clearly viewed as occupiers rather than liberators), I decided to have our communications platoon establish a center of operations at the Ad Duluwiyah police station, not realizing the danger inherent in such a decision.

Lt. Frank Blake II was my signal officer, and the man in charge of setting up the communications center. Before leaving, I told Frank to give me a call if there were any problems. I anticipated none. After all, we had encountered no firing or resistance whatsoever in Ad Duluwiyah. Benign hostility and unpleasantness from the locals, yes, but no combat.

"Give me a ring if you have any problems," I said to Frank, and I left him and several other members of the communications platoon with an interpreter and a Bradley Fighting Vehicle. About two hours later, as the sun was setting, I got a call at the base. It was Frank. He sounded nervous.

"Sir, there are a lot of police officers here, and we are outnumbered like five to one."

"What are they saying?"

"Well, my interpreter tells me they're talking about some serious anti-American stuff, and I'm not sure it's a great idea for us to spend the night here."

Frank was a smart and reliable young officer, but he was not a fighter in the traditional military sense of the word. The son of Home Depot chief executive officer Frank Blake Sr. (and the second cousin of actor Ben Affleck), Frank was one of those guys you'd sometimes see in Iraq and wonder how they possibly got there. He did his job and he did it well, with professionalism and enthusiasm, but neither he nor anyone else in the communications platoon had been trained with combat in mind. These guys were communications geeks, not warriors, and I had blindly placed them in a potentially lethal situation, some ten miles from Logistics Support Area Anaconda and two miles from our base at Samarra East Airfield—far from any swift assistance from American forces better suited to the ugliness of war. So we drove right over to the police station, and the moment we arrived I was filled with a sense of regret. The place was crawling with heavily armed Iraqi police officers, none of whom seemed particularly pleased to have a group of American soldiers in their midst. Quietly and calmly we packed up our gear and left the station; on the drive back I kicked myself for having been so reckless. I should have known better. We had just put a serious hurt on this town, in the form of Operation Peninsula Strike, and I'm sure there was no sense in their minds that we had "liberated" them from anything. But the truth is, I didn't understand the fight or the climate at this time. Utilizing the police station, which was centrally located, as a communications headquarters was technically sound, by-the-book army doctrine. In hindsight, it was a terrible decision for this particular environment. Fortunately, I had told all of my soldiers—from the lowest private to the highest officer—that they were free to raise the red flag at any time. "We're all in this together," I had said. "If you see something we're doing wrong, speak up." That's what Frank did. So nobody got hurt. If he had remained quiet—if he had attempted to be a good soldier, in the customary sense of the word—it's quite possible that lives could have been lost that night.

I slept little in those first few weeks—not simply because I was working so much, but because of the anxiety associated with being responsible for so many people. There was no one with whom I could share this burden. I had no close friendships within the battalion and I did not know my brigade commander. Some guys made a habit of venting through letters, e-mail, or phone calls back home. Marilyn and I communicated about once a month by phone, and that was it. The calls were typically short and focused on trivial matters and updates about the kids. The first time we spoke, in late June, I had called just to let the family know I was all right. Marilyn had recently taken charge of the battalion family support group, so suddenly, almost overnight, she had become best friend to roughly four hundred Army wives. It was overwhelming for her, and I sensed in her voice the same trepidation and anxiety I was feeling. But there was little we could do to help each other. At one point Marilyn asked me a question about a fairly large purchase that had appeared on one of our credit card statements (I had typically handled all family finances when I was home, but that was another task Marilyn assumed when I was deployed). This was a classic Iraq moment: here I was, eight thousand miles away, in the middle of a war, and my wife needed help figuring out a credit card bill. Of course, I was totally clueless and helpless to effect any change whatsoever.

"Honey, I have no idea," I said. "You're just going to have to deal with it. I'm sorry."

The precious satellite phone was a double-edged sword, sometimes providing brief contact for couples who missed each other desperately . . . and at other times providing an avenue for conflict in relationships already frayed at the edges. In either case it distracted soldiers from focusing on profoundly important and often lethal work. We had a single satellite phone for the entire battalion. By limiting calls to ten minutes and moving it efficiently from company to company, we could get it through eight hundred soldiers every two weeks. Many of the guys really looked forward to their one opportunity to use the phone. Often, though, it was an uncomfortable phone call because after they talked about the kids or whatever, there would be upsetting news. Even in the strongest relationships, the phone calls could end badly. In many cases they ended with violent eruptions, the result of soldiers having been dumped by their girlfriends or wives, or having been informed of some terrible financial development, like the spouse buying a brand-new and very expensive car—with cash, just emptied the savings account—as soon as the guy left for Iraq. Or maybe it was something as simple as giving away the soldier's dog now that he was gone, because she'd always hated the dumb dog anyway! The romantic notion is that family and friends on the home front never forget that you're fighting for them, and they wrap yellow ribbons around trees and remain faithful to the men and women in combat. The truth is a bit more complicated. The truth involves men like one of my key platoon sergeants, who discovered while in Iraq that his wife of fourteen years had packed up the car and driven their two children to Florida, where she'd dropped them in the lap of her in-laws and said, *Adios, time for a new life.* His response, of course, was to request time off to repair his broken family. The answer, rather obviously, was . . . no. It comes off as callous or heartless, but I needed this platoon sergeant to lead thirty men into combat every day. We were at war, and we couldn't afford to send people home to repair marriages. Eventually, though, we had to take his unit off patrol because he clearly wasn't up to the job. He was completely shattered by what had happened in his personal life. So on balance, I didn't like the phone; it brought mainly misery, as far as I could tell.

My brigade commander, Colonel Rudesheim, initially insisted that 1-8 Infantry establish its headquarters on LSA Anaconda, which was then home to fifteen thousand of some of the fattest and least fit airmen and soldiers in the theater of operation. Moreover, he wanted us to set up our TOC next to the Ohio National Guard military police unit, which included numerous female soldiers who made a daily habit of sunning themselves on top of the aircraft hangars in various stages of undress (you can imagine what that does to a typical infantry soldier who has been roaming the battlefield for two months). The entire base reminded me of something out of the old television show *M*A*S*H*. LSA Anaconda was the perfect place for combat infantrymen to become soft and distracted from the matters at hand, and there was no way I would allow 1-8 Infantry to be based there. Fred, however, was adamant, and went ballistic when I disagreed with him. Apparently, agreeing with Colonel Rudesheim on every decision, no matter how ill-informed, had been an endearing trait of my predecessor. It was not to be one of my stronger suits.

"There are no fighters on this base," I told Fred. "We'd be the only ones. And you know what will happen. You're going to put us on perimeter guard, and then you're going to expect us to guard the base, and also do operations from here, and there is no way we can get a feel for the fight while operating from this base."

Eventually, and to my surprise, Colonel Rudesheim relented. He gave me three or four days to find a suitable place to set up my units. We ended up in a little town called Baldah, halfway between LSA Anaconda and Balad proper, probably six or seven kilometers from the base, straddling the Tigris River. My executive officer (XO), Maj. Rob Gwinner, had found what seemed to be a suitable space in what could best be described as this region's seat of government, which some American civil affairs units had already rebuilt in the previous two months. We settled in the nicest building in the region, a structure already occupied by the mayor and some public officials. To me it made sense, logistically and tactically, so we immediately moved in and began establishing a perimeter.

A few days later, on July 5, Colonel Rudesheim stopped by to attend one of our operations briefings, and his reaction was not favorable. He couldn't believe that we had taken over the nicest building in the region (I also heard that he'd received complaints from the mayor, who was not happy about our presence), and in just about every way imaginable felt this was an inappropriate site for the headquarters of 1-8 Infantry. Fred expressed this opinion not in a personal exchange, but rather in the form of a public tirade, in front of fifty of my officers, most of whom had no idea whether I was even qualified to serve as their battalion commander. It was Fred's considered opinion that the battalion commander and XO were "stupid," that our decision to utilize this building as our headquarters was perhaps the dumbest thing he'd seen since he'd been in Iraq, and that he obviously couldn't trust us to do the simplest of tasks. Before storming out, Colonel Rudesheim said that we had three days to find a new site, or our new headquarters would be on LSA Anaconda, less than a half mile from his office.

I was speechless. Never in my career had I been humiliated like that as a commander. Oh, I'd been criticized, to be sure, but never as a commander had I been publicly dressed down in front of my officers. The reaction to this spanking was mixed. Rob Gwinner was incensed, as were several of the other officers. Some, I'm sure, were left scratching their heads, wondering whether the new battalion commander was a complete dork unworthy of their allegiance. As for me . . . I was embarrassed and hurt. More than anything else, I was angry, and I knew that deep in my heart I would never have a good relationship with Fred. I neither trusted nor respected him, and I knew the day would come when I would not be there for him. In light of subsequent events, one could argue that this strategy backfired rather spectacularly, but I could not help the way I felt. Fred was not suited for this guerrilla warfare, as our battalion met with success and attracted media attention (while ignoring his orders), I believe he became a jealous brigade commander.

The following night 1-8 Infantry experienced its first contact of the war, in the form of an RPG attack on our (now temporary) headquarters in Baldah. The shots were fired at dusk, from a distance of about three hundred meters, and while they failed to penetrate the building, they did produce an explosion that was loud enough to get our attention. With an RPG, there are actually two explosions: one when it's fired (the initial launch audio signature) and a second when the grenade hits its target. It's almost like you think you were fired on by two RPGS, but it's really only one. This being our first experience with an RPG attack, it was followed, predictably, by wildly inaccurate reports: eight insurgents and six RPG shots, or something like that. In reality, there were only two shots, both fired from the brush line across the Tigris. We returned fire and attempted to pursue, but nothing came of it. There were no casualties, no real damage, no insurgents captured or killed. But the point had been made. Baldah was a very small village and we'd been there only three days, but already we were unwanted. My response was to order a search of every home we had not previously visited. This amounted to some fifty or sixty homes, and a search that stretched into the early-morning hours. We confiscated some weapons and detained several adult males. Generally speaking, we ruined everyone's night, just to send a message that we did not appreciate being attacked.

On this point I diverged, again, from my boss, who, like some senior-level commanders in Iraq, seemed to believe that the best way to deal with a problem was to throw money at it. When LSA

Anaconda began to take mortar fire in the middle of July, Colonel Rudesheim's first inclination was to stop the violence through a course of appeasement: specifically, by meeting with the sheiks who owned the land surrounding the base (typically the land was rented to tenant farmers) and offering them cash payments to use their influence and have the firing stopped. What a classic and hopelessly misguided American solution to so many problems: just write a check! It wasn't a small amount of money. These were payments as large as $10,000, to approximately fifty different sheiks, just to have them stop doing something they shouldn't have been doing in the first place. They took the money, of course, and, predictably, the violence did not abate in the least. To the sheiks these feeble attempts to buy influence and favor amounted to a display of weakness on the part of the Americans. They took the money, did whatever they wanted with it, and, you might say, laughed all the way to the bank.

Within seventy-two hours we had found a new site to establish the headquarters for 1-8 Infantry: an abandoned, crumbling school in Balad city proper, adjacent to an old Iraqi army barracks compound (a good ten miles west of LSA Anaconda). The previous unit had stationed a company of soldiers there, and my plan was to use it as our headquarters, as well as the home for our Alpha Company. So I made a three-month down payment to the school's headmaster, and we moved in and began rebuilding and repairing the school. (In another twist of fate, we would discover that the headmaster had been a senior member of Saddam's Baath Party—not too surprising, since a lot of people in education and middle bureaucracy were, by necessity, card-carrying Baathists. But apparently this particular schoolmaster had been extremely active. Such was the price of doing business in Iraq.) The school became our headquarters: Forward Operating Base (FOB) Eagle was established, and is still being used four years later. The lease actually expired after three months, but by that time the headmaster had fled the area and we just naturally assumed control of the run-down school.

To adequately patrol its 750-square-kilometer area of operation, 1-8 Infantry relied heavily on the talents and energies of a small group of company commanders.

Bravo Company, led by Todd Brown, was farthest south, headquartered in an old ammunitions depot not far from LSA Anaconda. Captain Brown was a 1996 graduate of the U.S. Military Academy; he was also the first captain of his West Point class (top cadet leader) and, as I quickly surmised, ridiculously smart and competent. He had spent his first tour of duty in Italy, with the 1-508 Airborne Combat Team, and then had gone to a Ranger battalion. I had known Todd previously, since he'd worked for me when he was a young first lieutenant at Fort Carson. Captain Brown was not only an astute military mind, but an accomplished triathlete as well. At six foot one, with blond hair and blue eyes, and a lean, muscular frame, Todd looked every inch the tireless all-American soldier, and that's pretty much what he was. Technically and tactically proficient in small-unit actions, he was the kind of guy who couldn't sit still, who always felt there was some way to improve. Shortly after hitting the ground in Iraq, Todd decided to teach himself Arabic because he knew that he'd be able to more effectively communicate with the populace if he didn't have to rely entirely on the services of a translator. Indeed, Captain Brown's greatest strength was his ability and eagerness to relate with the community; he was blessed with exceptional interpersonal skills. While it was clear that Todd saw the big picture in Iraq, he also understood the importance of getting the details right. When I suggested that we build a mock village for training purposes, Todd went out and found the lumber and ply-wood and got the job done. He oversaw the construction of multiple training ranges. He knew how to effectively and safely clear a small room or a long alley. In sum, he was one of West Point's finest, and I was fortunate to have him leading Bravo Company.

A little farther to the north, just outside of Baldah, was Bravo Fourth Engineers (also known as Beast Company, also known as D Company, 1-8 Infantry) led by Captain Eric Paliwoda, our engineer commander. Eric ended up being my closest friend in Iraq. I had a slightly different relationship with Eric than I did with the other company commanders, in part because of Beast's status as an engineer company. These guys were soldiers, but they had not been trained as infantrymen—their secondary role was to fight; their primary role was to utilize their engineering skills in the pursuit of reconstruction. So I was highly protective of these men. Yet, I had no choice but to treat them as an infantry company. As I told Eric early in our tour, "We'll use some of your engineer assets to reduce ambush sites and maybe help us in other areas, but we're not doing a lot of initial bridging or building. My area is so wide open that I'm going to need you to fight, and I'm going to need you to train and fight like infantrymen."

That was fine with Eric. At six foot six and 215 pounds, he'd been a member of the track team (the discus event was his specialty) at West Point, from which he'd graduated in 1997. Eric and I had also crossed paths at Fort Carson, so we had some history, and I quickly became his mentor in Iraq. We called Eric the "Doctrine Monster" because he was so doctrinally sound; in terms of understanding what the Army taught and expected, from a theoretical standpoint, he was flawless. He was also technically and tactically competent, traits that served him well when Beast Company was patrolling in Baldah and Albu Hishma. Eric was primarily responsible for putting together the police force and city council in Baldah—enormously challenging and important tasks. These were responsibilities that did not apply to all of the company commanders. Todd Brown, for example, was concerned mainly with protecting LSA Anaconda. Basically, Bravo Company, 1-8 Infantry, using 135 soldiers and fourteen Bradleys, protected the fifteen to twenty thousand people who rarely left the base. That was Todd's job. Eric's role was more diverse: security, stability, and reconstruction. He had to know how to fight; he also had to understand the importance of sitting in on endless, boring city council meetings, and of mediating between opposing factions. Fortunately, Eric was suited to the task. He believed in what we were trying to do in Iraq, although I would later come to discover that his family did not share in this passion, and his service had created something of a rift. In this way, too, Eric differed from Captain Brown, whose military lineage was impeccable. Todd's father was a one-star general and chief of military history in Washington, D.C.; his father-in-law was a retired one-star general. Eric was more like me—a soldier of his own making—and we connected on that level. He had built me a rocking chair emblazoned with the words "Old Man" on it, and I'd often sit in that chair on a porch overlooking the Tigris with Eric by my side, dissecting the day's activities, deconstructing the fight in ways large and small. We'd watch the sun set over the river, and conversations about blood and battle would give way to more personal observations, like how much Eric missed his fiancée, Wendy, and how he couldn't wait to get back home and start a life with her. I liked Eric enormously, and I trusted and respected him, but there were times when his lack of experience and combat expertise caused me concern, so I tried to spend as much time as possible with him. He was supposed to be an engineer, after all, not a warrior.

I was usually stationed with Alpha Company in Balad. Alpha

Company was led by Captain Matthew Cunningham, a 1996 graduate of West Point, where he distinguished himself in the classroom and on the lightweight (150 pound) football team. Matt, like me, was a type A personality. His military specialty was urban operations and urban warfare—useful tools in Iraq. Matt was a naturally aggressive and energetic officer who vigorously supported my attempts to employ a more aggressive approach to the war. I admired Matt for any number of reasons, not least because of his ability to behave professionally under difficult circumstances. He and his wife, Amy, had one child at the time, a daughter who suffered from physical problems that were going to require surgery by the end of the year. Matt had hoped (and planned) to be back in time to be by his daughter's side when she went into Denver Children's Hospital, but that didn't happen. Instead, he remained in Iraq. If any of this weighed on Matt (and I'm sure it did), he didn't let on. Matt and his company were in charge of Balad proper, and he went about the job of eliminating violence and building a police force with the focus and ceaseless energy of a true believer; he was all about winning the war.

Farthest to the north, just shy of a small pro-Sunni town called Ishaki, in an old, abandoned army compound straddling Highway 1, about five miles northwest of Balad, was Charlie Company, led by Captain Karl "Clyde" Pfuetze. A graduate of Officers Candidate School at Fort Benning, Georgia, Captain Pfuetze earned his nickname because of what sometimes seemed to be a split personality. There was Karl . . . and then there was Clyde. Karl would talk to Clyde . . . a lot. Karl walked to the beat of a different drummer, and while I had no problem with his quirks and eccentricities, I did at times find Captain Pfuetze to be utterly exhausting. Leaders—the good ones, anyway—don't want to have to micromanage other leaders, but I had to keep a pretty good handle on Karl. His company was stationed in what I would consider to be the Wild, Wild West, and Karl operated as the new sheriff in town. Charlie Company's tactics, methods, training, and reports always seemed slightly askew. I worried about Charlie Company the most, and I worried about Karl. I worried about his hygiene (the worst I'd ever experienced), his mental state, and his tactics. At thirty-one years of age, Karl was a little older than some of the other company commanders, but he often seemed less mature. One of the mistakes I made as a battalion commander was in trying to develop Captain Pfuetze, despite his occasional insistence on taking unnecessary and unauthorized risks with his men. I should have realized that I could not develop him— during wartime, there is simply too much to do. As a matter of fact, you shouldn't try to develop anybody in a combat situation, and I probably should have just replaced Karl at the earliest opportunity. As they say in the army, If you can't *change* the people . . . change the *people*.

There were moments of breathtaking beauty in Iraq, and there were moments of abject horror. On more than one occasion the first gave way to the second. My battalion suffered its first serious injury during the first week of August, on a strange and surreal evening that began with hope and humanity and ended with chaos and violence.

Adjacent to Alpha Company's compound in Balad was a gorgeous five-thousand-seat concrete soccer stadium that Saddam had built. Soccer is the national sport in Iraq, of course, and this facility, with a neatly trimmed pitch and pristine goals, reflected its status. (There were times when we would be in the middle of nowhere, seemingly in places where only the prophet Muhammad had walked, and there, rising from the dirt, beyond all reason, would be a pair of soccer goals.) In an attempt to build a bit of esprit de corps among his men, and to foster goodwill with the citizens of Balad, Captain Cunningham organized Friday-evening matches between the soldiers of Alpha Company and a city team from Balad, composed mostly of players who were in their teens or early twenties. The games were typically spirited and competitive, although predictably the Iraqis emerged victorious most of the time. The locals had their own uniforms, while Alpha Company typically played in T-shirts and shorts—until one evening the Iraqis showed up with a gift: uniforms for the American soldiers!

The games went on without me for the longest time, simply because I was too busy and too concerned about the safety of my men to indulge in a game of soccer; I'd been in-country for nearly two months and hadn't taken off my gear. Eventually, though, I accepted the offer.

Although sportsmanship and camaraderie are at the core of any athletic competition, there were practical considerations that made it impossible to treat this as just another soccer match. The Iraqis loved playing the Americans, and they loved taking the Americans to the woodshed. Friday night was soccer night in Balad, the one night when the city really relaxed (Saturday was typically the one day off from work, and on that day most people went to mosque; Sunday was the first day of the workweek); however, it also usually marked the beginning of a cycle of violent activity, since many of the insurgents held day jobs during the week. A certain degree of caution had to be exercised when staging these matches, particularly when the battalion commander was involved. So we put Bradleys at all four corners of the stadium, facing out, on alert; additionally, two foot patrols actively circled the stadium. I couldn't imagine the backlash if one of our soldiers was shot while playing soccer. Good intentions notwithstanding, it would be a public relations nightmare, and there was no way I was going to let that happen.

Before the game began, one of the Iraqi players presented me with an Iraqi national soccer team jersey—a show of respect, he said, for the commander who had come to help liberate the Shias. And how could I not have been moved? How could I not have felt optimism at that point, playing soccer in front of several hundred local spectators, all cheering and chanting wildly as the sun set over the Tigris. It didn't matter that we were a little older and a little less fit than our Iraqi opponents. It didn't matter that they were running rings around us. For someone who loved sports, and who believed in its transformative powers, this was a night to cherish.

As fate would have it, though, a call came over the radio in the middle of the game, as I was running around in shorts and an Iraqi soccer jersey—in public without my combat gear for the very first time.

"Sir, we have a man down in Albu Hishma."

There it was, something close to the worst-case scenario: one of my soldiers wounded while I was out playing soccer. I put on my gear and drove straight to Albu Hishma, arriving at the scene of the contact approximately twenty minutes after I'd first received the call. A platoon from Bravo Company had been out on patrol; while working through a target (translation: searching the home of a suspected insurgent), they had come under fire from another home across the street. The platoon returned fire, and in the action Specialist Rossetti Faamausili sustained serious gunshot wounds to his left arm. By the time I arrived the sergeant had been treated by medics and was in the process of being airlifted out of the area. One of the insurgents, I was told, had been killed in the opening seconds of the contact; a second insurgent had been shot while trying to escape. This man was now in the center of a small circle of American soldiers, the four of them creating a defensive perimeter around the fallen Iraqi, whose chest and back were riddled with bullet holes, and whose weapon was close by. I entered the circle and put a hand to his throat; I was surprised to detect a slight pulse. The man was still alive, but rapidly bleeding to death.

I understood exactly what had happened. This was the first contact for this platoon, and the men were naturally scared and nervous—even now, in the quiet aftermath, it was apparent that they were ready to continue fighting. Moreover, they'd never seen anyone shot close-up before, never witnessed the gory consequences of combat. So they froze.

"Guys," I said, trying to remain calm. "You shot him, you didn't kill him, and now we have to try to save him. That's how it works over here."

I called in a medic and together we began applying pressure bandages to the Iraqi's wounds, to stop the external bleeding, but the efforts were woefully late and insufficient. He expired without regaining consciousness.

I did not lose my temper about any of this. The truth is, I was far more concerned about the injuries to Specialist Faamausili than I was about the death of an Iraqi insurgent. I was, however, committed to upholding the ideals that I had been taught, which meant fighting with lethal force one moment, and then, perhaps in the next instant, trying to save the person who had sought to kill me. Twisted logic, perhaps, but such was the code we lived by.

"Twenty minutes ago this guy was alive," I said to our soldiers, "and you sat there and let him bleed to death. That's not the way we do it. If you can't kill him, and the action is complete, then you have to save him. And you didn't. You let the guy bleed to death."

In an attempt to use the action as a learning tool, I ordered several of the men to assist with the application of bandages, so they'd have some practice working on a sucking chest wound (there would be no shortage of those in Iraq). That may sound callous, but I considered it the best use of a bad situation. Most of them were shaken by the prospect of having killed another human being; they were also repulsed by the prospect of touching a dead body. I thought it was important to lay out for the entire battalion precisely what I expected in these types of situations:

"When the bullets are flying, that's the time to eliminate the target. If you don't eliminate them—if you wound them, and then the action concludes—you are obligated in this battalion to try to save them, bandage them up and help."

It wasn't until an hour later, while conducting interviews with some of the townspeople, that I learned that our battalion's first combat experience had been even more disturbing. A civilian woman—a noncombatant—had been hit in the cross fire between the two insurgents and my rifle squad. Originally my translator had been told that the woman had been transported to a local hospital, but apparently that wasn't the case. Instead, I was told, the woman had been taken to her family's home, and had since expired. Worse, she was a young mother, with a baby less than two weeks old. This seemed almost incomprehensible, but as I would discover in the following months, the incomprehensible became ordinary in Iraq.

The woman's house was located just a few blocks away, so I left with my translator and a few soldiers from Captain Brown's company. When we arrived, I couldn't believe the scene. The woman was lying on a small patch of grass in front of the home, surrounded by friends and family, all of them wailing and crying and shouting at the Americans. I stepped through the crowd, had Captain Brown check the young woman's pulse; she was gone. We could see an entrance wound behind one of her ears, and a larger exit wound in the back of her head. I stood up and tried to address the mob calmly, but their anger was palpable.

My job, however, was not merely to express sympathy, but to defend the actions of my soldiers, and it was in this defense that I began to understand not just the complexities of war, but the almost impenetrable fog that would come to typify combat actions in Iraq.

Such is the challenge of waging a guerrilla war. On a single night—a night that had begun with such promise, with a soccer game against Iraqi teenagers—my battalion experienced the wounding of one of its comrades, the bleeding out of an insurgent, and the unfortunate death of a noncombatant. There was little I could say to the family members, who simply screamed and howled:

"Your soldiers came in and started shooting everybody!"

Our translator explained that we had killed two insurgents, and they were carrying weapons, so there was validity to our actions, but that did little to assuage their anger. It was a terrible scene, and one that would be played out, in one form or another, many times over the coming year. In reviewing this incident, I learned that my soldiers, who were working without a translator, had tried to help the injured woman, and indeed had placed her on the back of a truck that was supposedly going to take her to a hospital. For some reason, though, she was transported to her home, where she was placed in the grass and allowed to die with her family and friends all around her.

A few weeks later I visited the family, along with my translator. The news relayed to me on that day was shocking. Because the young woman had been killed by Americans, no one in the family would take responsibility for her baby. It was as if the child had been infected. They refused to feed the baby or care for it in any way. Ultimately, I learned, the child died of starvation. Why? Because no one was going to help a baby whose mother had been killed by Amercians. The ignorance and stubbornness of such a decision was beyond my comprehension, and it caused me to harden a bit. This was my first exposure to the insanity of the Iraq war, and a foreshadowing of things to come.

That evening was a metaphor for everything that went wrong in Iraq. In retrospect, I realize that we had limited resources, so we needed to have limited objectives. Four years later the fight would be centralized in Baghdad, and I think maybe the fight was always in Baghdad—if we could have saved the capital city, then perhaps we could have won the war, regardless of what was happening in Samarra, Fallujah, or almost anywhere else. Instead, we sent American troops into the countryside and into smaller villages and cities in a half-baked attempt to blanket the entire country, even though we hadn't nearly enough troops on the ground to accomplish such an ambitious task. We ended up conducting a grassroots democratic movement and a grassroots reconstruction campaign. We did the best we could, but maybe we should have just focused our efforts on Baghdad: pour all our resources into the seat of government and commerce, get the city back on its feet, and then let the Iraqis figure out the rest for themselves.

The 1-8 Infantry got pretty good at fighting the crazy war we were asked to fight, but I do know that we lost the village of Albu Hishma that night, less than two months into my command. Albu Hishma might have been pro-Saddam . . . or it might have been on the fence. I don't really know. I do know that when we left that village, around two o'clock in the morning, any hope of winning Albu Hishma was gone. The political war had ended. Not that I was over there to win the hearts and minds—I wasn't. If anyone had intended that to be part of the U.S. strategy, however, it was now gone. The hearts and minds were never going to be won in that village, because of our actions that night. Yet, our actions were just. The patrol was attacked; it responded by killing two insurgents, and in the cross fire an Iraqi woman was killed as well. In one night we went from feeling like liberators to . . . well, something else entirely. We left in our wake hundreds of angry and heartbroken people, and I don't think it's any coincidence that Albu Hishma, a hard-core Sunni town, would be a significant thorn in our side for the next year. The message they would send in that time was clear:

We don't want you here. We don't want your money, your freedom, your help. We want you to leave.

CHAPTER 6

With the dog days of summer came an escalation of violence, in the form of more frequent attacks and increasingly bold activity on the part of the insurgency. In the second week of August, Charlie Company headquarters, now based in the Ishaki community center, had sustained a significant predawn attack. The insurgents had launched RPGs from three different locations simultaneously, and although there were no serious injuries to American troops, it was apparent that the war, in this area anyway, had changed course. No longer were the insurgents content to ambush in small numbers; this was a sophisticated and brazen assault on a fairly large U.S. company headquarters. And as such it merited a response beyond a mere shrugging of the shoulders.

I decided to make the trip north to Ishaki to spend some time with Charlie Company. We left on August 19, a small group of soldiers from my headquarters element traveling in a four-vehicle caravan. We often traveled in this fashion, with precisely this number of vehicles and soldiers. In any battalion, typically, the command group element consisted of two scout vehicles (Humvees) and two Bradley Fighting Vehicles. The Bradley carrying the battalion commander was known as HQ 66; the Bradley carrying the battalion operations officer was HQ 33.

Our operations officer was Major Darron Wright, a tough-talking Texan through and through. As far as Darron was concerned, if it wasn't from Texas, or it didn't involve Texas in some way, it wasn't worth much. To Darron the world revolved around UT football, UT basketball, and the Dallas Cowboys. An ROTC graduate from the University of North Texas, Darron had the dirtiest flak jacket in all of Iraq—and not because he spent a lot of time low-crawling around the country; he just had a bad habit of spitting tobacco juice down the front of his flak vest. Although he stood just a shade under six feet tall, Darron was broad-shouldered and strong, a cowboy to the core. In the simplest of terms, Darron was a warrior. As operations officer he was responsible not only for the day-to-day fight, but for long-range planning as well. It was the fighting, though, that Darron relished; this was a kid who could almost smell out the contact. He had keen insight and intuitiveness as to how we needed to fight and kill the enemy. In that regard, in fact, I'd say he was more skilled than anyone else in the entire brigade. I saw a lot of men in action, and many of them were woefully inadequate. Not Darron. I had pretty good tactical instincts when it came to combat, but Darron was even better; he was the rare soldier whose senses seemed to improve in the heat of battle.

That said, there were times when Darron's eagerness was a detriment. A week prior to our trip to Ishaki, for example, Darron had violated one of my standing orders in regard to traveling with "white light." When the 1-8 Infantry patrolled at night, soldiers were forbidden from using headlights on any of their vehicles. The reason was simple: a vehicle using its headlights was an easy target. Of course, you sacrifice speed in the name of safety when you travel without white light, but I considered that to be an acceptable trade. Not everyone agreed, including, for example, my brigade commander, Colonel Rudesheim. Darron typically followed this directive, but not always. On one night in early August, while rushing to a joint intelligence operations briefing involving Special Operations Forces (SOF) at LSA Anaconda for a joint raid to kill or capture a high value target (HVT), Darron had authorized the use of white light. His patrol came under fire, and two of our soldiers were seriously injured. Darron regretted his decision, and actually broke down in tears as I chastised him for needlessly risking the lives of his men. I told him he had only one more chance; any other displays of disobedience to rules designed specifically to ensure the safety of our soldiers would result in Darron's leaving the battalion.

Occasional lapses in judgment notwithstanding, I trusted Darron and appreciated his abilities, and I was happy to have him with me that evening as we traveled along Alternate Supply Route (ASR) Amy toward Highway 1, on our way to Ishaki. Darron and I would take turns leading on these types of patrols, since the lead vehicle was the one most likely to experience the first round of fire in the event of an attack. Both Bradleys were manned by highly skilled and proficient gunners, which provided a level of comfort. Still, we knew by this time that a Bradley offered something less than complete protection, since the insurgents had already demonstrated that they possessed weaponry sufficient to gut a Bradley. A few months later, an American M-1 tank—one of the most secure fighting vehicles in our fleet—took a catastrophic IED attack along the Tigris River. The turret of the tank was blown sixty feet from the tank, and the entire crew was killed instantly. That was unnerving, for until that time most tanks were thought to be impenetrable—but they weren't. The typical Bradley, while fast and more agile, was significantly more vulnerable to attack; although we hadn't seen it up close, we knew by August that certain RPGs could penetrate a Bradley's armor—and a roadside IED could stop it cold.

On Highway 1, approximately halfway between Baghdad and Samarra, was a large rest area, complete with a sprawling marketplace and a mosque. This particular stretch of highway was a route popular with Shias making their pilgrimage to the Golden Dome Mosque in Samarra, so the rest area had been developed because of its proximity to the two cities (it also served as a highway exit into Balad). As we passed the rest area, with Darron's HQ33 in the lead, Darron got on the radio.

"You see those guys near the fruit stand?"

Indeed, there had been a group of young men standing at one of the markets as we passed, staring at our convoy. On a few occasions we would pass a group such as this, and one of the men would slide his hand across his throat, as if to indicate an impending execution. Sometimes this would signal an imminent attack; sometimes not. On this night there was no reaction from the group, but as we pulled away from the rest area, leaving the lights of the marketplace behind, and drove on through the blackness, a volley of RPGs hit Darron's Bradley. One of them penetrated the vehicle's armor, whistled into a back compartment, and ignited several rounds of ammunition. Remarkably, despite the fireworks, the communications sergeant stationed near the point of entry suffered only some minor injuries (basically just cuts and bruises). The attack was successful, however, in completely immobilizing the Bradley and cutting off all communications with its unit. Within seconds the entire convoy had ground to a halt: HQ 33, disabled, was at the front, followed by the two scout Humvees and, finally, my Bradley, HQ 66. Each vehicle was separated by a distance of roughly forty to fifty meters.

Unable to contact Darron, I got on the battalion command net, which was monitored by the company commanders, company command posts, battalion TOC, and, usually, the brigade TOC. So within a matter of seconds, everyone knew that we were under attack, and they scrambled to respond by launching forces within the vicinity. Of course, a lot can happen by the time reinforcement troops arrive, and this was a classic example.

Heavy fire (we later surmised the ambush force to have consisted of at least a half dozen insurgents) followed the RPG attack—a withering barrage from machine guns and other automatic weapons, most of it directed at the Humvee in front of my Bradley. Our standing policy at this time was to stop and fight, so that's what we did. Not everyone embraced this philosophy—in fact, the majority of units opted to run out of the kill zone rather than fight the enemy, especially in the early days. The strategy adopted depended largely on the attitude of the commander, as well as on the training and confidence of the soldiers (an infantry unit, after all, is trained to fight; a petroleum supply unit is not). I was a proponent of standing and fighting—of patrolling in platoon-sized elements, armed with sufficient combat power to simultaneously close with and destroy the enemy while securing the perimeter, and treating and evacuating the friendly wounded. To me, those were simultaneous actions rather than oppositional objectives. Typically, however, an American unit under attack would scramble out of the area before assessing casualties and treating the wounded. Securing the area was an afterthought. I was something of an anomaly. I figured, *We're the American army and we're an aggressive force, and if we let them get away, it only makes them stronger.* I have read many stories about the impact of cutting and running, and it just drives me nuts. I can't even relate to American bodies being dragged through the streets of Fallujah, and the military doing nothing about it. That type of scene was among my worst nightmares: to have any American soldier or contractor in my area of operation kidnapped or executed and then put on television, or even televised images of bombed-out U.S. military vehicles burning in the streets, with Iraqi civilians dancing around the flames. That never happened in my part of the Salah Ah Din Province, because I refused to allow it. Even on Highway 1, some units would leave their equipment and we'd come upon it, and it would be burning, and we'd secure the perimeter, and run everyone out of there.

Through my night vision goggles I could see the enemy—small green blobs about fifty to seventy-five meters in the distance, using palm trees and brush as a natural barrier, exchanging fire with the first Humvee. We began returning fire as well. The insurgents ordinarily would not stand long in the face of fire from a tank or Bradley, for the gunners were too accurate, the weaponry too sophisticated and lethal. Once squared in the scope of a skilled gunner, you were as good as dead. If you get hit at close range with a 25-millimeter round from a Bradley Bushmaster main gun, you basically just disappear. One of those rounds will tear a leg off or cut a body in half even at longer distances. At a half mile, one of these guns has a blast radius of more than ten meters, so you can easily decapitate a target without even hitting it. I've seen it happen: the head simply dissolves in a puff of smoke, leaving the body intact, still standing, for a few horrific seconds.

It takes time for the Bradley gunner to lock in on a target, however, so the chaos of the initial assault often involves a heavy exchange of small-arms fire—in other words, a shoot-out. From my commander's position in the Bradley, I instinctively emptied two magazines at the insurgent targets. Then my attention shifted to the second Humvee—the vehicle directly in front of my Bradley; I could hear yelling and screaming as the truck commander, Sergeant Raymond Quintana, scrambled to assist his gunner, Corporal John Wilson, who had been shot in the leg and was now perched helplessly in the gunner's hatch, directly in harm's way. Meanwhile, the driver of the Humvee, Private First Class Larry Bagley, slid out of the vehicle, clearly wounded, and fell onto the highway, fully exposed to the insurgents' attack. All three men had been hit by small-arms fire and were now desperately trying to stay alive. Stuck in the center of the kill zone, maybe twenty-five meters from the heaviest concentration of fire, they'd barely had time to react. The plan, it seemed, was to hit the lead Bradley with RPGs, immobilize it, cause the convoy to stop, and then rain fire on the vehicle closest to the ambush. On all fronts, the plan had succeeded.

Oddly enough, combat has a particular rhythm, and if you survive the initial contact, you can, if properly trained, react in ways you might never have imagined. As my gunner directed fire in the general vicinity of the enemy, I looked out at Bagley, his unconscious form slumped on the highway, the Humvee getting chewed up by machine-gun fire, and felt a surge of adrenaline rushing through my body. I can't explain this, really, and I certainly would not say it was the wisest course of action—battalion commanders are not supposed to take unnecessary risks—but I couldn't just sit there in my turret and give commands while watching one of my privates get eaten alive. I think you kind of strip your rank off in that scenario. We were both soldiers . . . trying to help each other. *We will do anything we can to save our wounded.* That had been my promise; that had been our code.

I told my Bradley gunner to lay down a base of fire, and suddenly I found myself running through the attack, the bullets whizzing past my head and bouncing off the pavement and the vehicles. *Ping! Ping! Ping!* Everything became surreal, the action almost in slow motion. I have trouble watching a movie like *Saving Private Ryan* now, for it strikes too close to home, with the bullets whistling through water, and the disorienting, deafening blaze of combat. My legs felt as if buried in sand as I ran through gunfire to the side of the Humvee. I didn't even try to fire my weapon, just ran as quickly as I could. My breathing grew louder, until it was almost all I could hear—even the crackling of gunfire and the rattling of bullets against metal and asphalt became little more than background noise. I grabbed Bagley around the shoulders and dragged him to the opposite side of the Humvee, so that the vehicle now provided shelter from the attack. Quintana, meanwhile, worked feverishly on Wilson, whose leg was bleeding profusely. Or at least it seemed to be bleeding—I couldn't be sure, since Quintana had been hit in the hand, yet there he was, focused on saving his comrade, getting Wilson out of the gunner's hatch and onto the ground on the other side of the Humvee, even as his own wounds gushed. Then there was Bagley, with a gaping hole in his neck, two square inches of flesh missing and providing a portal from which his life could flow.

I tried holding him, then yelling at him, anything to provoke a response; nothing worked. So while Quintana worked on Wilson, I applied pressure bandages to Bagley's wound, hoping we could get help from the medics before he expired. All the while the Humvee continued to be pelted by gunfire. By this time, though, the three soldiers in the first Humvee had dismounted and were using their vehicle as cover while returning fire into the ambush line; Darron's gunner in HQ 33 had also joined the fight, so it had become a more evenly matched battle. I was eventually able to get on the scout vehicle's radio and call in a medevac, while simultaneously burning through another clip of ammunition. I also called for more backup.

"Charlie Company needs to move!" I shouted to the battalion TOC. Partly out of anger, and partly out of tactical training, I had already begun to think about cutting off exit routes the insurgents might choose to employ. Moments after that call, the fire began to subside, a sure sign that the enemy had begun to flee. I picked up the night vision goggles and saw them moving with varying degrees of agility and speed. A few simply ran; others were dragging wounded behind them, slowly making their way up and over a canal embankment, until finally they were out of sight.

I wanted to go after them right away, but we had too small a group and too many wounded to close with and destroy the enemy with any degree of efficiency. I stayed until Charlie Company arrived and the wounded were taken out by Black Hawk. (This, by the way, was no small feat, because there were power lines along the right side of the highway, palm trees along the left side, and thick brush in the middle. And it was pitch black. So it took the bird two or three passes to land safely. I gained enormous respect for the chopper pilots in Iraq. Many of them seem to have ice water in their veins.) Wilson's knee was so messed up that he couldn't fully extend his leg—it was stuck at a forty-five-degree angle—so we had to put him on the top rack of the bunks that are used to carry wounded. Bagley went on the bottom bunk. Quintana stayed behind, his hand already bandaged up.

As the Black Hawk rose above us, I felt a wave of emotion. I came to discover that most combat experiences follow a predictable pattern. First is the shock of the initial attack, followed by resolution ("This is real—I'd better fight back!") and a series of instinctive responses. Simply put, you go into soldier mode—returning fire, seeking cover, giving orders, and closing with the enemy. It all happens within seconds. You care for your wounded soldiers, call for reinforcements, move to destroy the targets. Eventually, as the fighting subsides, a different set of feelings takes over, and anger is dominant. That's what I felt at this moment: a serious desire to exact revenge on the insurgents who had ambushed my unit and wounded three of my men.

This was the first time I had been involved in a prolonged, intense firefight, and I was proud of my response, and the response of my men. We had fought honorably. There is no way of knowing how a man will react when he faces combat for the first time, no guarantee that he will remember to do the simplest of things, such as firing his weapon. Some are frozen with fear; others (a precious few, thankfully, since they are often the most dangerous) are insanely drawn to the fire, and even seem to enjoy it. I came to believe that if a soldier survived his first contact with the enemy—his first firefight—then he stood a very good chance of surviving his entire tour in Iraq. But the rules of engagement were sometimes hard to grasp, as they are in any guerrilla conflict. When the enemy is ill-defined and intent on nothing so much as creating fear and chaos, the order and discipline of an army naturally begin to erode. Further complicating matters was what I considered to be the innate goodness of the American soldier, who has been trained to fight a particular type of war . . . a war that simply did not exist in Iraq.

Throughout the 100 Days of Hell, from July through October, we experienced a significant amount of contact with the rising insurgency, and one of the ways we attempted to counter this growing threat was to increase the use of trained marksmen—*snipers*. Most of these guys were incredibly talented and efficient, capable of putting a bullet between a man's eyes from a distance of four hundred meters—the army trains its marksmen well. I was always nervous about using them, because their work was exceedingly dangerous and frequently murky from a moral and philosophical standpoint. Nestled in trees or hidden on rooftops, the marksmen under my command were required to utilize redundant communication, meaning they had to stay in contact with both battalion headquarters and the nearest company headquarters. If either of those two forms of communication was lost, for any reason, the marksman would be withdrawn immediately.

That was just one of the issues. The other, equally pressing issue was related to the rules of engagement, which in Iraq allowed for the termination of targets under a variety of conditions. For example, anyone found digging by the side of a road or highway at night, under the cover of darkness, was considered to be engaged in nefarious activity—in all likelihood, this person was in the process of burying an IED, the purpose of which was to ambush and kill American soldiers. Therefore, soldiers were under standing orders to eliminate these targets. In simple, cold language, this means that the rules of engagement allowed for the execution of Iraqi insurgents under certain conditions, regardless of whether the insurgents were actively engaged in battle. From a tactical standpoint, this made perfect sense. From a moral and ethical standpoint, it was more complicated (although I must admit, after seeing the carnage of an IED attack, you begin to lose your moral ambivalence). On more than one occasion I received calls from snipers who were in position, with targets in their sights, asking for permission to pull the trigger. Each time, the sniper had spotted an insurgent clearly engaged in the burying of an IED. Yet, something prevented the soldier from executing the target in the prescribed and accepted fashion.

In one instance a team of U.S. marksmen, hidden in an orchard overlooking a highway, found a target with a shovel, digging at the side of the road at about two o'clock in the morning. Obviously it was well within the rules of engagement for the sniper team leader to go ahead and take the shot. Instead, his voice crackled over the battalion command net, reporting a target and requesting permission to fire. In reality, of course, he was almost asking for permission to *not* fire. It's one thing to shoot an enemy soldier wearing a uniform, carrying a weapon and shooting at you; it's quite another to shoot a young man, a kid, really, wearing civilian clothes and carrying nothing more lethal than a shovel.

"Permission to fire, sir," the team leader said.

I tried to stay calm. *Dude, just go ahead and shoot.* That's what I thought. What I said, however, was simply this: "Roger. Permission to destroy granted."

And that was that. The sniper fired and the target was eliminated. This type of combat, which isn't really combat at all, and certainly isn't combat the way it's taught at West Point, is disorienting to the American soldier, especially to the younger kids. Even the most zealous of soldiers did not sign on for this. I'll tell you something—the uncertainty wears off with almost disturbing alacrity. After two or three missions, most of the snipers began acting on instinct. Those who had experienced an IED attack . . . those who had witnessed the dismembering of their comrades . . . had no trouble pulling the trigger.

There is a desensitization process that takes place in combat. You do it once or twice, and you begin to understand what is required, and while it never ceases to be terrifying, it does become less daunting. One could argue that this isn't a good thing, for the more skilled the soldier, the more likely it is that he has become proficient at killing his fellow man. But such is the price of war. When we patrolled in the most dangerous places, like Samarra, I would be so scared or tense that I thought my heart might stop beating, but once the action began, the tension would miraculously release, and I would find myself falling into the groove of combat, and almost subconsciously doing what a soldier does. It was the part leading up to the fight that was always the hardest—the anticipation was more debilitating than the actual contact. Some of my worst nights were those that did not end with the exchange of gunfire, but rather involved ceaseless, nerve-racking patrols through quiet, darkened streets: *Will it happen at this corner? The next one?*

Funny thing about time when you're in combat: it passes imperceptibly. As the Black Hawk carrying Bagley and Wilson pulled away, I looked at my watch. It seemed as though the firefight had lasted only a few minutes, but in fact nearly an hour and a half had passed since the initial RPG that immobilized Darron's Bradley. Now, the air was filled with choppers—Black Hawks and Apaches—and our attention was turning quickly to the second phase of the fight: tracking down and eliminating the enemy. One of the chopper pilots had picked up movement away from the point of contact—a truck barreling east away from the highway. Was this truck carrying the insurgents we had just engaged? There was no way to know for sure, but what we did know was that there was no reason for any trucks to be out at that time (roughly 1:00 A.M.); as a matter of fact, with curfews in place and the prospect of being detained and interrogated, and perhaps even killed, hanging over their heads, very few Iraqis ventured out late at night. The exception, of course, was those Iraqis attached to the insurgency. After tracking the vehicle for a short time, the Apache pilot came on the radio.

"Sidewinder requesting permission to fire."

I hesitated only briefly. Sidewinder (the handle of our Apache support unit) had tracked the vehicle's progress from within one hundred meters of the point of contact. More than likely, the truck had been parked on the other side of the canal from where the insurgents had established their egress route. In other words, this was the getaway car.

"Permission granted," I said.

The Apache fired on the truck with Hellfire missiles—not the most accurate of weapons, but powerful enough to scare the crap out of anyone, even if they don't hit the target. That is precisely what happened. As the first missiles crashed into the ground, the truck came to a stop and its passengers scrambled out and began running through some thick brush near the canal. We moved in instantly, and within a few minutes had captured and detained one of the men. The other man we found at a farmhouse about a half mile away. When we arrived to search the house, all of the occupants were awake, which seemed rather odd given the late hour (although I suppose it was possible they had been roused by the nearby firefight). The scene at the house was almost comical: a simple Iraqi family, in various states of evening attire, all standing nervously, fidgeting, looking at each other and trying to say as little as possible . . . along with a man in a blood-spattered white robe.

Which one of these things doesn't belong?

The family members were clearly scared mute, although I'm not sure who they feared more: the American soldiers or the insurgent in their midst. Throw him under the bus, and they stood a chance of being terrorized by his friends and allies. Protect him and they were likely to be detained by the Americans. For them, there was no easy solution. This goes back to the tribalism of the Middle East: *my tribe against your tribe . . . unless both of our tribes are threatened by another country.* One of the greatest challenges we faced in Iraq was trying to convince the common citizen to stand up to the insurgents. Too often they chose what seemed to be the path of least resistance—allowing the insurgents to blend in, or even providing shelter for them—rather than picking up a shotgun and saying, "Not in my home."

In this setting it was pretty obvious what had happened, so we didn't detain or interrogate any of the family members; we simply removed the man in the bloody robe and continued our search, eventually capturing and detaining three more men at a nearby farming compound (at this site we also recovered some military equipment and RPGs). It was close to dawn by the time the whole thing began to wind down. Although two were wounded, none of the detainees was killed. I would be lying if I said that I didn't want to kill them, but that window of opportunity had passed. Our job, in the aftermath of the firefight, was to search, capture, detain, and, if there were wounded, provide aid. As much as we might have wanted to eliminate the targets, that was no longer an option—as long as they did not offer resistance, they were to be treated with respect. These were the rules of engagement, and they were nothing if not demanding and confusing.

When I returned to HQ that morning, I was at once exhausted and relieved. Major Rob Gwinner, my XO, would later tell me, "Sir, when you came back, you were quite a picture: dried, caked blood all over your uniform . . . on your face and hands. You were drenched in sweat and dirt and grime. The guys were ready to follow you into hell and back after that."

That wasn't my intent, of course, but I do believe that the best commanders are those who earn the respect of their men through their actions rather than their words. One of the main problems I had with Colonel Rudesheim was that, in my experience, he rarely left the safety and security of his air-conditioned office to go on nighttime missions; certainly he was never involved in a firefight where his life was on the line. Fred might have been a great peacetime commander, but in my opinion, he was unqualified for leading in this type of guerrilla combat.

If there is terror during combat and sadness afterward, there is also a feeling of vindication—at least when things go reasonably well. I had spent eighteen years in the Army, training every day with a narrow and specifically articulated purpose: to fight and

win our nation's wars and defend our country. Now, finally, I had
seen the elephant, and if we hadn't emerged with an overwhelming victory, at least we had acquitted ourselves admirably. We did
not give up; we stood and fought, and we survived. In the end, we
killed, wounded, and captured the people responsible. In the aftermath of that initial firefight I did not feel sad or grief-stricken;
neither did I feel like I wanted to kill every last insurgent in Iraq
and bring the country to its knees. I did feel as though we were in
the fight to win it, and I clung to the belief that winning was still
an option. Eventually that would all change, but for the time being I believed it to my core, and nothing about my first taste of
combat swayed that opinion.

Yet, fighting was only part of the job; at times it wasn't even
the most difficult part. As a battalion commander I was not
merely the leader of a fighting unit; I was a general contractor,
diplomat, law enforcement officer . . . and a dozen other things at
once. I was, more than anything else, a fixer, and the job was
never-ending.

As the sun rose on August 20, I took a shower, cleaned off the
mud and the blood, changed into a new uniform, and headed into
Balad for a meeting with a man named Abdul Hassan Mosa, the
chief technician at the Balad electric station. Abdul's job was to
help facilitate the restoration of reliable utilities to the citizens of
the province, and my job, on that day, at least, was to help him
accomplish this task. So, just a few hours removed from a fierce
firefight with a band of insurgents, I found myself sitting at a
desk, poring over diagrams, discussing kilovolts and substations
and energy transference, and generally playing the role of utilities
administrator. Like so many things in this broken country, the
process of bringing electrical power to the people of Iraq was
hopelessly archaic and inefficient. Not to mention corrupt. Some
neighborhoods seemed to be getting power all the time; some

were getting no power at all. Still others were getting power for short bursts of an hour or two at a time, only to be plunged back into darkness without warning. The people of Balad and surrounding areas understandably were not happy with this situation. Eventually I was able to arrange a meeting with the chief engineer for the entire province, who explained that the distribution of power—in other words, the amount of electricity that would be allocated to a given town, village, or neighborhood—was determined by a daily phone call from Baghdad.

"They tell me to throw a switch," he said. "And I throw the switch."

"That's it?"

He nodded.

"Show me," I said.

He brought me to a phone that looked like it had been manufactured in the 1940s. I picked up the receiver and said, incredulously, "Do you even know who it is that calls?"

The engineer shrugged, smiled. "Somebody in Baghdad. I just do what I'm told."

"Well, we're stopping that immediately," I said. Then I proceeded to explain the way it worked in a democracy—that we would, from that point forward, try to make decisions about things such as electricity and water in a manner that benefited the greatest number of people, rather than those who had the most money or influence. This was clearly a foreign concept, but we tried. We spent the entire day interpreting the electrical grid, ultimately working out a spreadsheet that would, in theory, result in a more equitable distribution of resources: instead of some residents getting twenty-four hours of power and others getting none, everyone would have access to electricity for approximately six hours per day. It worked for a while, but when I went back a couple months later, the system had already been corrupted. The

Army Chief of Staff General Schoomaker posing with Fighting Eagle soldiers at Forward Operating Base (FOB) Eagle on 21 August 2003. *(Courtesy of Capt. Frank Blake II)*

Finalizing raid plans with Capt. Eric Paliwoda, Beast Company commander, and Maj. Darron Wright, the battalion Operations Officer, in the vicinity of Alternate Supply Route (ASR) Linda on 7 October 2003. We are in the midst of closing in and detaining twenty-one insurgents that attacked a 1-8 Infantry patrol earlier that afternoon. *(Courtesy of Capt. Frank Blake II)*

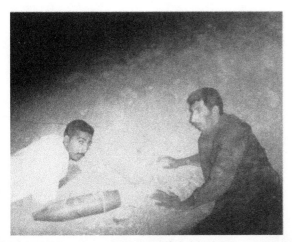

Iraqi insurgents caught red-handed by 1-8 Infantry scouts burying an improvised explosive device (IED) on 14 November 2003 less than a mile east of FOB Eagle along ASR Linda. Following the Rules of Engagement (ROE), the scout section could have killed these two insurgents on the spot but chose to detain them. *(Courtesy of 1-8 Infantry Scouts/Capt. Frank Blake II)*

I will never forget the faces of the young boys and girls of Iraq. They are no different than young kids in America. They want to play, be loved by their parents, and celebrate birthdays! *(Courtesy of Capt. Frank Blake II)*

Baking bread with the locals in Baldah, Iraq, 8 December 2003. Contrary to popular belief, it was not all about killing and detaining Iraqi insurgents. We spent a lot of time getting to know the people of Iraq.

In the pediatric ward of the Balad hospital on 17 January, 2004. Balad lost an average of eleven babies a week to severe dysentery, diarrhea, and subsequent dehydration. It was the number one cause of infant deaths. *(Courtesy of Maj. Darron Wright)*

Maj. Gen. Raymond Odierno, commander Fourth Infantry Division, Maj. Gen. John Batiste, commander First Infantry Division, Lt. Col. Nate Sassaman, and Col. Randal Dragon, brigade commander, First Infantry Division, in the 1-8 Infantry operations planning room, FOB Paliwoda, February 2004. I briefed General Batiste for over two hours, including a site visit to the Balad Police Station where from the roof I gave him an overview of what his division might face during Operation Iraqi Freedom II. *(Courtesy of Capt. Frank Blake II)*

I am checking locals for blast burns on their hands from firing RPGs minutes after being ambushed with three volleys of RPGs in the vicinity of Baldah, Iraq, late on 21 October 2003. The RPGs missed their intended targets and partially damaged the local mosque. *(Courtesy of Army Times)*

Congratulating a member of our first graduating class of the Iraqi Civil Defense Corps (ICDC) at a ceremony at FOB Eagle on 23 October 2003. We did everything we could to train and outfit these ICDC platoons, but they were woefully unprepared for what we were asking them to do. *(Courtesy of Army Times)*

Memorial service for Bravo Company Squad Leader Staff Sgt. Dale Panchot on 22 November 2003 at FOB Lion, five days after he was killed in action by a direct RPG hit to his chest in the vicinity of Albu-Hishma, Iraq.

The only picture I have of all the commanders together in 1-8 Infantry taken on 2 December 2003 (thirty days before Eric was killed). From left to right, Capt. Eric Paliwoda (Beast Company), Capt. Matthew Cunningham (A Company), Lt. Col. Nate Sassaman, Capt. Todd Brown (B Company), Capt. Karl "Clyde" Pfeutze (C Company), and Capt. Kevin Ryan (HHC Company).

Sheiks signing the Ramadan peace treaty at FOB Eagle. Iraqis hate to sign anything, since it makes them have to commit to something.

Probably the first fugas (a napalmlike incendiary) shot since Vietnam executed by the 1-8 Infantry days after the ambush that killed Staff Sgt. Dale Panchot. Our policy was to reduce enemy ambush positions, so we reduced one square kilometer around this position. In the foreground is the alternate enemy attack position that the Apache helicopters destroyed. After this action we were never attacked along this stretch of road again. *(Courtesy of Lt. Patrick "Omar" Bradley)*

The bridge leading away from Samarra and the Tigris River. The January Samarra incident happened about a mile to the east of this location. *(Courtesy of Capt. Frank Blake II)*

Platoon Leader Lt. Darren Amick *(left)*, Capt. Todd Brown *(right)*, and a destroyed insurgent mortar vehicle, 7 March 2003. I called for army air, then handed off the Apaches to Captain Brown, who pushed them to Lieutenant Amick. This is the Power Down management theory in practice. *(Courtesy of Lt. Darren Amick)*

The burned-out shell of the truck carrying the five old men returning from prayer service in the Albu-Jelli region killed by the Fifth Corps Long Range Surveillance Company. *(Courtesy of Maj. Darron Wright)*

We had 120 seconds to return fire once we had the Q-36/37 location data on the enemy mortar position. There was no time to call higher for permission. I insisted on quick counterfire, and it caused many insurgents to make hasty, ill-advised decisions leading to their demise or capture. *(Courtesy of 1-8 Infantry Mortars/Capt. Frank Blake II)*

All the good guys—here are the officers and the first sergeant of B Company, 1-8 Infantry that fought in Iraq at a get-together in Colorado. *(Courtesy of Capt. Todd Brown)*

Autumn 1965, right outside the Free Methodist Church in Mt. Vernon, Washington, with my dad, Marcus Sassaman. I learned compassion, empathy, and extreme competitiveness from my father. He was clearly my first role model. *(Courtesy of Marcus Sassaman)*

Coach Jim Young and I after the 1983 spring football game at West Point. He was a special coach, person, and mentor in my life. He definitely wanted to win! *(Courtesy of Marcus Sassaman)*

Gen. Richard Myers, chairman of the Joint Chiefs of Staff, the guest speaker at the Army Ball in Colorado Springs, Colorado, June 2004, my wife, Marilyn, and I.

Family portrait on December 8, 2007. *(Courtesy of Moments In Time Photography, mitstudio.com)*

rich neighborhoods would pool their money, pay off the utilities administrators, and get power for most of the day. Meanwhile, the poorer neighborhoods were back in the miserable position of surviving without electrical power for all but one or two hours a day. This would prove to be a common mode of operation in Iraq: in the absence of a legitimate and fair form of government, or even a capitalist economy, organized (or at least semiorganized) crime filled the vacuum. Saddam had been one of history's most notorious gangsters, and even in his absence, the gangster mentality prevailed.

By the time I collapsed on my cot that night, after more than forty consecutive hours without sleep, I could barely see straight. My head ached and my body cried for rest. Fatigue, though, was not a unique condition for anyone in our battalion. I remember seeing a tape of a segment that appeared on CNN, in which I was interviewed by Nic Robertson (one of the handful of journalists who earned our trust and respect, not only for his commitment to unbiased coverage, but for having the guts to spend enough time outside the wire with us to really understand what was happening). I remember little of the actual interview, except that I was so tired I wasn't even sure I was offering coherent observations. When I saw the tape, I was startled by my appearance: haggard, hollow-eyed, and yawning constantly. There is a scene in the report in which some of our guys are shown firing on a car that had raced through a checkpoint; moments later they are tending to the wounds of the men they had shot. Nic had also been with the 1-8 Infantry when we were attacked by mortar fire; he had stood by and taken notes as I tried to mediate a dispute between sheiks. (A foundation of trust had been established, allowing imams, sheiks, and local government officials to meet with me as their leader.)

"How do you guys do this? You must be exhausted."

I nodded. "We are. Every one of us. This unit is beat to death. And when we get home, you know what we're going to do? We're going to sleep. For days."

I had become something of a warrior king in Iraq, with all the attendant responsibilities, opportunities, and headaches. The position was utterly exhausting.

CHAPTER 7

As the battalion commander I felt for the longest time that it was my responsibility to reach out and make direct contact with the family of any soldier from the 1-8 Infantry who was wounded or killed in the line of duty. Too often this was a task left to someone far down the chain of command . . . someone who probably had no personal interaction with the soldier and might not have understood the circumstances that led to his or her injury. When a soldier loses a leg in combat, or when a family loses a son or daughter, the least they should expect is a personal phone call from one of the soldier's superior officers.

But there came a time when I could no longer make each and every one of those calls. It was too exhausting, too debilitating, and there were simply too many. The breaking point came on a late-summer day at Alpha Company headquarters. Each day we received delivery of a logistics pack (LOGPAC) from LSA Anaconda.

The pack included an assortment of supplies: food, ammunition, fuel, mail—just about anything needed to facilitate base operations. The arrival of the LOGPAC was eagerly anticipated not only by our soldiers, but by the insurgents as well; the increase in activity often provoked an antagonistic response. It was a simple and reliable formula: the more people who were clustered in one area, the more likely it was that a mortar or RPG attack would be successful.

On this day the first mortar hit shortly after the LOGPAC pulled into our compound. We ended up taking nearly a dozen rounds, and at some point in the onslaught, the driver, twenty-two-year-old Specialist Roy Allen Gray, was hit. Not directly, mind you—a mortar shell can do enormous damage even when it fails to come close to its target, and the chunk of shrapnel that embedded itself in the specialist's thigh was a classic and grisly example. Within minutes of the attack I was on the scene, along with Rob Gwinner and Doc Slicton. By that time, however, Specialist Gray was already unconscious. The shrapnel had not merely cut into his thigh; it had severed the femoral artery, an injury that often had fatal consequences on the battlefield, so rapid and massive was the loss of blood. We worked together for several minutes, Rob and several medics applying pressure bandages as Doc Slicton calmly issued directives. By the time he had been stabilized and airlifted to a hospital, Specialist Gray had lost more blood than I would have thought possible. It seemed incomprehensible that he would survive this injury; that his leg might be salvageable was out of the question. This, however, proved to be wrong, and it was a graphic example of the heroic and technically proficient work accomplished by medics on the battlefield, and by surgeons at army hospitals, that Specialist Gray not only survived, but kept his leg. I did not know at the time, however, that he would be so fortunate, and I certainly didn't know it when I called his family back home in Indiana three nights later to explain the circumstances that led to his being wounded.

Specialist Gray was the sixteenth soldier in my battalion to be wounded (none had been killed to that point), but for some reason—fatigue, maybe, or just emotional overload—I felt this one more acutely than the others. There was a certain rhythm . . . a drill . . . that was supposed to guide these types of conversations. It was my job to be reassuring, comforting, and complimentary, to convey to the family my (and, by extension, the army's) sincerest condolences, as well as appreciation for the job that the soldier had performed. I was expected to be strong and somewhat clinical, but something went wrong on this night, and about halfway through the conversation, as I explained the details of the attack, and the memory came back to me—kneeling there on the ground, watching the blood gush from the specialist's leg—I started crying. On the other end of the line, the crying suddenly stopped, and the parents began consoling *me*. This was unforgivable, unprofessional, unacceptable, and I knew it couldn't happen again. The moment I got off the phone I went to visit Major Gwinner. Unfair as it might have been, I had to hand off this particular job.

"Rob, there's no way I can make another phone call to an American family and explain why their son or daughter has been hurt as badly as he or she has. So there's a new rule: Every time someone gets hurt or killed in this battalion, you go into a battle drill where you not only call the family, but take care of all the effects and make sure that a memorial service is set up, and, if necessary, that a casualty assistance officer is assigned to go back with the body. I'm sorry. I just can't do it anymore."

Rob nodded. "No problem."

It's hard for me to explain why, after more than a dozen such calls, the duty suddenly reached critical mass—but it did. Part of the problem, I think, is that there was no closure for me in these matters. This kid's face still visits me in my dreams—his skin drained of all color, his eyes falling shut, blood pooling all around him. Yet, I never saw him again. It happened so often that way in Iraq. We became terrifically skilled at saving fallen soldiers, but a fundamental part of the process involved immediate evacuation to a facility capable of managing catastrophic injuries. Most injured soldiers were back in the United States, recovering at Walter Reed Hospital, within a matter of days, and then they were medically discharged from the service. So one of the problems of the fight, as a battalion commander, was that you got extraordinarily close to your soldiers, and when they were wounded, there was no farewell. They were simply gone, and the battle went on in their absence.

If you consider soldiers to be merely numbers—pieces on the chessboard—I suppose you experience their deaths and injuries in a less visceral manner. I wasn't like that. I always found it strange that the army had no concrete strategy for dealing with the emotional fallout that accompanied a fallen soldier. I admired the brigade commanders who understood that a battalion commander's workload and job description usually precluded visiting a wounded soldier, but who still took it upon themselves to embrace this admittedly difficult task.

I remember reading an article about Col. Dave Sutherland, a brigade commander who had been one of my mentors a few years earlier (I was his executive officer when he was a battalion commander). Dave had accumulated a vast array of tactical, diplomatic, and leadership skills that made him one of the army's most promising senior officers. He knew how to communicate effectively with soldiers at every level of the military—from general officers to privates. Navigating the waters of promotion is a tricky thing, and Dave had it mastered. I played the game for a while (pretty much until I got to Iraq) and then realized I wasn't cut out for it. I admired those who knew how to continue playing without sacrificing their souls, and Dave was one of those men. He made it a point to visit every soldier in his brigade who was wounded or killed in action. No matter where they were. If this sounds impossible, well, it isn't. It just takes an enormous amount of effort and resources. Colonel Sutherland had decided that this was a priority in his brigade, so anytime a soldier was wounded, he stopped whatever he was doing and immediately jumped on a plane or chopper and rushed to the point of contact or the nearest hospital (if the soldier had survived). The guy routinely went out of his way to express concern, compassion, and respect for his soldiers. That's why I admired him. Dave was all about taking care of his men—he was the reason I understood the importance of providing cold drinking water for my soldiers. He was the reason I tried to instill a sense of pride and professionalism in each member of the battalion, from the cooks to the mechanics to the young officers.

Dave Sutherland understood the value of boosting morale and connecting with the soldiers who fight and die for you. I believe that if I had served under Dave in Iraq (or under Col. Dave Hoag or Col. Jim Hickey, two other brigade commanders I respected and admired), my army career would have ended differently. As it happened, I had the misfortune to serve under Fred Rudesheim, a man who rarely visited soldiers in the hospital, and who was, in just about every way imaginable, my exact opposite—philosophically, tactically, and personally.

Fred had a taste for the fine life. Whether it was the Sunday-afternoon catered lunches he held for his battalion commanders—with white tablecloths, linen napkins, polished silverware, and fine foods and desserts—the fancy leather furniture in his private office, or the seemingly endless search for the best Persian rugs to adorn the brigade conference room, Fred was, by all appearances, reluctant to sacrifice any of his creature comforts in a combat zone. Here's an example of Fred's mind-set: After the chairman of the Joint Chiefs of Staff, General Richard Myers, finished his visit to 1-8 Infantry headquarters in late August, the chairman presented both Fred and me with beautiful pen sets inscribed with his name. After General Myers's aircraft had departed, Fred turned to me and smiled, and with the excitement of a little boy who had just found a shiny new bicycle under the Christmas tree, said, "Nate, a high-quality pen is the quintessential gift for me." I never forgot that, and even made sure to give Fred a "high-quality" pen set and remind him of that comment at his departure dinner held in Colorado Springs shortly after our return from Iraq. (The gift was meant to be symbolic and more than a little irreverent, though the intent may have been lost on Fred.)

Colonel Rudesheim had spent his early boyhood growing up in Panama. I surmised that many of his personal habits and much of his worldview were formed in that country, where Americans were powerful and Panamanians were not. I always felt like I was in the British Army around Fred. He not only wanted you to kiss his ring and remind you that he had the overall Iraqi national situation well in hand, but insisted that you attend to his every need. This was not entirely his fault; sadly, Colonel Rudesheim was the perfect by-product of the U.S. Army system of promotion. Arrogant, uncaring, aloof, uncoachable, and unable to relate to or have empathy for his soldiers, he was twice "promoted below the zone" (i.e., ahead of schedule) to his next grade, and therefore adopted the attitude of one who was an expert on all matters, military or otherwise. Fred was the epitome of a twenty-first-century army officer. I don't doubt that he had the potential to be an outstanding brigade commander, particularly in a peacetime setting; as a wartime commander, however, Colonel Rudesheim lacked the creativity (and the stomach) required to fight a growing, competent insurgency and instill a warrior ethos within his brigade. He was far more comfortable waxing eloquent in large command and staff meetings about the national picture in Iraq or redoubling efforts within his staff to host or entertain the next visiting general officer. In short, in all my years of military service, I had never run across a commanding officer who was so interested in his own personal gratification and desire to be a general officer. Unfortunately, after eighteen years of dedicated military service, the good Lord gave me a boss more dissimilar to me than anyone I had ever encountered.

Fred's lack of combat experience might have been tolerable if he had compensated with charisma. Even in that regard Fred was wanting. To witness Colonel Rudesheim presenting awards to soldiers was tantamount to watching paint dry. He was so clearly uncomfortable around the men—it pained him to make small talk, and he struggled mightily to find any common ground with his soldiers. Fred appeared far more interested in ensuring that his soldiers were in the right uniform than in having them live-fire their weapons before they left on patrol. He was a politician to the core, and his tactics were plainly the worst in theater. He spent no time trying to understand the Iraqi situation on the ground and even less going on night patrols with his subordinate units. While we heard of awesome tales of courage from Colonels Hickey and Hoag, who routinely accompanied their subordinate units on night missions, we never had the privilege of Colonel Rudesheim joining us on a nighttime raid, ambush, or major operation. He was usually back in the comfort of his elegantly appointed office, checking e-mails, hosting reporters, calling his wife, or watching movies on his laptop computer, while his enlisted drivers delivered dinners and snacks to his air-conditioned quarters. In my entire career, I had never witnessed a commander make so many ill-advised tactical decisions. He was clearly a fish out of water, and the brigade suffered from his incompetence. To me, Fred will always stand out as a shining example of how army officers should not be, and how we have failed to properly train a generation of senior leaders suitable for combat.

Fred could compose one killer of a memo; he knew how to host a dinner party and conduct an inspection. However, it is my considered opinion that as a combat brigade commander, Colonel Rudesheim used tactics that led to the maiming and deaths of several soldiers in his brigade.

I have few regrets from my service in Iraq. However, if I had to mention a couple they would be as follows: One, I wish the 1-8 Infantry had been even more aggressive and violent in our combat actions against Iraqi insurgents; two, I wish I had followed Major General Odierno's directives for increased lethality in our combat actions from the start, and ignored the filtered, innocuous, and risk-averse orders issued by Colonel Rudesheim far earlier in the campaign. If I had, then my battalion would have suffered fewer casualties. I know that in my heart, and I will have to live with it for the rest of my life.

Under different circumstances, I suppose, Fred and I might have found a degree of common ground; at the very least, we would have peacefully coexisted. After all, I was neither an anarchist nor an iconoclast. I hadn't survived in the army for nearly two decades, and risen to the rank of battalion commander, without possessing at least a shred of diplomatic ability. I knew how the game was played, and for a while I thought I might be able to play it well enough to reach the rank of general officer. Iraq taught me something, however. I didn't care that much about receiving titles or awards or medals. It helped me realize what was important, and what type of man (and officer) I wanted to be—a man who wasn't willing to sacrifice his dignity or risk the safety of his own men for the sake of his own career. This realization led to an irreparable fracture between myself and Colonel Rudesheim; ultimately, I believe, it led to my downfall.

For most of the summer of 2003, our battalion had been experiencing insurgent mortar fire on a regular basis. The violence did not dissipate until we began to flex our military muscle. General Odierno had already authorized the use of artillery for counterfire throughout the division, but Colonel Rudesheim was reluctant to endorse this philosophy, largely because he feared the collateral damage that might result from such action. Well, collateral damage is one of the costs of war. You try to minimize it, of course, but it's going to happen. War is imprecise and unpredictable. It is, in a word, terrible. If you aren't willing to accept collateral damage as a cost of doing battle, then you shouldn't engage the military in the first place. I remember Fred asking at a meeting of battalion commanders, "Why can't we take care of this problem? I just don't understand why we're continually getting mortared."

In what can only be considered an act of career suicide, I looked across the table and said slowly and surely, "I can tell you why, sir. It's because you won't fire the artillery."

Fred leaned forward in his chair as the room fell silent. "Gentlemen, we're going to take a little break. I'd like to talk with Colonel Sassaman . . . in private."

What ensued was a fairly heated and open debate between two officers with wildly divergent opinions on how to fight the war in Iraq. First, Fred warned me never to challenge his authority again in front of other commanding officers. I didn't respond, but rather went right to the point of contention.

"Sir, we need to be able to fire artillery. Because you're holding back, we can't win this thing. And people are going to get hurt." That, of course, was precisely what happened, until finally, during a mortar attack in mid-August, I gave the order to "return fire."

The battalion TOC responded with a note of concern: "Sir, we have to clear that through brigade."

"Screw brigade," I said. "Return fire. Now!"

So we did. We wounded a few of their guys, captured all the enemy mortars, and suffered no casualties on our end. From that day on, whenever we came under enemy mortar fire, we responded in kind. We never again asked brigade for permission to fire our mortars.

Sometimes even common sense proved elusive to Fred, as in his directive regarding travel along roads and highways. Early on we would deliberately drive down the middle of these routes (as noted) simply because it was safer and tactically sound. It provided us standoff, better fields of fire, and force protection. IEDs typically were positioned right on the shoulder of the road, and anyone who had spent more than a few days in Iraq understood and embraced the concept of avoiding the side of the road. But there was a period in the fall of 2003 where we felt some pressure to abandon this strategy. The Iraqis were accustomed to driving at sixty or seventy miles per hour, and American military convoys usually traveled at half that speed, so it wasn't unusual for traffic to be backed up for a couple miles when we hit the highway. Inevitably, perhaps, this led to the more aggressive Iraqi drivers using the shoulder as a passing lane or crossing medians into the flow of oncoming traffic in a desperate and frustrated attempt to outrun the convoy. There were accidents and IED explosions that resulted in the killing of Iraqi citizens. It was wild and chaotic, but it was preferable to the alternative: driving on the proper side of the road and serving as an easy target for the insurgents.

Or so it seemed. Fred disagreed. During one of our stuffy British-style Sunday luncheon meetings, Fred asked the battalion commanders, "Who is driving down the middle of the road?"

I figured the answer was the obvious: everyone. So I raised my hand. Of course, no one else did.

Fred shook his head in disgust. "I want you to stop doing that; it backs up traffic for the Iraqis."

Incredulous, I tried to reason with him. "Sir, you realize I've had two guys injured because of IEDs and RPGs fired right from the side of the road. One lost his foot, one lost his leg. If we drive down the middle, at least it gives us some standoff room from an attack—plus it gives us a better field of vision as we scan."

Agitated, Fred said, simply, "Pick a lane, Nate."

"But, sir . . . that's preposterous. Nobody does that."

By now he'd had enough. "Colonel Sassaman, I'm giving you a direct order. Don't drive down the middle of the road."

That was the end of the conversation. Afterward, when asked about how to proceed when traveling, I told my guys, "It's business as usual. Stay away from the shoulder."

So it went between me and Colonel Rudesheim—a pattern of disrespect and disobedience having now been established, I gave orders based on instinct and experience, rather than on consideration for the chain of command and traditional army protocol. I had crossed a line, and I knew it, but I didn't care. By now it was apparent that in my one year of combat duty, as a battalion commander, I was going to be working for a man who did not believe in fighting; who felt that we should be prosecuting the war with a policy of appeasement—where we paid people to stop attacking us, instead of just eliminating the attackers. I couldn't do that. At heart I was still a ten-year-old boy who couldn't stand getting his butt kicked on a basketball court. I couldn't gear it back . . . couldn't settle. For me it was a fight to the death; for Fred it seemed all about settling and moving on to the next promotion.

I'm not saying that Fred was unique in his perspective. Far from it. General David Petraeus, who would become commander of the Multi-National Force in Iraq, was, by most accounts, one of the army's most gifted and successful officers. I know that as head of the 101st Airborne Division in Iraq, he believed in a softer, gentler approach, so that the Iraqis would believe that U.S. forces were there to work with them rather than to fight against them. Similarly, there was no shortage of battalion commanders willing to accept Colonel Rudesheim's policy of appeasement, especially if it meant they could avoid the fight. I believed in a harder approach—my battalion was one of the few that actively and regularly patrolled in the cities. I taught my guys to fight, and to protect themselves and the citizens of Iraq. Yet, whenever we returned from a patrol, we would be subjected to an interrogation: *Why did you return fire? Why didn't you ask permission from brigade? What type of weapons did you fire? Who were the targets?* It was pathetic.

I guess people just saw the fight in different ways. Many divisions didn't bother to fight at all. One of the great revelations (I think it will be viewed, historically, as a blunder) of the Iraq war is that there was no consistent tactical strategy between battalions, brigades, and divisions across the length and breadth of the entire theater. There was even less communication between ground commanders and civil affairs officers.

By the middle of July, pressure increased from higher headquarters to begin civil projects. Though very little money had been released to battalion commanders, it was made clear that progress made on the civil front was just as important as tactical successes on the battlefield. So, in short order, a process was set up in which civil affairs officers from assorted units competed for dollars to begin any number of civil projects that were not synchronized in any fashion or order with the current tactical missions or overall reconstruction strategy. Not only were these officers running rampant all over ground commanders' areas of operation, they were clearly operating outside of the intent of some of the ground commanders. There was a time in the fall of 2003 when a civil affairs team from LSA Anaconda had worked a separate deal with the mayor of Albu Hishma to rebuild a school in the community. This singular event represented how unattached and renegade civil affairs officers seeking projects "to pad their records of achievement" worked at cross-purposes with military commanders' operational efforts on the ground. What the civil affairs team did not realize was that the base where they lived, watched television, ate their meals, and spent nights in the officers/noncommissioned officers club (LSA Anaconda) was routinely mortared by insurgents supported and housed in Albu Hishma. It was a place where I was not going to spend a dime of American money until I saw an end to the bloodshed and attacks against allied forces along Alternate Supply Route Linda into LSA Anaconda. However, since the civil affairs team had no operational clue and was not attached to the brigade or battalion that owned the land, it had no idea it was acting in opposition to my intent for that particular Sunni community.

Some time later, a *New York Times* reporter asked me if I was going to tear down the school the United States had built for that community even though the insurgents had killed more Americans in and around their community than any other in my area of operation. It was a good question, but I said we would not destroy the school, since the Iraqi people would take care of that later (jealous neighboring communities routinely bombed and destroyed other communities' civil projects). I did make the Iraqi police clean up the anti-American graffiti on the school every time I drove past. The major unattached civil affairs units were never on the same page as the ground commanders in Iraq, and the only synchronization that did exist was between battalion commanders and the small (two- or three-people) civil affairs team directly assigned to their units.

Major General Odierno visited the brigade headquarters in August 2003 to lay out guidance for the simultaneous rebuilding effort of Iraqi cities, towns, and communities across the division area of operation. The guidance was simple: "Spend money." And with those two words, I saw more U.S. currency pass from American hands into Iraqi hands than I ever saw exchanged by businesses stateside. First, I was aghast at the complete lack of controls on the contracts and projects and the process that approved either; second, there were no priorities. It was left up to us on the ground to decide what we should work on, though it was relatively easy to figure out: hospitals, clinics, schools, police and fire stations, orphanages. Yet, it seemed odd that we would be making these decisions without an overarching rebuilding strategy from the State Department or the Department of Defense.

In one of my initial meetings with Sheik Ahmed, the mayor of Balad, I asked him and his council for their top ten priorities for civil projects in their community (I was trying to hand over some ownership of the rebuilding program to the local government). Their top priority was . . . roads! They wanted paved roads for all the streets in Balad! Hospitals, clinics, schools, water-treatment plants, power plants, sewer plants, marketplace improvements, mosque makeovers, police stations, fire stations—all of these were viewed as secondary concerns. Why? Simple—they knew they could get a $50,000 road project approved by the

Americans, receive all that money up front, and then spend $5,000 for the road project while pocketing the other $45,000 for other uses. It did not take long to figure out that Sheik Ahmed was far more interested in building the Badr Corps (one of the rival military arms of Shia Muslims) with these dollars than in improving the tread life of his constituents' car tires.

For the U.S. forces, it was more impressive to display an array of civil projects in your area of operation to visiting general officers than to work through a synchronized rebuilding plan that helped Iraqis first with water, then with sewage treatment, then power; unfortunately, those projects were far less glamorous than reporting the number of miles of new road that had been paved or the sheer number of schools rebuilt, regardless of whether the Iraqis needed them or not. It was the ugly American ideal of throwing money at the problem to solve it, and to make matters worse, just as some ground commanders were appeasing their Iraqi constituents with boatloads of money, others—like myself— were trying to use this tool in a carrot-and-stick fashion to destroy the will of the local insurgent cells, only to be undermined time and time again by misinformed and misguided civil affairs officers whose only purpose was to spend as much money as possible in their short tour in Iraq.

Spend money . . .

Tragically, that pretty much summed up the extent of the "Iraqi Marshall plan" for all battalion commanders in Iraq.

Because our brigade commander appeared not to be committed to winning, it put me not only in a foul mood, but also in a pretty tough spot. Fred was aware of this, and eventually, in mid-October, decided it was time for another father-son chat. It happened at the Fourth Engineer Battalion headquarters, following another of our endless meetings. Fred and I went for a walk, and I distinctly remember him removing his helmet as he spoke, an indication of the intimate nature of the encounter. I sensed by this time that Fred was not comfortable with my battalion's aggressive approach to the mission—notwithstanding our record of success. The 1-8 Infantry had adopted a thoroughly offensive mode by now, fighting from Thursday through Saturday, then refitting on Sunday through Tuesday—planning the next round of targets, assimilating information, and training. On Wednesday we'd conduct final rehearsals, and then we'd begin the next round of offensive operations on Thursday. We had become highly successful in terms of killing insurgents and capturing detainees and equipment. We had found and confiscated the single largest weapons cache north of Baghdad since the war had begun— hundreds of thousands of rounds of ammunition, RPGs, mortar rounds, AK-47s . . . all in pristine condition.

I actually believe that with a modicum of support—say, two tank companies—the 1-8 Infantry could have taken Baghdad. (I don't mean to diminish the efforts of those who went on to fight and die in the capital. I'm talking about a particular time and a particular window of opportunity, a window that has long since closed.) We were that aggressive, that tactically intelligent. We were having that much success. We had broken the code on how to win the war, and indeed we *were* winning—at least in our area, and at least for a while. On all fronts—political, economic, social, cultural—we could claim significant and obvious gains. The Balad police station was up and running, with a thousand officers working on our behalf. Militarily speaking, we were on the offensive; as a result, the number (and frequency) of insurgent attacks was rapidly dropping, and the enemy was dissipating . . . fleeing to different (and less resistant) areas, such as Samarra, simply because it didn't want to deal with us anymore. To attack the

1-8 Infantry was to invite a death sentence. It was that simple. I make no apologies for it. The results, I believe, speak for themselves.

On a single day in the first week of October, LSA Anaconda experienced six different mortar attacks from an equal number of locations, simultaneously coordinated at 0600 local time. It was the most sophisticated and ambitious attack we had experienced. My response was to return fire without hesitation, in an overwhelming display of strength and aggression. Within two hours we had tracked down all six firing locations, seized mortar tubes and rounds, and captured or killed several insurgents. Basically, this happened because we swarmed all over them before they had a chance to leave. That was the last time, at least during my command, that LSA Anaconda experienced that type of attack. It just never happened again.

By almost any reasonable measure, the 1-8 Infantry was extraordinarily productive, but I think Fred was frustrated and annoyed by our radically aggressive approach, and by the pace of our work, which was undeniably swift. He was satisfied with our efforts in reconstruction because, in fairness, that's where his heart was; that was his passion. The combat, however, seemed as if it was distasteful to Fred, and I'm sure he was concerned that something would eventually go terribly wrong. Why, he wondered, was I so eager to engage the enemy? A soldier who doesn't fight, he noted, is a soldier who gets home in one piece. I couldn't disagree; technically speaking, it was an argument without holes.

"If you never patrol, no one will ever get hurt."

I didn't even know how to respond, so I didn't. I just walked and listened, with a sick and empty feeling in the pit of my stomach, for I knew that this was not intended as a dialogue. Fred was merely affirming what I had already suspected: that in many ways the 1-8 Infantry was alone in this fight, and that the only way we would have the full support of our brigade commander was if we agreed to cease hostilities and take a more measured and peaceful approach to our jobs—changes that I was certain would lead to more soldiers getting killed or wounded. I couldn't do it. From the time I was a little boy I had been taught that anything worth doing was worth doing well; winning, I had been led to believe, was important. My father had told me this. So had my coaches and mentors at West Point. Now I was hearing something else entirely:

Winning does not matter.

You don't need to do your best.

And the sad part is, he was right. In the end, no one really cared.

CHAPTER 8

It is not the critic who counts; not the man who points out how the strong man stumbles, or where the doer of deeds could have done them better. The credit belongs to the man who is actually in the arena, whose face is marred by dust and sweat and blood; who strives valiantly; who errs, who comes short again and again, because there is no effort without error and shortcoming; but who does actually strive to do the deeds; who knows great enthusiasms, the great devotions; who spends himself in a worthy cause; who at the best knows in the end the triumph of high achievement, and who at the worst, if he fails, at least fails while daring greatly, so that his place shall never be with those cold and timid souls who neither know victory nor defeat.

—PRESIDENT THEODORE ROOSEVELT
APRIL 23, 1910
PARIS, FRANCE

From the first weekend in October 2003 until the beginning of the monthlong Ramadan holy period (which began in late October), the 1-8 Infantry aggressively took the fight to different high-value targets while simultaneously laying the groundwork for Balad's first city council and mayoral elections.

The previous one hundred days had been highly active, and we had begun to gain the trust of some of the locals; as a result, tips and information started to work in our favor. We found that by combining that information with our own intelligence, we had enough tactical work every week, and we began to conduct a series of highly successful operations that either destroyed or captured key cells, and facilitated the capture of several influential planners and financiers. On October 17, 2003, four months to the day after my assumption of command, the city of Balad conducted its own city council and mayoral elections under the security of the 802 officers and soldiers of the 1-8 Infantry. More than forty thousand voters had been registered; we secured twelve different polling sites at schools in each of the districts, and the lawyers of Balad oversaw the casting of ballots by more than thirty thousand voters (compare that with the less than 50 percent of the eligible voters who typically turn out for a presidential election in the United States). Five council members from each of twelve different districts were elected, and at the end of the night, in a packed, smoke-filled community hall, hundreds of Iraqi citizens looked on as history was made in this small corner of the earth. The city of Balad had elected a new mayor, as well as fifty-nine men and one woman to its city council.

This was, without question, the finest day I had in Iraq; and in the ensuing days and weeks, as we worked with the city council in Balad and those of the surrounding communities, it became evident that there was a strong sense of governance among the new council members and mayor—they were clearly eager to do the right thing for their people, and to embrace the responsibilities that came with being elected. The Iraqis, I discovered, loved to vote, and to exercise their newfound freedom. Simply put, they welcomed the opportunity to have a voice in determining their own future.

With Ramadan came a dramatic change in tactical policy—one that set our military efforts back considerably. The decision had been made that during Ramadan the United States' forces would cease patrolling all cities in Iraq and limit patrols to the city outskirts and primary travel routes. Additionally, we would not actively engage in offensive operations but would fight only if we were attacked first. In retrospect, this was a spectacularly disastrous military policy decision—the only way to defeat an insurgency is to live in the city and resist any open defiance of authority and fight back, for the guerrilla enemy will always take the path of least resistance to find a weaker, passive area to conduct its insurgency operations. This gigantic step backward resulted only in relieving the constant pressure we had applied on the insurgents, and thus allowed them to regroup, rearm, and reequip to fight another day.

This represented yet another miscalculation by the theater commanders and division commanders (and, presumably, by the senior policy makers in Washington). They had assumed the war was over when the president had landed on that aircraft carrier off San Diego; everyone would be home by August, they said. Then they said we'd be staying a bit longer, but the situation was under control. Now, in the face of irrefutable evidence to the contrary, they had decided that the Iraqis were ready to take over stability and security of their areas, at least in the short term. If they passed the test, well, we'd all go home.

The test failed, of course, and to me this represented Vietnam redux: You take Hamburger Hill and you give it right back. You lose a company of men on the hill, get them medevaced out, and then the next day you receive orders to move to another hill. What happens? As soon as you leave that hill, the North Vietnamese army moves in and occupies it. The same thing happened in Iraq during Ramadan. We forfeited many of the gains that had been made, and along the way lost the respect of the Iraqi citizens and gained the contempt of the insurgents. Admittedly, the respite was welcomed by many American soldiers, for it represented a chance to take a deep breath after so many months of aggressive patrolling. Leaders on the ground, however, hated it. In our battalion, at least, we were placing constant pressure against the insurgency, and for that reason we were winning. It was like having your hand around the enemy's neck and squeezing it . . . and then suddenly releasing it. Not only did you lose control, but you also lost the pulse of the overall situation: where the cells were operating, which cities seemed to present the most danger, and what individual targets to attack next. After so many months of acquiring information and wresting control and power from the insurgency, we were thrown back into the dark. Without access to the intelligence gleaned through routine (though undeniably dangerous) patrols, we had no way of knowing what the enemy was planning, or whether it had any intention of adhering to the Ramadan "treaty."

Skeptical of the policy, I insisted that the sheiks in my area (more than 130 in all) sign a peace treaty stating that they would control their respective areas and would not allow attacks on American forces; if there were any insurgent attacks, then the policy of U.S. forces not patrolling or conducting missions in the villages and cities would instantly disappear. Well, we should have known this would be a difficult period when on the first day of

Ramadan, the International Red Cross headquarters building in Baghdad suffered multiple bomb attacks and major explosions, severely crippling the efforts of the Red Cross, the only nongovernmental organization in-country at the time. This, sadly, merely foreshadowed things to come; as the insurgency escalated, American forces vacillated in their response, and the entire brigade experienced an increase in casualties.

The Iraqi insurgents weren't the only ones who violated the spirit of the cease-fire. The army made mistakes as well. In early November, five elderly Iraqi men were killed in the Albu Jelli region of my area of operation while returning from a prayer meeting at a local mosque. I hasten to add here that they were not killed by any soldier affiliated with the 1-8 Infantry. Rather, they had been engaged by a long-range surveillance company (LRSC) for Fifth Corps (stationed in Baghdad), a unit that for some reason (unbeknown to me) had been inserted into our area of operation.

I led a three-day investigation into the deaths of these men, and here, in summary, is the result of that investigation. These were basically just five old men, with an average age of more than seventy, going about their business. They were not insurgents. They were not aiding or abetting insurgents. They were civilians coming home from a prayer meeting, in a heretofore peaceful region; we had experienced no contact whatsoever in Albu Jelli. (Our battalion had experienced hundreds of contacts by this point, so we were intimately aware of the hot spots—this wasn't one of them.) The truck carrying the five elderly Muslims, who lived not 150 meters away, came under fire from the LRSC. All five men were killed during the attack (remember—this was at a time when we had been forbidden to conduct offensive operations); afterward, two thermite grenades were tossed into the cab of the truck, not only ensuring that everyone was thoroughly dead, but that the truck and all evidence would be incinerated.

Everything about the incident smacked of impropriety, so I insisted upon an investigation. I reviewed photos of the scene and combed the attack site for physical evidence. I also spent the better part of three days on-site, speaking with locals and family members about what had happened. It was never made clear to me why these soldiers fired on the truck carrying the elderly men. I don't know if they were surprised or felt threatened in some way (although that seems unlikely); I only know that they opened fire with lethal intent. Later, as the investigation intensified, the LRSC would claim that it had been fired upon by someone in the vicinity, and that the soldiers presumed the shots came from the truck. I have my doubts, not least because of a lack of physical evidence. Not a single round of AK-47 ammunition was found at the site of contact. There were no weapons, no shells, nothing (aside from that which was used by the Americans). Moreover, this LRSC was a group infamous for employing questionable military tactics—like moving into different areas and shooting people up, and then just leaving. I submitted a statement to the U.S. Army Criminal Investigation Division (CID), and I sent documentation to Colonel Rudesheim requesting that a formal Article 15-6 investigation be conducted. I was a warrior and a soldier, and I understood, perhaps better than most, that collateral damage was a regrettable but unavoidable aspect of war. Nevertheless, something about this incident struck me as odd. It was the first case I'd seen where I felt civilians had not been caught in the cross fire, but murdered in cold blood. It almost seemed as though the old men, who could not possibly have posed any sort of legitimate threat, had been shot for sport.

At the very least, I explained to Colonel Rudesheim, this was a clear violation of the laws of land warfare, and as such it merited further investigation. Everything about it was inappropriate—from the lack of evidence indicating any type of firefight, to the fact that the LRSC soldiers had bolted immediately after the contact. It smelled of a cover-up. I spent the better part of three days sifting through statements, cleaning up the site, and meeting with local villagers from Al Mazare'e (the actual village in Albu Jelli), who were understandably infuriated, and who wanted to know what the Americans were going to do about the deaths. In the end I put a detailed report together and presented it to Colonel Rudesheim, along with a word of warning: "Sir, you know how this works over here. It's an eye for an eye."

For any number of reasons, the whole sordid affair turned my stomach. First of all, we were in the middle of Ramadan, and we weren't supposed to be conducting any type of offensive operation. Second, Fred had never told me that this particular outfit had been inserted into my area of operation, and he must have known the unit had arrived. Typically this LRSC unit operated under the control of Fifth Corps, but it was considered a mobile corps asset, like a Ranger company; simply put, these guys could not possibly have moved into our area without the brigade commander knowing of their plans. For the duration of their mission, whatever it was, they reported to Colonel Rudesheim. Even stranger, though, was the fact that an LRSC unit rarely, if ever, conducted offensive operations. Their job, by definition, was to perform long-range surveillance. The whole thing stank to high heaven. I believe American soldiers killed those old men that night, and I said as much in my report. The brigade commander disagreed. He told me he spoke with the company commander and was satisfied that the action was clean. There was just one problem: the company commander wasn't even on the ground the night of the contact. To my knowledge, Fred did not even go out and look at the scene at the time. I did. I'm quite sure it wasn't a clean action. It was an unprovoked attack on a group of elderly civilians, and I knew before I'd even completed my investigation that a consequence of this action would be retribution . . . revenge.

An eye for an eye.

In all candor, I was less concerned with the unfortunate deaths of the five men than with the effect their demise would have on my soldiers. I knew this would be viewed as a clear provocation, and that my men would immediately come under attack, respect for Ramadan notwithstanding. That is precisely what happened. Fred didn't seem to care. Rather than reporting the suspicious nature of the attack to division command, Fred dealt with the matter on his own. To my knowledge, General Odierno never knew that five old men on their way home from prayer service were killed by an LRSC unit. In light of future events, including a far less egregious offense on the part of my soldiers that would ultimately contribute to the premature conclusion of my military career, this seems more than a bit ironic. Perhaps that's just a coincidence. There are victims in war, sometimes innocent, sometimes not. The line between right and wrong can be blurred to the point of invisibility.

Familiarity breeds contempt; predictability breeds confidence. Part of the Ramadan strategy involved a centralized brigade plan, in which a series of observation posts throughout the brigade would be manned in synchronized eight-hour shifts. This was Colonel Rudesheim's baby, and he nurtured it with all the enthusiasm of a proud parent. I remember my guys one night were less than one minute late arriving for a shift, and Fred began screaming at me, questioning my ability to follow the simplest of orders. Previously, battalion commanders had been in charge of security for their own areas, but now the brigade directed which units would man which observation posts; brigade also dictated the firepower (in my area it was two Bradleys) allotted to each post—again, breaking the platoon-size patrol precept I felt was necessary for combat power outside the wire. As a result, observation posts across the brigade's area of operation would undergo a simultaneous change of men and equipment every eight hours. It worked like clockwork—and it was rigid and predictable to the point of being almost suicidal.

I should have been more aware that this was a foolish and dangerous policy, and I should have challenged Colonel Rudesehim on its merits. The nature of an insurgency is to watch your pattern of movement. They want to see your habits: when you eat, sleep, patrol; when supply trucks arrive and depart. For better or worse, the American army is terrific at forming and revealing patterns. We get into routines and we stick to them. We want our dinner pack or our logistics pack coming in at 1400 every day because it's easier that way. Habitual behavior takes little or no ingenuity. We remember the routes, we know the times. The less we have to change, the more comfortable life is for everyone involved.

Including the enemy.

On the morning of Monday, November 17, at roughly 0600 hours, I woke to the sound of a squawk box, and the news that one of our units was in contact with the enemy. I scrambled off my cot, ran for the door, and jumped into my Bradley. Before we could even get moving, Sergeant First Class James Harkness shouted over the brigade net, "We've been hit! We've been hit!" My heart sank. There is no worse feeling for a commander than to hear that one of your men has been wounded. And within a few seconds the news worsened, as Harkness reported, "We've lost one."

I drove to the front gate of LSA Anaconda and found my path blocked by a wall of delivery trucks and cement mixers. This was just another of the endless series of army ironies. Here I was, on the Mother of All Army Bases, with National Guard units protecting the entrance and exit points . . . and I couldn't get out to help my men because a convoy of trucks had arrived to help feed and nurture this ever-expanding base.

"Get these trucks out of the way!" I screamed into the radio, at the brigade XO. Before he had a chance to respond, though, we simply burst through a barrier and flew out of the compound. I kept waving at people, shouting at them to get out of the way, and I kept yelling into the net, letting them know that we were taking alternate routes to avoid the ridiculous truck traffic . . . and that we'd be bringing in wounded shortly. Usually we would have flown in a medevac chopper, but the action had taken place just five minutes away from LSA Anaconda.

"Clear the area!" I screamed. "We have casualties on the way!"

This was as dire a situation as one could encounter in Iraq—a deadly ambush and a subsequent recovery and evacuation of wounded—but there seemed to be no urgency to it, no realization that an actual war was going on outside the wire. On the base—inside the wire—it was life as usual, with supply trucks coming and going, Iraqi contractors delivering supplies, and soldiers filling their stomachs and counting the minutes until they could go home. For those who didn't fight, life on LSA Anaconda was usually no more exciting or risky than it was back home at Fort Carson or any other Army base in the States. Those things—the little things that reflected a lack of a unified mission or perspective on the war—drove me nuts: the gate officer yawning as I waved my arms wildly and implored him to let our Bradley pass; the radio operator at the end of a twelve-hour shift, casually taking the report from a unit that had come under fire, sleepwalking through his job ("Uhhhh . . . can you guys give me that grid again?") as a fellow soldier bled to death.

What had happened on this morning was that SFC Harkness was moving his squad and two Bradleys from one observation post near Albu Hishma to another at precisely the appointed time, just as he had done dozens of times in the previous three weeks, since the beginning of Ramadan. The insurgents, of course, had been watching this pattern of behavior and knew precisely what we were going to do, so they had established a fairly sophisticated ambush employing multiple rocket launchers and heavy-machine-gun fire from an embankment on the other side of a canal, about 150 meters from the road. As the squad was moving, RPGs began to fly. Rather than trying to run through the assault, the squad did as it had been taught: it stopped and prepared to fight. As the men were beginning to dismount their vehicles, one of the Bradleys took a direct hit from an RPG. The round pierced the vehicle's armor and sailed directly into the chest of Staff Sergeant Dale Panchot, killing him instantly. (Captain Kevin Ryan, one of my commanders, saw Dale's body later, in the hospital, and told me he was astounded by the wound—a hole nearly two inches in diameter, straight through his body, as if someone had tossed a baseball through his chest. Until that moment, despite all the carnage I had witnessed, I hadn't really understood the awesome power and lethality of an RPG.) It was a direct hit, a one-in-a-billion shot that ended Panchot's life in a heartbeat. Two other soldiers had been wounded by shrapnel, and now Harkness was on the net, explaining that he was trying to return fire, but he found himself in an untenable position. He lacked the manpower and resources to treat the friendly wounded and return fire. Forget about pursuing the enemy. This was crisis time.

"Bravo," I said. "Just get your wounded out of the kill zone. We're on our way."

Thus began perhaps the most violent day in Iraq for the 1-8 Infantry.

The ambush involved a group of eight to twelve insurgents and was initiated by a half dozen RPGs. We began to clear the area as soon as we arrived, and it wasn't long before one of our choppers spotted the enemy trailing away. Alpha Company was already on the scene, and Bravo was on its way, so we had a significant accumulation of manpower prepared to fight. I dismounted my Bradley at almost precisely the location where the patrol had been hit, and began moving with Alpha Company. We had crossed a canal, scrambled up an embankment, and were steadily cutting a path through the tall grass of a nearby field, working our way back toward the village of Albu Hishma, which was probably five hundred meters northwest of the point of contact, when a series of mortar rounds rumbled into the ground. This was one of the more sophisticated attacks my battalion experienced—a coordinated effort between at least two groups of insurgents. One group had evaded capture and moved out in the wake of the initial attack, and as we went off in pursuit, another group fired indirect mortars on us. It was pretty impressive, I have to admit—at least in comparison to the typical insurgent ambush.

So we immediately launched counterfire; I also authorized the Apaches to move into the location from which the mortar fire had originated, because it was on the other side of the village—perhaps an additional kilometer to the northwest, in an area of high, dense vegetation—too far to reach swiftly by any means other than helicopter. In an instant, the Apaches lit up the site of the mortar fire; then I ordered the demolition of an abandoned building that was located right next to the ambush site, figuring that it had probably been utilized in some fashion by the insurgents as they planned or executed their attack; and if not, well, a few Hellfire missiles would send a message: we were killing the ant with a sledgehammer. Unfortunately, the first Hellfire missile was not the most accurate of shots, and missed its target by nearly a mile, erupting a little too close to the village for my comfort.

"Sidewinder," I said. "You just put that first missile into the—"

The chopper pilot cut me off. "Sorry, 33. Bad missile."

"My ass it's a bad missile, Sidewinder. You miss one more like that, and you're gone. You will never support 1-8 Infantry in the fight again. Is that clear?"

"Yes, sir."

"Good. Now go ahead and fire your second missile and get off the station, so the next Apache can come in and finish this thing. But you'd better be dead on with this last one."

He was. The building imploded as the Hellfire roared in. The next Apache followed on its tail, and as the first chopper rotated out, the second fired two more missiles, reducing the building to a pile of rubble. Meanwhile, a vehicle attempted to run through a checkpoint we'd established on the outskirts of the village, and was instantly blanketed in small-arms fire, wounding several passengers (all insurgents) and killing one. I shouted orders and tried to take in a dozen different sights at once. It was complete sensory overload—the earth shaking from a combination of Hellfire missiles and exploding mortar rounds; the crackling of small-arms fire; the crying and cursing of men in combat. In the middle of this madness, I saw a small Iraqi woman exit her home—a humble little mud hut—balancing an empty water basin on her head. The fireworks seemed not to faze her in the least as she walked purposefully and steadily to a hand-drawn well down the street and filled her basin with water. Then she turned and walked home, never once quickening her pace, never once looking up at the skyrockets overhead, never once flinching at the rhythmic popping of automatic weapons. She simply closed the door without looking back, and all I could think was that no single image better represented the insanity of the war in Iraq. This woman's life was going to go on, regardless of the circumstances outside her home. It was early in the morning, and at this time of day, every day, she filled her basin with water. Today would be no different. Let the crazy village boys fight it out with the American soldiers if they wanted. Let them kill and be killed. She had better things to do. Whether there was strength or honor or sadness in this attitude, I couldn't say for sure. It was just . . . odd. Almost surreal. Maybe she thought there was no way she'd be caught in the cross fire; maybe she didn't care. I have no way of knowing. It was just another of those things that happened in Iraq that left me shaking my head in wonder.

In a larger sense, I suppose, if one chose to put a positive spin on things, it could be argued persuasively that this woman's resolve represented the will of the Iraqi people. She was going to get her water because that's the way the world worked for her. Regardless of what was happening, she would survive; same thing for the Iraqis as a whole. They would survive and move on and endure because that is what they had always done, for centuries longer than the United States had even been in existence. These were people who had already been through hell in so many ways—particularly during the thirty-five years of Saddam's rule. How much worse could it possibly be now?

If, however, there was a dominant emotion I experienced that day, it would have to be anger. Panchot was the first soldier in my battalion to be fatally wounded, and his death signaled for me the crossing of a threshold. Although I hadn't voiced this sentiment aloud (because it didn't need to be voiced), my primary goal was to bring every soldier in the 1-8 Infantry home alive. I thought this was an attainable goal. I don't mean for that to sound selfish; it wasn't about me. It was about the lives of the men and women under my command. It's also true that preserving the lives of your soldiers is an objective that does not necessarily dovetail neatly with a campaign of aggressive patrolling and fighting. Colonel Rudesheim had tried to make this point in our conversation back in October:

"If you never patrol, no one gets hurt."

We were soldiers, and I believed in the job we were doing, and in the way we were doing it. Still, there is no way to prepare for the loss of one of your soldiers, and Panchot's death, so sudden and violent, rocked me to the core.

That very day we rounded up approximately two dozen sheiks who controlled that particular village and the surrounding area, and I questioned each of them at the base—in great detail. Most of them seemed to understand how angry I was, and a few even seemed to be sympathetic to our situation, but it was hard to say for sure. There were so many layers to these kinds of exchanges, so much feinting and posturing and double-talk. Some of the sheiks were detained for nearly three weeks as we tried to sift through various leads and misinformation. I kept them in the back of our headquarters, along with some of the highest-ranking officials on the city council. The intent was to gather intelligence that would help us track down the insurgents behind the attack, but I don't deny that there was a punitive purpose as well. For me, this was the beginning of a gradual shift toward the dark side. I didn't tell Colonel Rudesheim about the detainees—I'm sure that he would not have approved of my methods—but I wanted to send a message. The mayor, deputy mayor, police chief—all were punished for the lapse of security and the breaching of a peace treaty that had led to the death of Staff Sergeant Panchot. Not that anyone took responsibility. Rather, it was the same old story—"outsiders" had come into the area, and the sheiks and the city council had no control over them whatsoever. I suspected, however, that the attack had not been planned or executed solely by outsiders. The manner in which they had used the terrain and planned the attack indicated a familiarity that could not have been acquired in the short term.

The ambush of November 17 also led to one of the more controversial events involving the 1-8 Infantry: the "imprisoning" of Albu Hishma. One day after the ambush we began to wrap the entire village in barbed wire, and closed all but one entrance and exit, which was guarded by American soldiers. Every male in the village between the ages of eighteen and sixty-five was given an identification card, and anyone who wished to enter or leave the village was required to present his ID. A curfew was installed, which sometimes conflicted with the agrarian nature of the Iraqi economy. The Iraqi citizens, not surprisingly, found this process degrading and responded with anger and hostility of their own. They compared themselves to Palestinians, who sometimes endured the same sort of indignity.

I can't say that I blame them. At the same time that I was reading Tom Friedman's *From Beirut to Jerusalem,* in an effort to educate myself about the history of the Middle East, I was giving orders that reflected an apparently oppressive occupational force. I couldn't help but wonder what we'd gotten ourselves into. Yet, I understood that on some level these draconian measures were necessary, and even though it was not my idea to wrap Albu Hishma in barbed wire (the order came from General Odierno), I enthusiastically discharged those orders. Within one week, Albu Hishma was under martial law.

Like it or not, I was the sheriff.

CHAPTER 9

There is a paranoia in the military, attributable primarily to an adversarial relationship with the media, that leads to questionable decisions and public relations blunders. Too often the American people were presented sanitized, superficial, or downright fraudulent versions of events that occurred in Iraq (or, in one notable case, Afghanistan)—as if they were children who couldn't bear to hear the truth about the war their country was fighting. Mistakes were made on the battlefield. Is that a shock? Frankly, I find the administrative and policy errors that corrupted the entire initiative (such as failing to deploy troops in sufficient numbers in the early days of the war) to be far more disturbing and, ultimately, damaging than the mistakes that occurred in combat. Again, this is one of the realities of war; it is an imprecise and bloody business. Don't think for a second that we didn't accidentally shoot some of our own soldiers in Germany in 1944; we did. We also dropped bombs on our people, and on German noncombatants.

In every war the United States has fought, in fact, soldiers were struck down by friendly fire, and civilians were wounded or killed. That includes the supposedly "good" and "noble" conflicts, such as World War II. At least we were there to win the fight, and with that resolve came an understanding that despite our best intentions, some very bad things were going to happen.

The army seemed to go out of its way to present everything that happened during the Iraq war in a positive light, even if it meant blatantly misrepresenting the actions of specific soldiers. The truth is, not everyone is wounded or killed in the line of duty; not everyone is killed by enemy fire, and to suggest otherwise diminishes the sacrifice of every soldier who represents his country. The long, laborious cover-up surrounding the death of Pat Tillman, for example, only served to cheapen his memory. It was enough that he had forsaken a lucrative and glamorous career as a professional athlete in favor of selfless military service. It was enough that he gave his life on the battlefield. That he was killed by American forces in the haze of a mission that went bad is, to me, not particularly surprising. Given the fallout that ensued, it was not something that should have been hidden. Nor was there any need to portray Jessica Lynch as anything other than what she was: a soldier who was wounded and captured, as opposed to a "heroic" young woman who went down with guns blazing. I don't know why the Army is so desperate to identify its heroes and villains in this manner, and I don't know why it doesn't share its mistakes along with its triumphs.

Despite incredible advances in technology and telecommunications, despite the awesome power of the Internet, the American people have actually been privy to less of the horrors of war during the Iraq conflict than they were during Vietnam. Whether this is because the media are not doing their job properly, or because the military has some sort of stranglehold on their actions, I can't say for sure. There were times when I almost felt as though some type of conspiracy were in place—an agreement to keep everyone happy. Certainly, in general, I felt that the mainstream media opposed the war and thus presented a biased and often inaccurate account of what was happening—this, despite the fact that only a precious few reporters dared stay long enough, or delve deeply enough, to get the story straight.

I always wondered what would happen if audiences in the United States were shown videotape of the carnage—mangled, charred American bodies along the side of a road in the wake of an IED attack. Maybe that would disgust people and make the army's job even more difficult; then again, maybe it would give pause to those who opposed the war or those who agreed with a policy of appeasement.

You still want to win this thing by winning hearts and minds? Well . . . take a look at this.

You just show a few Americans who have been bound and gagged and had their heads chopped off by an insurgent, and there's no telling what response you might provoke. Perhaps it exceeds the boundaries of decency to project such images around the globe, but it's happening nonetheless, and I'm not sure why we're so squeamish about it. Whether Americans respond to scenes of their countrymen being executed by saying, "Let's kill the terrorists" or "Let's bring everybody home—now!" is almost beside the point. Regardless of the outcome, I'd rather they have a clear understanding of what is happening in Iraq, and what we endured while we were there.

To civilians and senior officers alike, I used to say, "You really need to get some American blood on your hands before you start questioning commanders on the ground and how life should be over there. Fight your way out of a couple of ambushes, hold the hand of a friend as he dies, and then come talk to me."

The army did a horrible job of telling its story. Granted, there is a natural (and perhaps even healthy) wariness between the media and the military, but certainly more could have been done to present a clearer vision of life on the battlefield. I was something of an anomaly: I welcomed the media and spoke bluntly about our work. Maybe I was too open, but I think my approach was preferable to that of Secretary Rumsfeld, who would stand up at a press conference and tell the *Washington Post* and *New York Times* what he thought, and expect them to print it as gospel. Because of his arrogance—*I'm the secretary of defense, and I'm saying it, so that's the way it is!*—the army took a beating and did nothing to defend itself other than to blame its problems on the "liberal media" for failing to get the story right. Rumsfeld was just flat-out ignorant in terms of how he saw the media in this conflict. Al Arabiya, Al Jazeera—every single night they broadcast lie after lie, atrocity after atrocity. If there was an action in Mosul, it was on the Internet or television. It didn't matter how big or small the action might have been. If U.S. forces shot up one car at a checkpoint, it was broadcast in all its ugliness; meanwhile, when the insurgents committed the inhuman act of bombing a Red Cross building in Baghdad, it went virtually ignored. I'm not saying we should have embraced propaganda or utilized a similarly one-sided approach. I'm just saying that when it came to the disseminating of information, we got smoked.

The fear of saying or doing the wrong thing can cripple an army. Certainly in Iraq there was an unwillingness to accept collateral damage as a price of engaging in battle, and the tendency to hide mistakes or to compensate with a checkbook was particularly disturbing.

One such incident occurred in late November, and involved

the Third Battalion, Twenty-ninth Field Artillery. The battalion was located at Samarra East Airfield, which is where we had started out back in April, when I first took command of the 1-8 Infantry. The battalion was used primarily for counterfire whenever the enemy would attack in our area. Using more than two dozen howitzers, and working in conjunction with a fairly sophisticated radar team, the battalion would typically return overwhelming fire within thirty to sixty seconds of an initial strike. This was by design, since the window of opportunity often closed quickly, as the enemy wasn't fond of waiting around to be shot after an ambush or mortar launch.

By this point the brigade, in general, had achieved a significant degree of competency in returning accurate, lethal fire. Mortar fire was particularly valuable, since we no longer waited for clearance before firing. As soon as we received grid coordinates pinpointing the location of the enemy, we simply fired. Immediately. As competent as our soldiers had become, however, there were variables that added to the challenge of unleashing accurate counterfire. Chief among these was the weather. Every twelve hours meteorological data was updated and entered into the battalion's computerized artillery system, but the slightest change, if not properly accounted for, could result in the target being missed—sometimes by a wide margin. On this particular night a stiff wind, probably twenty-five to thirty miles per hour, had begun to kick in. November, December, and January are raw months in Iraq—temperatures falling into the thirties and forties at night, with lots of wind and rain. The dusty roads of summer become muddy trails, travel becomes treacherous, and fighting takes on a different set of challenges.

Beast Company, 1-8 Infantry's engineering company, had taken fire early on the morning of November 24, with three mortar rounds hitting the base at approximately 0600 hours.

That's typically the way it worked—rounds would come in just before daylight, as the insurgents used the last thirty to forty-five minutes of darkness to fire and get out of there before they could be easily or clearly identified in the daytime. Third Battalion returned fire in support of Beast Company, but apparently the action was taken without the artillery having been updated with the most current meteorological data; as a result, the rounds landed, on average, five hundred meters short of their intended target—in some cases, they fell as much as seven hundred meters short.

The consequences of such a misfiring can be disastrous, and so they were in this case. My first indication that something had gone awry occurred with the arrival of a local man at our base. He was crying and waving his arms, shouting something about the Americans having killed a bunch of people near his village (Al Mazare'e). I had no idea what he was talking about, since I did not yet know that Beast had been fired upon, or that counterfire had been launched by Third Battalion, Twenty-ninth Artillery Regiment. Beast was already in the process of questioning villagers located in the area where the original mortars had been fired, so that's where I went. When I arrived, I found soldiers from Beast involved in a heated discussion with villagers who were trying to explain that several people had been killed by American fire roughly a half mile away. None of it made sense, so I asked one of the villagers to lead me to the site of the damage.

By the time I arrived, most of the dead had been taken away by their families and the wounded had been transported to Balad Hospital, but it was obvious that something had gone terribly wrong. Four Iraqi civilians had been killed; five others were seriously wounded. One large family, in particular, had been devastated by the blasts. The Ahteemi family lived in a farming compound, and when one of the first rounds entered the home and ripped apart a section of the first floor, terrified family members began streaming outside. They had no idea what was happening and were simply trying to protect themselves, but they wound up rushing straight into the line of fire. Mr. Ahteemi, I later discovered, had four wives and more than a dozen children. One of his wives was killed in the onslaught; another was seriously wounded. Four of his children were killed; three more were injured.

It's almost impossible to put into words the horror of a scene such as this, and the sadness that envelops you as you walk through a farm and see the body parts of children who have been blown to pieces . . . or the helplessness of explaining to the survivors that you intended no harm, and that it was all just a terrible accident. Yet, you do it . . . time and again. After a while you become steeled to it.

After the site had been cleaned, I drove back to the base and released everyone who had been detained as part of the investigation into the incident, because they were all just part of the Ahteemi clan; none of them had been involved in the original attack on Beast Company. They were just distraught relatives. A family in Iraq, you see, is not merely the nuclear unit—it's the first and second cousins, aunts and uncles, grandparents and great-grandparents. They all live in the same area, farm the same land, share the same resources. So we had made a bad situation worse by capturing and detaining all these people who had nothing to do with the attack, and who were, in fact, visibly shaken by what had happened that morning.

After ordering the release of all detainees, I went down to Balad Hospital to visit the wounded and meet with members of their family. It wasn't the first time I'd been through this sort of thing, but I must admit that this particular incident was more disturbing than most, for a variety of reasons. The mother who had been killed was in her early forties, not much older than I was at the time. The three children who had been killed were roughly the same age as my children. The survivors were in rough shape. One of Mr. Ahteemi's wives had shrapnel wounds to her torso and face; the children were all crying, in part out of pain, but probably as much because of the emotional trauma of what they had experienced. The most seriously wounded was a twelve-year-old girl named Ma'rwa Ahteemi, whose legs and spine had taken the brunt of the blast.

Ma'rwa just lay in her bed, wailing and moaning, and the sight of her in that state, a poor, helpless child who had done nothing to deserve this fate, filled me with overwhelming sadness. For a soldier, there is almost nothing worse than the death or maiming of a child. That is why I urge any president who would commit American sons and daughters to fight in a foreign land to seriously consider the consequences of his actions. Please understand that a lot of terrible things are going to happen in the course of a war—worse things than you can ever imagine. People are going to be killed and maimed, and some of them will have nothing whatsoever to do with the battle being fought. There was a time when wars were fought without consideration for such things, when the object was simply to slaughter as many people from the opposite side as was necessary to achieve victory. This included combatants and noncombatants alike. We are, thankfully, a more civilized nation than that today, and I know of no American soldier who is unmoved by the prospect of a wounded child—but it happens . . . and it will always happen when countries go to war.

Every so often in Iraq I would feel a huge sense of sadness and grief; but part of the job—part of the challenge of leading soldiers into combat and helping them stay alive—was to put these feelings aside. As I stood there in the hospital that day, watching Ma'rwa Ahteemi cry out in pain, I wanted nothing more than to walk over to her and hold her in my arms. I wanted to respond in the natural way that a father would respond, but I couldn't do that. For one thing, I was an American military officer, a soldier in uniform, and nobody wants to hug a soldier in a uniform after her family has been shelled and wounded or killed. More to the point, what could I have said?

It'll be okay . . .

No, that would be a lie. Nothing would ever be okay for Ma'rwa. We had changed this girl's life—irrevocably and forever. You have to understand that an Iraqi woman does not hold the same status in her society that an American woman holds in her society. It seemed to me that Iraqi women were viewed by the men in their country as second-class citizens—at best. In some cases, they seemed to be considered of less value than the animals that were raised on their farms. This point was driven home to me early during my deployment, when I saw an old truck rumbling through Albu Hishma, on a cool, rainy day. In the cab of the truck was a man and a small boy, maybe four or five years of age; I presumed they were father and son. I do know that the back of the truck was filled with people—four adult women and perhaps fifteen children, all female. They were jammed together, some sitting on top of each other. All of them were wet and shivering. As the truck rolled by, I signaled for the driver to stop. He rolled down his window.

"Dude," I said, incredulously, through my translator. "What's up with all the women in the back? Why don't you at least allow a couple of them to ride in the front?"

The driver laughed. Then, speaking as if the passengers were farm animals on their way to market, he responded. "Sir . . . the women need the fresh air."

Meaning, I guess, that women, at least in that particular region, did not share the front seat of a vehicle with a man, and that a four-year-old boy ranked higher than all nineteen of the

females put together. And that's just the way it was. I have heard
people argue otherwise, but as far as I could tell, women in Iraqi
society had few rights and even fewer privileges. They served a
few very specific purposes, most notably cooking, cleaning, and
breeding. A woman unable to perform those basic functions was
of little use to anyone. That is the thought that went through my
head as I looked at Ma'rwa Ahteemi, with her broken legs and
shattered spine. A woman who was injured in that way, paralyzed
from the waist down, would be utterly useless. She would be an
outcast, with no function whatsoever. She couldn't bear children;
she couldn't clean a house or prepare a meal; she couldn't work
on a farm. That little girl's future disappeared in Iraq the day she
took shrapnel in her spine, and the realization that American soldiers had been responsible for her fate saddened me beyond
words. Ma'rwa would have a very difficult life, at best, and there
was virtually nothing I could do about it.

The army's answer to such mistakes was to pull out a checkbook and try to place a dollar value on the damage that had been
done. I understand, of course, that this is not a unique approach in
Western (particularly American) culture, where litigation often
results in financial compensation for the loss of life. In this arena,
however, it seemed even more perverse. Each life was deemed
worthy of a certain payment, depending on the age of the victim
and the circumstances surrounding his or her death (i.e., the degree of perceived negligence or error on the part of the U.S. military). In the case of Mr. Ahteemi, I believe the final payment was
approximately $15,000. That was how much the U.S. govern-
ment was willing to pay this man for the loss of three children
and one wife. It was, in my opinion, a twisted response to the
coldness and brutality of war. On principle alone, I was opposed
to monetary compensation for collateral damage—the idea of
placing a dollar figure on human life seemed at once grotesque

and weak, and the process always left me feeling sick to my stomach (often I was the officer responsible for issuing these payments).

Attempting to secure proper medical care for those who had been wounded by our mistakes was another matter. Following the errant bombing of Mr. Ahteemi's home, I asked Colonel Rudesheim and some of our doctors to visit the wounded at Balad Hospital, with the hope that some of them might be transferred to a U.S. MASH facility at LSA Anaconda. Being in Balad Hospital was like being in an American hospital in the 1940s; the equipment was relatively new, but the technology was decades behind that which was commonly utilized in the United States. The doctors could do almost nothing for Ma'rwa and her family, and they readily acknowledged as much. So I put in a request to have some of our people examine the wounded, and to my surprise it was honored. American physicians visited Balad Hospital and decided that Ma'rwa should be transferred to the MASH facility. She eventually ended up going to the United States and getting some superb care to try to restore some of the function in her upper body. In short, she received the best medical care possible and probably made the most complete recovery that could be expected given the severity of her injuries, but she did not regain the use of her legs. Though she went home with a wheelchair that her family could not possibly have afforded without American assistance, I have little reason to be optimistic about the long-term outlook for her life in Iraq.

As for Mr. Ahteemi, his grief soon gave way to greed, and he began pestering me endlessly about receiving the $15,000 he was due. "You should know, Muqadem Sassaman" (Muqadem is Arabic for lieutenant colonel), Mr. Ahteemi had said to me shortly after the bombing, "that with this money, I will be able to get a new wife." He paused and smiled. "A fine young woman."

That, I guess, was part of the arrangement—when you married, you gave the wife's family a certain amount of money. So, far from being distraught over the death of one of his older wives, Mr. Ahteemi was excited about the prospect of trading up. Moral objections aside, I was primarily concerned that he wouldn't be able to manage his resources; he was a poor farmer from an agricultural area who had never had access to so much money in his life. I was worried that he wouldn't use the money to rebuild his home and to help the surviving children. So when the check arrived, I drove Mr. Ahteemi to a local bank and helped him set up an account. Now, in this particular bank (and in most Iraqi banks at the time), there was no interest to be earned on the account. It was not like a typical American bank. You simply put the money in a safety-deposit box. In this way, it would at least be safe from thieves, of which there was no shortage. Sometimes, in fact, multiple families would share one home and steal from each other. It was my hope that by establishing a bank account for Mr. Ahteemi, I was helping him have the best chance to use his money wisely.

It wasn't until more than a month later that I stopped by the bank again and discovered that Mr. Ahteemi's account had dwindled to less than $2,000. So I visited his home, along with my translator. Mr. Ahteemi was not home at the time, but one of his wives told us she was concerned about her husband's behavior. He'd bought himself a car and some nice clothes, in addition to a new wife. Some of the money had been used to rebuild the home (which was a prerequisite to receiving payment), but everything else had been spent on himself.

"You must do something about this," she said. "He's not taking care of the children."

I just listened and nodded; there was, of course, nothing I could do.

Several months later, when I returned to the United States,

I received numerous inquiries from journalists who had gotten wind of the journey of Ma'rwa Ahteemi. I understood their interest. Ma'rwa's story was moving and compelling in its own right, but it also represented something larger. What better way to simultaneously illustrate the horrors of war and the triumph of the human spirit than to focus on a seventy-pound girl whose body has been broken, but whose will remains strong? For a change the U.S. military handled the matter in a way that was appropriate . . . even admirable. Rather than simply throwing money at the problem—buying silence through appeasement— we rolled up our sleeves and got our hands dirty. Although I was immersed in problems of my own at the time I conducted interviews regarding Ma'rwa, I tried to speak candidly about what had happened, and why I had tried to make sure that she received the best possible care. "We'd made a mistake," I told one reporter. "And we were trying to help the family out."

Most of the stories, while acknowledging the quagmire that the Iraq war had become, seemed to offer grudging respect to the soldiers and doctors and politicians who tried to take care of Ma'rwa. I can't imagine that a better response could have been achieved by pretending the bombing wasn't our responsibility, or by simply further padding the bank account of Ma'rwa's father. Admit your mistakes . . . publicize your triumphs. I still believe that's the best policy, and the response to Ma'rwa's story would seem to support that notion.

At the same time, I don't mean to imply that this was a tale with a neat or happy ending. It has no ending yet, and I have no reason to believe that Ma'rwa, for all of her strength and courage, will find a fulfilling life back in Iraq. The last I knew, she had returned to the family farm. Life on that farm is not easy under the best of circumstances; I can't imagine what it must be like for Ma'rwa.

I have been, for most of my life, an optimist, but Iraq sucked much of that out of me. I would like to believe that Ma'rwa has found a measure of happiness, but I can't believe that is the case. Mr. Ahteemi got a new car and a new wife, but before long the money was gone and it was back to business as usual. The same old dreary life—only now he had four fewer children, and one who was severely disabled.

That is the reality of war, and it is the price of bringing democracy to Iraq.

CHAPTER 10

Despite the similar names, Samarra is hardly the city of the Good Samaritan. In fact, in December of 2003, when the 1-8 Infantry was ordered to leave Balad and drive north to Samarra, to lead an action known as Operation Ivy Blizzard, the city was among the most violent and ravaged in all of Iraq.

Operation Ivy Blizzard provided keen insight into the lack of coherent, consistent viewpoints among U.S. commanders on how to effectively attack the insurgency—even between battalions fighting in the same combat brigade, there seemed to be no sense of a shared vision. It was the story of an American tank battalion commander, Lieutenant Colonel Ryan Gonsalves, who appeased the Iraqis and generally avoided fighting the insurgency to limit collateral damage. As a result, the First Battalion, Sixty-sixth Armor Regiment had failed to establish legitimate authority (the crucial first step in the formula for a successful campaign in Iraq) in this predominantly Sunni city; in fact, the 1-66 Armor had suffered combat losses that had forced the battalion to leave its base on the outskirts of Samarra and reestablish a base of operations deep in the hinterlands, miles from the city center. This was a devastating setback, since, as previously noted, it is virtually impossible to defeat an urban-based insurgency from beyond the city limits. Ivy Blizzard was an operation clearly designed to use American might to regain control of Samarra, an insurgent-infested city whose occupants routinely defied American authority and had been emboldened by their previous successes over the 1-66 Armor.

I was never more afraid in my life than during nighttime patrols through the streets of downtown Samarra; it was only a matter of time before the RPGs, machine-gun fire, IEDs, and sniper fire would ring out, breaking the unbearable tension that precedes a combat action. Though I have seen news reports depicting the Sunnis' "love" for Samarra's Golden Dome, Shiite Mosque (which was bombed in 2006, allegedly by al Qaeda), I believe the primary reason for their affection, at least in late 2003, stemmed from the fact that insurgents could launch RPGs or sniper fire from the mosque without fear of retaliation; they knew full well that U.S. soldiers were forbidden to return fire in the vicinity of the mosque, or to conduct raids within its walls. We were so concerned about causing any damage to the building that we deliberately and needlessly placed our soldiers in dangerous, even life-threatening situations. This was yet another example of a dubious military decision that bordered on Vietnam-era lunacy: allowing enemy forces a safe haven to plan, equip, and fight without any concern about retaliation from U.S. forces. I, for one, had no problem with the bombing of the Golden Dome Mosque; indeed, given a window of opportunity and the freedom to conduct such a mission, I would have ordered my soldiers to blow it to bits in late 2003.

I had mixed feelings about moving to Samarra. It was clearly an honor to have been designated as the battalion most capable of leading Operation Ivy Blizzard. This, to me, was not a small thing. Despite my ongoing philosophical disagreements with Colonel Rudesheim over how to prosecute the war (and his seeming belief in a policy of appeasement and nonconfrontation was one that was shared by some senior officers), this invitation, which came directly from General Odierno, validated all the hard (and frequently courageous) work that had gone into the previous months. No one really wanted to give voice to the obvious: the 1-8 Infantry had been chosen specifically because of the violent and aggressive approach it had employed in bringing security and stability to Balad and the surrounding area of operation—but it was clear, nonetheless. General Odierno had faith in us as a combat battalion, and knew that we were capable of cleaning up the mess that Samarra had become.

At the same time, I found it frustrating that after finally gaining a measure of success in our own area, we would be leaving (if only for approximately two months). Moreover, while it was nice to be recognized for our work, I considered it annoying that I had to risk the lives of my soldiers because another battalion had proved woefully impotent. Gonsalves and the 1-66 Armor had been up there for eight months, and their campaign, such as it was, had been an unmitigated disaster. Why? Because they had followed Colonel Rudesheim's lead and adopted a timid approach to their work. They were unwilling to fight, and their restraint not only had proved ineffective in winning the trust and respect of the Iraqi people, but had actually resulted in both the insurgents and the citizens holding the Americans in contempt. By refusing to use the weapons at its disposal, the 1-66 Armor had made a bad situation worse, and it seemed unfair that someone else had to fix their problem.

Nevertheless, that was our role, and if there was a bit of hypocrisy in General Odierno identifying the 1-8 Infantry as the main effort in Operation Ivy Blizzard (at the same time that our brigade commander was riding me incessantly about dialing back our aggressiveness), it was not really surprising. When muscle was needed, the 1-8 Infantry was summoned. It had happened during Operation Peninsula Strike, and it happened during the hunt for Saddam, when the 1-8 Infantry was handpicked to lead an air assault raid into Albu Tallah. We had become aggressive and violent; we'd also become very good at the business of fighting, and everyone knew it.

We left Balad on December 11, two days before Operation Ivy Blizzard was scheduled to begin. When Saddam was captured on December 13, however, the ensuing storm of publicity necessitated a delay; the operation eventually began on the fifteenth. Samarra, we quickly determined, was a far different and more dangerous place than Balad. It was, in my estimation, a city of criminals and terrorists. Since the start of the war, the Iraqis had repeatedly said there were three cities we'd never effectively control: Fallujah, Ar Ramadi, and Samarra.

"Why?" I asked.

"Because not even Saddam could control them."

That was true. Rather than relying on the tools of tyranny (fear and torture being the most obvious) that worked so well in most of his country, Saddam, ever the pragmatist, settled for good old-fashioned bribery in these cities. Among the many power brokers in Iraq was a group known as the "sheiks of the nineties," so called because they came by their titles not through the traditional methods of lineage, but rather through the largesse of Saddam. The dictator would appoint certain men as sheiks (as often as not they were gangsters who already held some sway over the population); then he would put them on his payroll, with the understanding that they would keep the populace under control. On some level, you had to admire the strategy. Saddam was smart enough to know that he could never manage these places through military action (not without enormous risk to his own status), so he brought the mob under his umbrella in time-honored fashion: by buying them. While the sheiks held lofty and evocative titles, they were really nothing more than well-paid, bloodthirsty henchmen, and it was their job to make sure that Saddam's rule was maintained. The sheiks of the nineties had access to Saddam's money, power, and police force. They were a semiautonomous branch of Saddam's government, a freewheeling death squad whose only role was to maintain order—by any means necessary. Samarra was crawling with sheiks of the nineties, and I can't imagine that they didn't find the 1-66 Armor's lack of fortitude contemptible; by the time we arrived, they owned the city.

In fairness, the turmoil in Samarra wasn't entirely the fault of Lieutenant Colonel Gonsalves. All parties would have been better served by flip-flopping our battalions: the 1-8 Infantry should have been in Samarra all along, and the 1-66 Armor should have been in Balad. As it was, we had our most passive unit stationed in a nasty, battled-scarred city. The tanks of the 1-66 should have come down to our area. They would have done a respectable job of traveling up and down the various alternate supply routes, taking RPG shots without ever fighting back, and Colonel Rudesheim would have been happy. Although it was a tall order, I know the 1-8 Infantry would have quickly been able to clean up Samarra.

Instead, we were brought in as a Band-Aid. Samarra was an urban fight, the 1-66 Armor was getting its butt kicked, and Gonsalves desperately needed infantry assistance—soldiers who were willing to patrol the city streets on foot, break down doors, and make their presence known. This was not an assignment without risks. The Samarra City Council had warned Gonsalves: *If you come back here, we'll kill you.* So the 1-66 remained ensconced on its base, outside the city limits, watching helplessly as the insurgents wreaked havoc. The whole place was a complete disaster. There was no American-led city council; no significant security and stability had been established—ever. They just continued to get pounded until, inevitably, two soldiers were killed in mortar attacks.

Whereas the 1-8 Infantry's base headquarters covered a footprint of approximately one square mile, the 1-66 had jammed itself into a footprint of roughly six hundred square meters. The first time I had visited, a few months earlier, it had occurred to me that if a round ever landed in there, people were going to be seriously hurt. At FOB Eagle there was room to breathe—room for a mortar shell to crash feebly into the earth and hurt no one—but not in Samarra. Since the 1-66 would not patrol, but would simply sit at observation posts and scan the area, its soldiers became easy targets. Attacks became more frequent until, finally, the battalion simply packed up and moved out of the city. When the 1-8 Infantry arrived in December for Operation Ivy Blizzard, 1-66 Armor's headquarters was an old agricultural warehouse area, just off of Highway 1, a good fifteen miles from Samarra.

To me, this represented not merely capitulation on the part of American forces, but a complete and utter failure on the part of the 1-66 Armor. Now, I'm sure that if you talked to that battalion commander today, he'd spin things in a different way—he'd argue that his unit won the war in Samarra. Things have worked out well for Ryan Gonsalves. He's been promoted to full colonel, and I'm sure he'll command a brigade one day, but he, just like Fred Rudesheim, was not a fighter, and he was not part of the winning organization that I thought the U.S. Army was all about. Rather, Colonel Gonsalves is cut from the same conservative and self-promoting mold that typifies the upper levels of Big Army, and the fact that his behavior was rewarded is one of the reasons I ultimately decided to leave the military.

As home to the Golden Dome Mosque (and the minaret), Samarra was an enormously popular destination for Shias making religious pilgrimages. There was just one problem: the city itself was overwhelmingly Sunni. Samarra, then, was in a state of constant tension and friction, based on hundreds of years of religious intolerance. There is no separation of state and religion in Iraq; it's one and the same. That's why a Muslim democracy will never look like an American or European democracy, and it's unrealistic to expect otherwise. (I always felt the best that could be hoped for was some type of parliamentary system.) In Iraq I developed a deeper understanding of the differences between "faith" and "religion," especially organized religion. I always got the sense, particularly on the Sunni side, because they're a little bit more fundamentalist, that it was well within the accepted parameters of some groups' beliefs to shed blood in the name of Allah—to purge the world of the infidels that could infiltrate their religion or water it down. None of the sectarian violence that plagued Iraq is surprising at all. The fracturing of this country is more deeply rooted in religious differences than in anything else, and U.S. intervention, halfhearted and ill-conceived, actually facilitated retaliation and violence on a level not previously known. We came to Iraq to help get rid of Saddam and liberate oppressed Shias, but twelve months later, radical Shias were killing our soldiers in the streets of Sadr City. So I'm not saying it was Sunni fanatics alone. The real struggle for U.S. forces, I always thought, was to try to avoid driving the traditional Muslim family, whether Shia or Sunni, into the radical camp—the camp that wanted nothing more than to kill Americans. It was a constant battle.

Nowhere did the battle seem more hopeless than in Samarra. The city itself reminded me of something you might have found in Germany or England in World War II—a battered metropolitan area that had survived multiple bombings. Highly concentrated and densely urban, Samarra was smaller than it appeared on a map. The streets were narrow and laid out in a grid, with roundabouts dictating traffic flow in all directions and giving the city a bit of a European flavor. Bordered by the Tigris River, Samarra covered a space of perhaps ten square miles; beyond the city boundary was desert.

For all its violent fundamentalism, Samarra was not untouched by Western influence. Just a few doors down from the Golden Dome Mosque, for example, was a local branch of the Arnold Schwarzenegger Gym, the popularity of which was apparent to even a casual observer. The men in Balad (and in most of the southern part of Iraq) were generally slight and unimposing. There weren't a lot of tall guys, and those who did crack the six-foot barrier were typically skinny to the point of appearing almost frail. Samarra was a different story. The streets were teeming with thugs—barrel-chested men with thick arms and pronounced brows. The first time I walked by the gym and peered through the window, and saw some of these guys pumping stacks of steel, I knew we were in for a different kind of fight, and indeed, it was. Anytime we were at a routine checkpoint, stopping young men, they came out swinging. They didn't like being told what to do, and confrontations were common.

In Balad, if we wanted someone to open the trunk of his car, he would usually just nod and comply. In Samarra, as often as not, the response was a stream of epithets hurled in angry Arabic. We detained people by the score, but there was no effective way to deal with much of the hostility and chaos that ruled in Samarra. Since the inception of the war, no American force had taken charge. American authority had been defied since day one, and now, having run 1-66 Armor out of town, the locals were more emboldened than ever. The place was infested with insurgents who wanted nothing more than to fight and kill American soldiers. It was a serious mess, which is why division command decided to launch Operation Ivy Blizzard: in the hope that we could finally provide some support and stability to the region, train a police force, and maybe use some money to rebuild schools and hospitals. In that way, perhaps, we could foster enough goodwill to turn the tide in a city that had been all but forsaken.

By the time the 1-8 Infantry reached Samarra, a degree of cynicism had infiltrated the ranks. I tried to refrain from voicing my growing concern over the army's lack of commitment to the war effort, and instead tried to focus on the job at hand. That's what Operation Ivy Blizzard was to me: a job. Not a "cause" or even a "mission." Just a job. By now we knew that we'd be leaving Iraq by the early springtime, so it was unlikely that we'd spend more than the next sixty days in Samarra before returning to Balad. There was only so much we could accomplish in that time frame, but I was committed to doing the best I could. For a while it had seemed as though there was real purpose to our work, but much of that spirit of nobility had been drained by now. In my heart, I questioned whether it was possible to turn things around. Winning, which once seemed a legitimate possibility, now seemed to be almost beside the point. After the death of Panchot and the bumbling of 1-66 Armor that resulted in my soldiers being summoned to what was essentially a meat grinder, I had become a far more skeptical commander.

As it happened, Operation Ivy Blizzard was a rousing success, in part because the capture of Saddam had led to an influx of information and intelligence, and a general breaking of ranks among the insurgency. We hit more than fifty targets in the first seventy-two hours alone, and encountered virtually no opposition. It was almost too easy, too smooth . . . as if the insurgents had known of our plans and decided to flee the city for a while. Regardless, I was immensely proud of the way we performed; everyone was crisp and professional in their communications. We were at the top of our game, taking down targets in methodical, tactical, military fashion—in a manner that would have made a lot of commanders feel good about what they were doing.

Following the initial wave of the operation, an eerie calm settled over Samarra. We got into a routine of heavy, consistent patrolling. Our units were in the streets, 24-7, demonstrating a presence (and a willingness to maintain order) that had been sorely lacking since the start of the war. At the same time, a military police battalion went to work on a different front—trying to get a large group of Iraqi Security Forces trained—and civil affairs teams cobbled together plans to spend money in the city and rapidly rebuild the police station and city council building. It seemed, on the surface at least, as though real progress had been made, and in relatively short order.

Even as the situation improved in Samarra, things were beginning to unravel in our former area of operation. We had left Balad on December 11; Operation Ivy Blizzard had begun on the fifteenth. Three days later I received word that seven police officers had been killed in Balad. Whether it was true or not, I couldn't say for sure, since the flow of information from the region had become slow and unreliable in our absence. Typically, people from Balad would come to our base during hours of limited visibility and slip us notes. In this way, we'd keep abreast of any problems that might be developing in the region. Unfortunately, the new unit in Balad was unfamiliar with this process, so any information that came to the gate was turned away. After about a week of being rebuffed, people from Balad began driving the hour and a half north to Samarra in an attempt to find the 1-8 Infantry and give us the information, thinking maybe we'd be able to help them in some way.

In one of these routine messages we received word of the seven murdered police officers in Balad, so I dispatched the XO and the Alpha Company commander in a patrol to verify the communication. If the rumor was true, it represented a distinct shift in the climate of Balad. We'd been gone only a week, and already, it seemed, the gains we had worked so hard to realize were being forfeited.

Sadly, we soon learned that the report was true; even more disturbing was the realization that the deaths could have been avoided, and probably would have been avoided had our unit not been dispatched to Samarra. Here's what happened: The police had discovered an IED near a farmer's market on a main thoroughfare into the city. Following standard protocol, the police officers had cleared the area and then visited FOB Eagle to ask for assistance from Second Battalion, Third Infantry Regiment (the unit that had taken our place while we were in Samarra). Initially, they received no response from 2-3, in large part because no relationship had been established between the soldiers and the police officers. This was a unit that had come in on a temporary basis; it would spend two to three weeks in Balad before beginning its own fight in Mosul. The soldiers knew nothing about the police force in Balad, and so ignored the possibility that the officers were telling the truth when they said they had found an unexploded howitzer round on the side of a city street. The police officers, frustrated to the point of agitation, and concerned that innocent lives would be lost, decided to take matters into their own hands and attempted to defuse the round. The bomb exploded while they were working on it, killing seven officers, including the deputy police chief. No offense to Colonel Fadhil, the chief of police, and an effective leader in his own right (until he was assassinated, anyway), but up to this point, it was the deputy police chief, Lieutenant Colonel Nasser Hamied Ahmed, who had really been doing much of the heavy lifting. Matt Cunningham had been working tirelessly with the deputy police chief to create a functional and effective police force, and now he was gone, leaving a void that would be difficult, if not impossible, to fill. In the six months that we had been patrolling in Balad, nothing like this had ever happened, and I couldn't help but think that this disaster was attributable in large part to the sudden exodus of the 1–8 Infantry.

Shortly thereafter, a firefight at a checkpoint near Balad claimed the lives of four members of the Iraqi Security Forces that we had trained. This was a major checkpoint on Highway 1, and we typically ran it jointly, with U.S. soldiers and Iraqi Security Forces operating side by side. I viewed these men as I viewed my own soldiers. They risked their lives in support of our mission, and we treated them accordingly. When they were wounded, they were medevaced to U.S. MASH facilities and received care from American physicians. The deaths of these four security men, coming on the heels of the killing of the seven Iraqi police officers, left me angry and frustrated. In a span of two weeks, eleven people had been killed in an area I still considered to be my responsibility.

Meanwhile, I was in Samarra, a city that had fallen suddenly and strangely quiet. Not that I was naive enough to think Samarra had been tamed. It was more like the city and the insurgency had taken a collective deep breath. I hated these periods of inactivity, for they tended to provoke complacency in a soldier. In Samarra, an area we did not know particularly well, this was an attitude with potentially deadly consequences. Despite the lack of contact, Samarra was an eerie and tense place, especially at night. The narrow city streets, lined with three- and four-story buildings (perfect for snipers), many of them empty or strewn with rubble, added a palpable air of danger. While curfew was strictly enforced in

Samarra, it wasn't unusual to see young men out after hours, wandering alone, and you knew their intentions weren't benign. Tactically and militarily speaking, Samarra was a city of challenges, and clearly it was a place better suited to the skills and aggressiveness of an infantry unit. Still, I didn't want to be there. We ended up pouring more than $7 million into the city in roughly two months; we trained a security force of more than one thousand Iraqis; we rebuilt infrastructure. Then we left. The entire time we were there, I worried about what was happening back in Balad.

As Christmas approached, I was beginning to wonder whether we'd ever see any real combat action in Samarra. Our guys were living in a huge warehouse, with no heat, no creature comforts to speak of, and no real affinity for the work they were doing. So I decided to try to bring some holiday cheer to the troops. I ordered Christmas music to be played over the loudspeaker in our headquarters—round the clock. At first it was kind of nice, but after a while I think it drove everyone nuts. I didn't care. We were a world away from our loved ones, fighting a war that seemed increasingly to have no focus, no support, and I was determined that, at the very least, my soldiers were going to experience Christmas. The cafeteria was decorated, and I arranged schedules in such a way that most of the battalion—perhaps 80 to 90 percent—would have Christmas Day off. We would have someone dress up as Santa Claus, and the officers would sing Christmas carols to the soldiers. We'd even have a candlelight service on Christmas Eve. This could be traced back to my childhood, being raised in the Free Methodist church—I wanted to have something formal, to recognize Christmas, and to celebrate. Yes, it was rainy and muddy and gloomy, and we were all far from home, but we would do the best we could to recognize the holiday and express gratitude for the small gifts that had come our way.

The holiday, however, did not go exactly as planned. I was on patrol on the outskirts of Samarra on Christmas Eve, when we were rocked by a massive explosion. The blast had occurred about a mile and a half to the south, in an area known as the Samarra Highway 1 Bypass, yet the force was startling even there, so far away. I knew right away that this was an IED explosion, and a big one at that.

We jumped into our vehicles and drove straight to the point of contact, arriving within minutes. The devastation was instantly apparent. The bomb had hit a small convoy from the Triple Nickel (555th) Engineer Battalion, with one of the three vehicles sustaining catastrophic damage. Charlie Company had already begun moving in on several groups of bystanders as we went to work trying to help the wounded. (In an IED situation, almost nobody stood around and watched. If you were an Iraqi, and you knew there was going to be an ambush or explosion, you knew enough not to be anywhere near the blast. If you were, there was a reasonable chance you'd be killed, detained, or captured—regardless of whether you had anything to do with the ambush. American forces were going to return fire, and then detain anybody even close to the site, whether involved or not, just to gather information.)

As Charlie Company began the interrogation process, our physician's assistant, Wayne Slicton, went to work on the wounded, but there was little he could do. There were three soldiers in the first vehicle. A sergeant first class had been driving. Next to him, in the front passenger seat, was a major. Behind them, in the rear of the Humvee, was a captain. In any combat action, survival and success are determined by a combination of skill and luck. In the case of an IED attack, skill doesn't come into play. It's all a matter of geography and timing. An IED is basically just a bomb buried beneath the dirt. Sometimes it's a single shell, sometimes it's a series of shells. Each shell is approximately two feet in length and six inches in diameter, and in this case packed with thousands of steel ball bearings, each about the size and shape of a marble. When the IED is detonated (this happens manually, by someone standing nearby, or through the use of a cell phone), the shell casing is ripped apart, and the ball bearings are propelled in all directions, becoming, in effect, thousands of miniature cannonballs that tear into anything in the vicinity with roughly the speed and force of a jetliner.

In this particular case, the blast originated from beneath the passenger side of the Triple Nickel vehicle. The front end had been sheared away, but it was the captain, sitting in the rear, who seemed at first to have taken the brunt of the attack, the force of which was so strong that it had torn his torso away from his legs. The captain had been wearing a lap belt, but all that remained in the seat were his legs and feet. He'd literally been cut in half. The major had also been killed instantly. Indeed, the bomb seemed to have landed on his lap. There was nothing left of him. Just bits and pieces, bloody fragments of a human being. Of the three, only the sergeant first class had survived the initial explosion, and he was in bad shape as well. Wayne worked furiously to stabilize him, but his injuries—hundreds of shrapnel wounds to his head and torso—were just too severe. He expired before we even got him on the medevac bird.

One of the things you don't hear about an IED ambush is the aftermath. Americans have seen little of the combat that is so common in Iraq, and even less of the carnage that follows a firefight or IED explosion. They don't see what I saw that day outside Samarra; a group of soldiers walking around for the better part of an hour, wearing latex gloves, scooping up body parts and filling three heavy plastic bags with remains, trying our best to leave nothing behind.

Nor do they witness the infighting that sometimes occurs, or the flaring of tempers that comes with trying to handle an ambush with professionalism and detachment. Colonel Rudesheim arrived on the scene while Doc Slicton and I were working on the wounded. As the rest of the engineer unit wandered around, dazed and confused (they were not a fighting unit, and I'm pretty sure this was the first time they'd ever been attacked), and Charlie Company tried to establish a perimeter and begin interrogating witnesses, I saw Colonel Rudesheim shouting at some of my men. Apparently, he felt that our guys had been a bit rough in the handling of the Iraqi witnesses, even though an aggressive interrogation was standard procedure around these kinds of attacks. It strikes at the core of a soldier to see a comrade cut up like that, whether you know him personally or not. Restraint was always advised, but things happen in the heat of combat, and it's actually pretty rare for anyone to be hanging around in the vicinity of an ambush—unless, of course, he had something to do with its execution. I know only that this was yet another surreal scene—Doc Slicton covered in blood, working to save the one soldier who still had a slight pulse, while just a hundred meters away my brigade commander interfered with an interrogation out of concern that one of the witnesses was not being handled gently enough.

It wasn't until later that day that I spoke with Fred about this (and I'm sure that interaction, blunt and acrimonious, did little to improve my standing in his eyes)—not until the bodies had been removed, the medevac had pulled away, and the entire scene was cleared of debris. I wanted the site to appear almost pristine, in part out of respect to our fallen soldiers, but also because nothing burned me more than televised images of Iraqis celebrating U.S. military casualties, or jumping up and down, waving frantically as American army vehicles burned in the background. So I always tried to scrub the scene of any contact, to make it seem like business as usual. There was nothing I could do to change what had happened, and all I could think about as we tied up the body bags and pulled away was this: Sometime in the next few hours, three American families were going to get the news that their loved one—a husband, a father, a son—was gone, and I could not imagine what that would do to a family, to get that kind of news on Christmas Day. Not that there was a *good* day to receive such a message—but Christmas? It just seemed so . . . tragic.

That night, back on the base, chaplain Leif Espeland conducted a Christmas Eve service, which now seemed to have a bit more poignancy. Afterward, I lay in my bunk, tossing and turning, images of the butchered Triple Nickel unit burned into my brain. Unable to sleep, burdened by anxiety over things beyond my control, I decided to go for a walk, maybe chat with the guys on the perimeter. We had a few different gates in and out of the base, and I wanted to make sure not only that they were secure, but that the men guarding them knew I appreciated their efforts on Christmas Eve. It just seemed like the right thing to do.

The first gate was located only about fifty meters from Highway 1, and as I looked out toward the road through night vision goggles, I was stunned to see a late-model GMC Suburban parked less than halfway between the gate and the highway.

"Dude," I said incredulously to the specialist who had been on sentry duty. "When did *that* show up?"

The first thing that came to mind, of course, was the possibility that I was staring at one seriously large and lethal vehicle-borne IED, one capable of blowing the entire gate back to Balad and then some.

"Uh . . . I don't know, sir," the specialist stammered. "It was out there when I got here."

I radioed the TOC and summoned the men who had been on

guard duty the previous shift. One of the soldiers explained that he had seen a group of what appeared to be American contractors drive up in two identical GMC Suburbans.

"They dropped this one off," he said, gesturing toward the gate.

"Uh-huh . . ."

He shrugged. "Then they drove off in the other one."

I couldn't help but laugh. "Soldier . . . you didn't report that to anybody?"

He shook his head. "No, sir. I'm just supposed to monitor activity in and out of the base."

"And . . ."

"Well, they never came in."

There was no point in debating the matter further. Instead I gathered several officers and a squad of men to help me investigate the scene. Normally I might not have considered this to be that big a deal, but after the day's events, I was a little nervous about the vehicle being booby-trapped. Stranger things had happened in Iraq, after all. Far stranger.

We looked all around the outside of the Suburban, using flashlights to check the undercarriage, wheel wells . . . anyplace a bomb might have been tucked. Then we opened the door, and what do you know? Stuffed into the backseat was the body of a man—at first glance, probably an Iraqi—with entry wounds clearly visible on his head. One of the back windows had also been blown out, indicating that, in all likelihood, this poor fellow had been the victim of a drive-by shooting. This was not a particularly unusual discovery. Over the course of the previous year I had picked up nearly a dozen private contractors who had been left to die in their vehicles along Highway 1. They always drove the same vehicle: a brand-new (or almost new) white GMC Suburban. Why such an ostentatious vehicle (and color) was chosen, I have no idea. It fairly screamed, "Americans on board!" Same thing with the shiny new Land Rovers favored by the Special Forces. Nobody in Iraq had anything like that—they all drove beat-up little compact cars, dented and rusting, at least ten years old. Driving a white Suburban was like driving around with a bull's-eye on the hood of your car. Unlike the guys in the Land Rovers, who at least had been trained in the art of self-defense, the contractors in the Suburbans were little more than prey on the open road.

Attacks on contractors were common, and their response to the violence was rarely inspiring. Typically, they would just drive as fast as they could, in caravans of two or more vehicles, and hope that they could outrun any trouble. After an attack, the survivors would hop into one of the remaining operational vehicles and speed away, leaving behind the dead and seriously wounded. There was no loyalty at all with these folks—their efforts and concerns were purely mercenary. Anytime we found one of them, we made sure that he received medical care (if he was alive), or that his body was returned to the States. In part this was due to respect for their families, but it also stemmed from my fear that the insurgents would take possession of a dead American contractor and publicly mutilate his remains for the purpose of propaganda.

In this particular case, the deceased contractor was an Iraqi national who had been employed by one of the large American contracting companies (his identification badge was still hanging around his neck). We spent a few hours removing the body, packing his valuables, contacting his employer, and then checking every inch of the truck to make sure that it hadn't been infected with some type of IED. Then we dragged it inside the base and cleaned it up. Then came the real problem: figuring out what to do with the body of the contractor. I imagine the poor guy had a family, but we had no way of knowing. All we could do was wait for his

American employer—or someone from division headquarters—to retrieve his remains. Unfortunately, no one seemed eager to take on that responsibility, and the body became something of a hot potato. With no other option, we were reduced to placing the body inside a metal container in a storage room at my headquarters. Believe it or not, there it sat until sometime the following afternoon, on Christmas Day, when the private contracting company sent a truck down to pick up the body.

It wasn't that I lacked compassion for the contractors. For the most part, I felt sorry for them. Not all of them, of course—the degree to which I respected their work and the challenges they faced depended largely on the circumstances that had brought them to Iraq. Consider, for example, Jean-Philippe, a Frenchman making $140,000 a year as a personal detachment security expert for one of the many European energy companies that had seen the reconstruction of Iraq as a cash cow. If Jean-Philippe wants to make ten or twelve grand a month by driving around in a Suzuki, with no vested interest in the outcome of the war, other than to line his own pockets . . . well, I'm not digging him too much. To me that's purely mercenary. Most of the contractors earned far less money while doing much more dangerous work, and I usually felt that they had been pressed into this type of work out of desperation. In some cases, I suppose, they were interested in supporting the war effort; more often, though, they were men who had found themselves in difficult financial situations, and this job, dangerous as it was, presented a potential solution to their problems.

Make no mistake—it was a crappy job. The typical contractor drove an 18-wheeler in the middle of a seventy-five-truck caravan—typically with a military Humvee at the front and at the back. They had no real security whatsoever. In the event of an ambush, there was little they could do to protect themselves. At least these guys were trying to do an honest day's work—helping with reconstruction or bringing supplies to areas in desperate need of assistance. However, the contract "security experts"? The idiots running around in the white Suburbans? Those guys were dumb as rocks, and I had a hard time working up much emotion when they careened into trouble—which happened all the time. They would use speed as their best weapon, flying up and down Highway 1 at eighty, ninety miles per hour. Many of them were killed in traffic accidents. Some were killed in traffic jams—they'd be sitting at a stop light, in the middle of a city, and insurgents or terrorists would see the white Suburbans, jump out of their sleek black window-tinted BMW cars, and open fire. Just for the pure thrill of it all. When this happened, the unfortunate victims were on their own. No one was going to stop and help them—least of all their fellow contractors.

Sometimes I felt more sympathy for the Iraqi national contractors than I did for the American drivers, because they faced the greatest risks. These men were considered traitors for helping the Americans, and if they were stopped or ambushed, they were as good as dead. I remember visiting a driver in the hospital after he had been shot at a checkpoint erected by the insurgents. Several Iraqi nationals were killed during the ambush, but this man had survived, despite taking two bullets in his torso. I found out he was from southern Iraq, yet here he was, hundreds of miles to the north, working at one of the most dangerous jobs he could find, doing whatever he could to support his family back home. I'm sure he went right back to work when he was released from the hospital.

Of course, sometimes the contractors fell victim to garden-variety thieves. On more than one occasion we raided homes, and in the course of our search discovered goods that had obviously been stolen from trucks on their way to an American base PX. We'd find cases of Pampers, Johnson & Johnson foot powder, or women's clothing from Sears or Kmart. One guy had a closet filled with piles of Jaclyn Smith blouses! I just looked at the guy.

"Come on, man. Give me a break."

He smiled and shrugged his shoulders. He wasn't a killer, just a plain old hijacker—and not a very good one at that.

I spent most of Christmas Day walking around on the base, talking with soldiers, shaking hands, making sure everyone had a chance to eat a big and reasonably well-prepared meal (we started serving at nine in the morning and did not finish until ten o'clock that evening). I hadn't slept at all the previous night—between the ambush on Triple Nickel and the discovery of the white Suburban, Christmas Eve had been one of the longest and most bizarre days of my life, and I found myself wandering about in something of a fog. The madness of the war had been illustrated in ways that left me on the verge of tears one moment, and stifling laughter the next. There was no logic to it, no reason or order. On the other side of the world, my wife was celebrating the holiday with our family. My children were opening presents and playing with their new toys. Whether they wondered what their dad was doing, or even remembered what he looked like, I didn't know. I couldn't bear to ask. I'd sent Marilyn an e-mail message a couple weeks earlier, informing her that our unit would be on an important mission, and I'm sure she knew enough about the war to understand the implication of that message.

There was no need for me to call on Christmas Day. No good would have come of it anyway. I was alive, with sanity intact. That was enough.

CHAPTER 11

It didn't take long for the police in Balad to obtain the identities of the terrorists responsible for the IED attack that had left seven of their fellow officers dead. Rather than responding to this information on their own, they reached out to American forces at FOB Eagle, and predictably were rebuffed. Gordy Flowers, battalion commander for 2-3 Infantry, our replacement unit in Balad, was a solid officer and capable leader, but he had his hands full. His soldiers were ensconced on the base, relatively (and understandably) content to bide their time until they were reassigned. They were new and unfamiliar with the area, and while they engaged in some daytime patrols and tried to get their feet wet, it was fairly obvious that they had not embraced the assignment with any great degree of enthusiasm. There were no efforts to meet with the mayor, no interaction with the police force. Checkpoints were no longer being jointly manned by the Iraqis and Americans. They were trying to get acclimated to their surroundings, but the process was laborious, largely because the 2-3 Infantry knew it was not long for Balad. Why invest heavily in a mission that isn't really yours?

I understood that sentiment, for it colored my view of our time in Samarra, but I can fairly say that the 1-8 Infantry did a commendable job on that assignment. A previously unknown level of stability and safety was achieved, and though the impact of our work dissolved shortly after our departure, I was proud of the effort we gave and the professionalism we brought to the assignment. Whether the 2-3 Infantry was similarly motivated during its stint in Balad is debatable. I don't think there was any negligence on the part of the battalion commander; nor do I question the unit's training or capability. I just think they were facing a learning curve so steep as to be insurmountable given the time frame in question.

Having already experienced the deaths of seven officers following a lack of assistance from 2-3 Infantry, the police in Balad were naturally pessimistic about the possibility of enlisting the unit's help in tracking down the perpetrators. Rather than wait for 2-3 Infantry to develop a plan of action, they reached out to our battalion, despite the fact that we weren't even stationed in Balad at the time.

The leader of the insurgent cell responsible for the bombing was a man named Fouzi Younis, who had been on our blacklist for quite some time. We'd been trying to track Younis down and pick him up for months, with no success whatsoever. According to the police, however, he had been tracked to an area of Balad known as the tomato paste factory district (so called for the simple and prosaic reason that it was an industrial area where tomato paste was processed and packaged). A combination of U.S. intelligence and information supplied by the Balad police force revealed that Younis had been operating an eleven-man cell out of this area. While the police were neither equipped nor inclined to handle a raid of this magnitude on their own, they were eager to help American forces capture and detain Younis and the other insurgents. I took this information to the brigade commander, and suggested that it was a good opportunity for the new unit—2-3 Infantry—to develop some rapport with the locals while executing an important and likely fruitful mission. Admittedly, there was an element of danger involved, but with careful planning, there was no reason for anyone to get hurt.

Colonel Rudesheim disagreed. "They don't have enough experience," he said. "It's too dangerous, and they're going to be leaving soon, anyway. Why don't you guys go down and take care of it?"

Interestingly enough, I think that Flowers and his battalion actually wanted to execute the raid on Younis's cell. But Fred Rudesheim was nothing if not conservative, so he authorized an exception to policy, granting permission for the 1-8 Infantry and its Alpha Company (which had patrolled that area of Balad) to return, temporarily, to its prior area of operation and conduct a raid on eleven targets (each insurgent constituting a single "target") in the tomato paste factory district. The raid would be a joint effort between American forces and the Iraqi police officers from Balad, and it would be conducted late on the night of January 2 (and well into the morning of January 3).

As usual for this period of time, I had mixed emotions about the assignment. On the one hand, I resented the constant shifting of territory. *Where do you want us? Up here in Samarra . . . or down south in Balad? Make up your mind.*

On the other hand, I really wanted to help the Iraqi police officers. We had trained them and worked alongside them for months, and our sudden departure had resulted in seven of them being murdered. The least we could do was help them bring to justice the insurgents responsible for this act. Call it revenge if you want, but it was an appropriate response. On a more personal level, I was ready to leave, anyway—I wanted to help restore order in Balad, where the investment in time and manpower had been far greater for the 1-8 Infantry than it had been in Samarra. Whatever gains had been made in the previous six months, clearly they were now being lost at an alarming rate. The police force obviously wasn't functioning particularly well, and the entire region had been subjected to an escalation of violence unthinkable just a short time earlier. On a professional as well as a personal level, I was enormously frustrated. I'd spent more than six months building relationships in the Balad area, establishing stability and security, and in a period of just two weeks, that order had already begun to crumble. When security begins to crumble, everything falls with it—that much had been demonstrated repeatedly throughout the country.

By the time we moved south on January 2, two more American soldiers had been killed on the outskirts of Balad—again, in what would have been the 1-8 Infantry's area of operation. That brought the death toll to thirteen—in less than three weeks. The numbers spoke for themselves, validating not merely the performance of the 1-8 Infantry, but the aggressive approach we had adopted. Our success in Balad, juxtaposed with the complete chaos that coincided with our departure, stood as irrefutable evidence that a policy of appeasement was hopelessly misguided and impotent. I never felt that my soldiers were the only ones capable of bringing stability and security to the region; but we were the only ones who made a serious, consistent effort.

Far from experiencing any self-righteous indignation over this turn of events, I felt mainly sick to my stomach at the unnecessary loss of life. I shared my disgust with Colonel Rudesheim in a heated discussion that not only transcended the accepted boundaries of military protocol (i.e., the privileges of rank were ignored), but did little to foster any goodwill between me and my boss. I didn't care. The deaths of the Iraqi deputy police chief, Lieutenant Colonel Nasser, and his six officers had been a huge setback in terms of running the largest police department in the province. And the four Iraqi Civil Defense Corps (ICDC) officers? That didn't help, either. After all, we were trying to recruit young Iraqi males to fight for freedom; when four of these officers are whacked at a checkpoint on Highway 1, it doesn't help convince another batch of highly qualified recruits that they should join us in our cause. The job, under those conditions, just doesn't seem to be worth the risk. As for the most recent deaths—two American engineer battalion soldiers killed in IED attacks on the Ad Duluwiyah bridge—well, what more needs to be said?

The tomato paste factory was one of the largest employers in the province. It was a massive complex located in a hard-core industrial part of Balad, with company-owned housing situated directly across the street. Most of the factory workers resided in these apartments, including, we had been told, the eleven members of the insurgent cell who were the targets of our operation.

We arrived at our old FOB Eagle headquarters around 1300 hours (1:00 P.M.); the raid was scheduled to begin approximately ten hours later, at 2300 hours. I checked in with the 2-3 Infantry, to make sure they knew that my company had returned, which they did. This had all been cleared ahead of time, and everyone understood that the mission had been assigned to my battalion, and that we'd be operating in this particular area. We were to be left alone, primarily to avoid the possibility of friendly-on-friendly problems. I had started rummaging through some things in my old office, trying to catch up on paperwork that had accumulated in my absence, when Eric Paliwoda walked through the door.

I hadn't seen Eric in probably two weeks. I had wanted his

entire engineer company to join us for the duration in Samarra, but the brigade commander had felt otherwise. Colonel Rudesheim felt Eric should be in Balad, where he could serve as an adviser for the new battalion commander. Well, there was no way that made any sense at all, since the battalion commander was a lieutenant colonel from Fort Lewis, and he wasn't about to take any advice from Eric—or any other captain, for that matter. Forget that Eric had been in-country for a while and surely knew more about the fight on the ground. In combat, unfortunately, it's rare for a senior officer to accept recommendations from an unknown junior officer. Regardless, after spending less than a week in Samarra, Eric was sent back to Balad, where he suffered the ignorance of his superior officer with typical grace and good humor. I had missed having him around the last few weeks, and it was good to see him here.

Eric was my guy. I'd been his mentor for some time, dating back more than three years, to previous assignments in the States. It was pure luck that Eric had become commander of the engineer company attached to my unit, and my experience in Iraq led not only to a greater respect for his abilities, but to a deepening of our friendship. Eric was extraordinarily capable and professional, and he never lost his desire to learn and to grow. He respected my experience and maturity (at the time, I was forty; Eric was twenty-seven), and eagerly sought my advice on any number of issues. But he was a highly accomplished young officer in his own right, and there were times when I felt like I was learning from him as much as he was learning from me. Yet, I was very protective of Eric and his men simply because they were engineers. True, I didn't treat them like engineers—we didn't ask them to build bridges or lead reconstruction projects—but neither did we expect them to fight like infantrymen. They traveled in armored personnel carriers (with less protection on the sides of their vehicles than we had on our Bradleys), and were assigned to their own territories, negotiating and working with their own city councils and security forces. They had their own little piece of the battle, and they did quite well with it. Still, it never left my mind that Eric's was an engineer company, so whatever he knew, whatever skills and expertise he possessed, might not be sufficient in the event of a firefight. Beast Company was learning on the job. So I constantly checked on Eric and monitored his progress. He was a promising young officer and a loyal friend, and ours was one of the rare military friendships that managed to transcend rank.

Funny thing about Eric: he never removed his flak vest or helmet. He was careful that way. I was too—most of the time. We were at a local Iraqi community dinner in a remote area one night when Eric noticed that I had shucked my vest. He shook his head.

"Sir, don't take your stuff off."

"Eric, relax," I said. "We're out in the sticks. Nothing is going to happen here."

Sure enough, on the one night (out of my three hundred–plus nights in Iraq) that I neglected to wear all of my protective gear, someone tried to take me out. Unsuccessfully, thank goodness, but leave it to Eric to remind the old man that there was no such thing as a safe place in Iraq. He was an outstanding soldier . . . and a good friend.

"I've got a few things I have to finish here," I said to Eric as I leafed through the papers on my desk that January afternoon in Balad. "Give me about twenty minutes or so, I'll come out to your hooch, and we'll catch up."

He nodded and left the room. I couldn't have known then that we would never speak to each other again.

Eric had told me that our headquarters base had been facing increasing pressure from the insurgents. Four mortar rounds had landed on Christmas Day; three days later, on December 28, eight rounds came in. The response? Nothing. This just goes to show that the insurgents respected nothing so much as violence and power. If they attacked, and you did nothing, then the next attack would be even worse. The escalation would continue until you did something about it. To me, it was no different from coping with a schoolyard bully. You couldn't stem an insurgency with hugs and kisses. You could not extend an olive branch in response to a mortar attack. It simply didn't work, and any attempt to prove otherwise was swiftly and vividly demonstrated to be feeble. As if to prove the point, eleven rounds landed within our FOB Eagle compound on New Year's Eve. And on January 2, the day I returned from Samarra, the number of shells that pummeled our base was . . . fourteen. That was unprecedented. (Prior to that point, the single greatest number of rounds that had penetrated our base in one day was seven, and that had been way back in September, when Specialist Gray had been wounded.) I knew when the first one hit, at around 1530 hours (3:30 in the afternoon), that the enemy had lost all respect for the occupants of this base.

As the sound of the first blast reverberated, we went into battle mode, exercising a drill perfected through endless repetition. In the 1–8 Infantry, the response was swift and strong. We returned mortar fire and dispatched units to the origin of the attack. Rather than running from the fight, we ran to it. Before I even left the base, I knew that someone from the engineer company had been wounded. At first, I didn't know who it was, or how badly he'd been hurt. Within two minutes of the first explosion, a second followed. Word of more injuries, more wounded, spread quickly.

As I ran outside, I saw a group of people crowded around one of the wounded, and as I drew nearer, I recognized him as Eric. He was unconscious, and clearly hurt badly. There was pandemonium at the base as more shells ripped into the ground. Part of me at that moment wanted nothing more than to stay with Eric and make sure that he was put on a helicopter and safely medevaced out of there; another part of me was far more interested in finding and killing the people who were mortaring our base and who had hurt my friend.

I leaned into Eric. "Hang in there, man."

We were on the move, busting out of the base and talking on the brigade net. This provoked a bit of confusion—since I hadn't used the brigade net down in Balad in more than three weeks, the response to my voice was not *Yes, sir, Colonel Sassaman,* but more like *Who the heck are you?* In fairly short order, however, we began to communicate effectively, and soon we arrived at the spot from which the mortar fire had emanated, but not before more rounds had hit the base and four soldiers had been wounded, one of them critically—and not before the insurgents had managed to escape. The site was vacated by this time, leaving only a small group of soldiers from Alpha Company to clean up the mess and file a report. No one from the local unit had even bothered to join us in the hunt. They weren't properly trained or equipped to battle an insurgency. They hadn't been in-country long enough, and obviously had no inkling of what the fight entailed. So it was left to us—1-8 Infantry—to make matters right. Even with choppers in the air, scanning the landscape, just a few short minutes after the assault, we found nothing.

It wasn't until I returned to the base, at around 1930 hours, that my worst fears regarding casualties were confirmed. As I walked through the front doors of the school that served as our headquarters, I saw Kevin Ryan, my headquarters and headquarters company (HHC) commander, standing next to the 2-3 battalion chaplain. Kevin's presence alone was enough to cause concern, since he spent most of his time at LSA Anaconda. There was no reason for him to be here, at this hour, unless something extraordinary had happened, and he needed to speak to me about it. The chaplain's presence only served to make matters more distressing.

I looked at Kevin . . . and he looked at me. And I knew.

"Eric?"

Kevin nodded.

Oh, no . . .

The rage and grief boiled over instantly, and I lost it. I threw my helmet down a hallway. I took off my flak vest and kicked it against a wall. I wanted to destroy anything within reach, including my own uniform and equipment. This was not the most professional response, but I couldn't help myself. I just could not believe that out of all the guys in the battalion who might be killed, it would be Eric Paliwoda. Not that there was any reason why it shouldn't have been Eric, of course. War plays no favorites. I took this one hard, sitting there crying, yelling, pounding the walls for a good hour or so. Thankfully, most of this happened in solitude—everyone, including the chaplain, had cleared out the moment I tossed my helmet, figuring, I suppose, that it was best to just let the old man grieve in private, in whatever manner he deemed appropriate. I was a forty-year-old battalion commander. I was not supposed to act this way, but one of my best friends— one of the soldiers under my command—had just been killed. I'd never experienced anything like that before, and the impact was more pronounced than I ever would have imagined.

I found out later that Eric had been killed by a tiny piece of metal that had penetrated his heart. The metal was likely shrapnel from one of the first few mortar rounds. It was ironic that he had died here, since Eric had been opposed to moving to this base in the first place. His company had been working out of Beast FOB, but division command had decided to collapse some of these smaller company bases into what were known as "enduring bases." Eric didn't want to move, but since his base was slated to disappear, he had no choice. So he wound up on our base. I just could not believe that the one guy who was going to be taken away from me was this guy—my friend—who didn't want to be on the base in the first place, who always wore his helmet and his flak vest, who was the commander's commander, always out in front, doing everything the right way . . . a guy who was a great role model for his enlisted NCOs and officers alike. I heard that he had been bending over, tying his shoes, when the blast occurred. It all sounded so . . . random.

I assigned another of Eric's close friends, Captain Tim Knopf, to serve as a casualty escort, and told him to accompany the body for the duration of the trip, no matter how long it took. Sometimes a casualty escort will go only as far as the United States, or to the hometown of the fallen soldier. Tim went all the way to West Point, where Eric was buried. While Tim was en route, we tracked down Eric's parents, who had been on vacation, and broke the news. We also informed his fiancée, Wendy Rosen. The thing I remember most about this, though, is the story that Tim related upon his return. He'd been at brigade headquarters when he'd overheard the brigade executive officer talking about the attack that had killed Captain Paliwoda.

"Too bad about Eric," the officer had said to Tim. "He was a good troop."

A good troop . . .

I found the comment offensive. Eric probably would have just laughed it off. He was a good troop—and so much more.

CHAPTER 12

The tomato paste factory raid went off without a hitch, and very nearly as scheduled. Life during wartime, I guess. Aside from a shift in starting time (the raid was pushed back to 0200 hours on the morning of January 3) and a decision to pull Eric's engineer squads off the mission, events of the previous day had little impact on this particular action.

Matt Cunningham and Alpha Company led the raid, largely because they were familiar with the territory. We divided the attack unit into three different platoons and, with the assistance of some Iraqi police officers, moved methodically through the neighborhood, simultaneously hitting house after house, taking down one target after another, and bringing all detainees to a collection point in an alleyway behind one of the homes. Most of the targets were subdued and detained without incident, although resistance was offered at one of the first homes entered, resulting in the killing of one insurgent. A similar contact near the end of the raid resulted in the death of a second insurgent. Although the most valuable target of the evening, the suspected ringleader, Fouzi Younis, was nowhere to be found (and his relatives, not surprisingly, weren't willing to share any information as to his whereabouts), it was a successful mission conducted with cool professionalism, fatalities notwithstanding.

On the afternoon of January 3, just a few hours after the tomato paste factory raid, while traveling back to Samarra, I received a call that a unit from Bravo Company had been ambushed near Power Line Road, on the southern side of the city. They had been conducting a routine patrol when five privately owned vehicles (POVs) had pulled up roughly two hundred meters away and formed a semicircle. In an instant, a handful of insurgents jumped out and began firing RPGs at our Bradleys. The shots came from the flank—as if the Bradleys were ducks in a shooting gallery. Unfortunately for the insurgents, the lead Bradley was occupied by the master gunner for all of Bravo Company.

The lead Bradley had stopped when the first RPG shell exploded; as we had so often stressed, this was a time to fight rather than run. The gunner turned to face the insurgents and then fired lethal rounds into two of the vehicles, basically incinerating them (and their occupants). In that exchange of fire, however, several businesses along the side of the boulevard had ignited, and that was the scene I encountered as I arrived: buildings smoldering, charred remnants of POVs, soldiers from Bravo Company efficiently patrolling up and down the street, knocking down doors in search of information. Three Iraqi insurgents lay in the street. Two already were dead; a third had a slight pulse but clearly wasn't going to make it. I looked at him, and thought back to the first time I had seen something like this, when some of my soldiers had failed to help a wounded insurgent, and the man had bled to death as I worked on him with our medic. I had felt an obligation then to help the wounded, to play by the rules (such as they were)—but now . . .

I moved slowly and methodically, not particularly disturbed by the sight of an enemy soldier—a terrorist—dying at my feet. Rather than digging in and getting my hands dirty, I walked away and found a medic.

"Take care of his wounds," I said. "Do the best you can."

Within minutes the man had bled to death on the sidewalk, and I felt . . . nothing. Three insurgents had been shot to death and two others had been blown to bits. I was okay with that. My men were alive, and that was all that mattered. In fact, I was ready to hand out Army Commendation Medals for Valor to the gunners who had done such an exemplary job of defusing this ambush. There is no question in my mind that if our gunners had not retaliated, swiftly and lethally, then American soldiers would have been killed. As usual, Colonel Rudesheim disagreed. Having moved his headquarters temporarily from the comforts of LSA Anaconda to FOB Brassfield-Mora (sixteen kilometers from Samarra proper) for Operation Ivy Blizzard, Fred immediately heard about the contact on Power Line Road and when he arrived on the scene, he wasn't happy.

"Why all the collateral damage?" he asked.

I didn't even know how to respond, but by now I was growing accustomed to the fact that Fred's outlook could not have been more different from mine. He was putting the Bradley crew through a routine of twenty questions, second-guessing their actions, while I was prepared to pin medals on their uniforms.

The following day I found myself at the door of an Iraqi family, offering a payment of $6,000 as compensation for the death of an elderly man who had suffered a heart attack during a raid that had been conducted by American soldiers from the 1–8 Infantry. Whether the man's death could be attributed directly to the actions of our soldiers was debatable, but I had been ordered by Colonel Rudesheim to appease the family with cash. Given the fact that my best friend had been killed just two days earlier, one could reasonably argue that I was not the right person for this goodwill mission, but I wasn't offered a choice. So my attitude as I approached the home was something short of generous. I was frustrated beyond words that I had to pay off a family because their grandfather had died of a heart attack while my soldiers were merely doing their job; however, general army policy dictated these types of reparation payments—that's just how it worked over there.

With these payments, typically, came much hand-wringing and crying, and occasionally a harsh exchange of words. On this particular visit, one of the younger male members of the family got in my face and began screaming at me, and I have to be honest: there was a fleeting moment in which I thought about putting a bullet in his head. Instead, I got in his face and, with an interpreter by my side, explained to the best of my ability that he wasn't the only one in the room who was hurting.

"I know you're upset about your grandfather. I'm upset about my friend, but I'm paying you $6,000; what are you doing for me?"

Now, I understand how that sounds. It is callous and contemptible; but it reflects precisely what I felt in my soul at that moment. I was still the good Christian man who had come to Iraq seven months earlier, but my spirit was broken. This encounter, and my handling of it, represented a significant departure from the way I was raised and taught to be. In a very real sense, I had crossed over to the dark side. In retrospect, of course, I understand the anger and pain this family experienced. Sometimes, even now, all these years later, when I sit at dinner at my house with my wife and children, I find myself reflecting back on these moments, and I wonder how I would react if a bunch of soldiers bashed down my door and marched into my house. If they were to bind my hands with flex cuffs and drag me out in front of my kids and my wife? If my dad were sitting there having dinner with me and had a heart attack because he was upset about it? I don't have to think about it for long. I'd probably want to kill every one of them. The truth is, that's not going a long way toward bringing democracy to anybody.

We acted with force because force was the only thing that seemed to work . . . the only thing the Iraqis seemed to understand. That very same day, in the same village not far from Samarra where I was delivering the compensation money, I stopped to talk with a group of men. One of the men was missing a portion of his right arm. It appeared to have been lopped off just below the elbow.

"Ask him what happened," I instructed the translator. I was curious, since I'd seen this sort of thing before—amputees, mostly middle-aged or older, were scattered about the country, and I always assumed that their injuries were related to the Iran-Iraq War. But that wasn't the case here. The man launched into a remarkable story about the day Saddam came to visit his village. The dictator had been driving through town with his motorcade, on his way from Samarra to Highway 1. The village residents had been instructed to line the motorcade route and wave enthusiastically to Saddam as he went by.

"But I hated Saddam," the man explained. "Hated what he did to my country and my people. So I did not wave."

To the man's shock, the motorcade stopped in front of him. Two of Saddam's henchmen jumped out, grabbed the man, and dragged him over to the hood of one of the cars behind the motorcade. One man held his arm in place while the other used a hatchet to hack off his right hand. The entire brutal incident, executed in full view of the village populace, took no more than a minute.

"They told me, 'That's what happens when you don't wave,'" the man recalled with a shrug.

Maybe that's how you maintained order in Iraq. I'd like to believe otherwise, but there were times when it seemed as though nothing else—only fear and violence—had any effect whatsoever.

On January 5, 2004, Fred and I had a heart-to-heart conversation, and it wasn't pretty. In the past, I had always felt reasonably comfortable in opening up with my battalion or brigade commanders. Early on—probably within the first month of my command—I had tried that with Fred, and it proved to be a mistake. He made it very clear that he was not interested in any kind of personal friendship with his subordinate officers. He was the brigade commander, and I was the battalion commander, and I should limit my contacts with him to a professional basis only. In this particular conversation, however, I chose to ignore the usual rules.

In the wake of Eric's death, Fred had stopped by to see how things were going with my battalion in general, and with me in particular. Things were not going well—at least not for me. I let Fred have it—with both barrels. I told him that I resented having to clean up the mess left behind by 1-66 Armor. I resented the fact that in the nineteen days since my battalion had shifted its focus to Samarra, all hell had broken loose in the southern half of the Salah Ah Din Province. As a result of our replacements not having any local expertise, combined with the Army's fondness for a "whack the mole" strategy (moving successful units from one crisis area to another, without staying long enough to have a significant, lasting effect), two American soldiers had been killed in my former area of operation, along with seven Iraqi policemen and four ICDC officers. Now I had to return to Balad and use whatever was left of our time—probably six weeks, two months at the most—to get the house back in order so that I could hand off to a new unit: 1–77 Armor, which would be arriving from Germany.

I communicated these thoughts and feelings not in a professional manner, but with bluntness and anger. I even went so far as to blame Fred for the death of Eric Paliwoda. "If you had let Eric fight with me in Samarra, instead of staying behind and advising the new battalion, he'd be alive right now," I said.

Maybe, maybe not. The point was, I had grown so frustrated by Colonel Rudesheim's version of how to prosecute the war that I could no longer withhold my feelings. I suggested that his tactics of appeasement, which diverged sharply, confusingly, and maddeningly from General Odierno's recommendations to fight, had contributed to the death of Staff Sergeant Panchot as well. The gist of the conversation was this: *I do not understand why you are trying to get my soldiers killed.*

On January 7, following a formal change-of-command ceremony, during which Captain Matt Shirley took over 1–8 Infantry's only engineer company, I presided over a memorial service for Eric Paliwoda. It was held in the same airplane hangar where Dale Panchot had been eulogized a month and a half earlier. After the ceremony I led a command and staff meeting, which concluded with this proclamation:

"Things are going to get a lot more violent in the 1–8 Infantry's area of operation, and if you don't think you can handle it, or come along and participate, then this is a good time for you to go ahead and walk out the door. Because, gentlemen, we are going to fight like we have never fought before. We are going to fight right up until the day we leave. If you think we're going into cruise control mode for the last sixty days, forget it. We're going to turn it up—starting right now."

Then I hopped in my Bradley and traveled to Samarra, crying for most of the two-hour ride up Highway 1. As I watched the sun set, I felt nothing so much as sadness: over the death of my friend, the loss of a great young officer, and the apparent hopelessness of the war. I shared none of this, of course, even though I was not alone in the Bradley. The gunner was in his hatch, scanning, doing his job; the driver was doing his. I was on top, with my head sticking out of the Bradley, sunglasses shielding my eyes from the desert sun, and hiding my tears. The battalion commander can't cry, after all. That's not allowed.

About twenty minutes into the trip, as we approached the Samarra bypass (the same spot where the three engineer soldiers had been killed on Christmas Eve), I got a call from Major Darron Wright. "Eagle 6, this is Eagle 3," he said. "Need you to stop in and speak with Attack 6 at the mess hall prior to your 1900 with Colonel Rudesheim."

The reason for my trip back to Samarra was to take part in a transition meeting update with Colonel Rudesheim, in advance of 1-66 Armor taking responsibility (once again) for Samarra. Following the meeting, I planned to drive right back to Balad. My schedule was tight, but apparently Matt Cunningham (Attack 6) needed to speak with me—before I met with Colonel Rudesheim.

"Okay," I said. "Have him meet me at the mess hall at 1850."

I dropped my stuff at the TOC and headed over to the mess hall, where I found Matt and Lieutenant Jack Saville, an Alpha Company platoon officer. After filling a plate with food, I joined them at their table; as soon as I approached, I knew something was wrong. Typically, we were pretty loose under these circumstances.

This was wartime, after all, and the formal stuff was best relegated to closed-door meetings. The mess hall was a casual place, as far as I was concerned. Both Matt and Jack, though, remained standing at parade rest as I placed my tray on the table. They stood at attention, heels locked, eyes straight ahead.

"Guys . . . what's going on?"

"Sir," Matt said. "We have to tell you something. . . ."

Over the course of the next few minutes I got the short version of a story that would evolve and expand into an epic involving more than a year of criminal investigation, litigation, political posturing, and backstabbing. In my possession I have more than seven hundred pages of court transcripts and documents devoted to the various proceedings stemming from this incident. It became a story, like *Rashomon,* told from so many points of view, and with so many conflicting timelines and agendas, that eventually it became nearly impossible to separate fact from fiction.

As battalion commander, there is no denying that it happened on my watch. I accept that responsibility. It is also true that I was there, personally, for none of it. I was neither a participant nor a witness. I knew only what I was told, and this was the beginning.

On the night of January 3, Lieutenant Saville's platoon had detained two Iraqi males who were driving a white truck in the northern part of Samarra (perhaps not coincidentally, near the Samarra Drug Industries [SDI] Complex, a drug manufacturing plant). The incident had occurred shortly after the 11:00 P.M. curfew. Rather than bringing the two men back to the base, which is what they should have done, Jack's platoon cuffed the two men and took them to a bridge near the Tharthar Dam, overlooking the Tigris River.

Matt did all the talking, quietly, soberly. Jack never said a word. There were perhaps a hundred soldiers in the cafeteria at the time, but only three of us shared this particular table, so we were able to speak freely. As the story unfolded, I began to sense the seriousness of what I was hearing.

"And . . ." I said as Matt paused.

"Well . . . the detainees were forced to jump into the river, and now allegations have come forward that one of them got out and walked away safely, but the other drowned."

Although the platoon in question was under Matt's command, he too had been absent when the incident occurred, but Jack had been there. In fact, he had been in charge.

I turned to Lieutenant Saville. "Jack, did anybody drown?"

"No, sir!"

I moved closer to his face. "Jack . . . are you sure nobody drowned?"

Lieutenant Saville looked me straight in the eye and nodded. "Sir, the last time I looked down, and I was in the trail vehicle, the last vehicle to go by, there were two Iraqi men walking down the street in the other direction. They were both soaking wet, and they were very much alive."

Almost as if pretending not to have heard what he said, I asked Jack once more, "Lieutenant Saville—did anybody drown in that river?"

He stiffened. "No, sir!"

I turned to Matt. "You know, the way Fred feels about your company, this is really going to be a mess."

He nodded. Matt understood the implications. Colonel Rudesheim despised Matt, perhaps even more than he despised me. I had never seen a brigade commander who was so engrossed in the affairs of a company commander, but there was history between Fred and Matt, and the bad blood worsened during their time in Iraq. Their relationship had reached its nadir on September 11, 2003 (the second anniversary of 9/11), following a particularly effective and aggressive raid on a top target. Matt's company had confiscated a large cache of computer equipment, telephones, financial records, and cash—in U.S. dollars—from the mansion of a man named Dr. Jassim, who was considered one of the top financiers of insurgent activity in Iraq. After clearing the mansion of all occupants, Matt had ordered the launching of several missiles into the mansion, effectively destroying it. This did not go over well with Colonel Rudesheim, who had already come to the conclusion that collateral damage was unacceptable. Fred would be the perfect commander for Operation Iraqi Freedom 25—sometime in 2028 or so, when we're trying to work through all the political solutions, but he was a terrible combat commander for the first year of the fight, primarily because (although he may have seen it differently) he seemed to me to detest combat and aggressiveness, or contact of any sort—all the things we needed to win this fight. So when Fred arrived at FOB Eagle TOC to be debriefed by Matt, he was really upset that Matt had used AT-4 missiles during the raid. Why, he asked, had it been necessary to fire missiles into the home?

Without missing a beat or cracking a smile, Matt replied, "Sir, the missiles were symbolic. We destroyed the twin pillars of that mansion just as the terrorists did the twin towers on 9/11."

Standing right next to Matt, hearing all of this, I could barely contain myself. My immediate thought was that I could not have said it better. (Matt later said it was just the first thing that popped into his head.) Fred was not amused.

"Colonel Sassaman," he said. "I'd like a word with you."

Fred proceeded to voice his extreme displeasure with Captain Cunningham, whom he described as "a renegade." Furthermore, Fred added, "If you don't get a handle on him, I will."

So, by the night of January 3, Matt's head had long been on the chopping block. Fred had been trying to get rid of Matt for months, and this incident, true or not, would likely have terrible repercussions for Matt, and for Jack as well. I did not yet understand the implications for my own career.

"Matt," I said. "This is something that will get you relieved of your command." I turned to Lieutenant Saville. "Jack, you're probably done."

The irony (one of many, actually) in all of this was that Jack Saville was my best platoon leader. He was a West Pointer, bright and capable and energetic. The way I saw it, he had simply made a bad call—one that paled in comparison to some of the horrendous leadership decisions I had witnessed in Iraq. Since no one had gotten hurt (or so it seemed, anyway), I decided to protect my men.

"All right, here's what we're going to do. We're going to leave it between us right now. I have to go up and meet with Fred, and see where this whole thing is at."

If this was the beginning of my attempt at a cover-up (as has been speculated), it was feeble, at best. I had no idea that the wheels of military justice had already been set in motion.

When I walked into brigade headquarters, I inadvertently stumbled upon a conversation between Lieutenant Colonel Gonsalves and Colonel Rudesheim, the essence of which was this: *How much should we pay the family of the Iraqi man who drowned in the Tigris River?* They stopped talking, rather abruptly, when I entered the room.

"Sir, do we even have a body?" I asked. "Do we have any evidence whatsoever that anybody actually drowned before we pay a family in Samarra $8,000?"

Fred dismissed my skepticism and turned the conversation to more mundane matters: the transfer of authority in Samarra from the 1-8 Infantry back to the 1-66 Armor. At the end of the meeting, as I stood to leave, Fred asked me what else I knew about the night of January 3, and the incident at the Tigris.

"Sir, I just spoke with Matt Cunningham, and the truth of the matter is, they saw two Iraqis walking down the street when they left the reservoir."

By the end of the meeting, I had come to realize that I was one of the last men in the brigade to know that my own guys had pushed these two detainees into the water. (I had been in Balad, first for the tomato paste factory raid, and then to deliver the eulogy at Captain Paliwoda's memorial service.) Now, I know that some people will suggest that a lack of communication is an indication of a poor command climate, but I had a pretty good command climate, and eventually my soldiers did tell me what had happened. They just weren't going to get on the airwaves and tell me about it when I was down in Balad, dealing with Eric's death, helping with a change in company command.

Regardless, a bad decision had been made, and now it was up to me to deal with the consequences.

"I want you to know," Fred said before I left, "that if your soldiers were involved in pushing those men into the water, they will be court-martialed."

I nodded, although none of this made sense to me. We were going to court-martial our own soldiers without even having a body; and we were already prepared to write checks to the "grieving" relatives. To me it seemed odd that suddenly we were taking such a drastic and hard-line approach to what amounted to nothing more than a poor display of leadership. As I reflect back on it, I don't think it's out of the realm of possibility that my soldiers were scapegoats. The timing of the incident hurt. Revulsion over the Abu Ghraib prison scandal (in which detainee abuse was well documented) started to gather steam around this time, and my battalion was caught in the middle of it. I would not be surprised if someone relatively high in the chain of command had issued a policy change—written or otherwise—regarding the handling of detainees, in reaction to the wildly inflammatory nature of the Abu Ghraib detainee abuse case. I do not think such a change was motivated by goodness or honor; rather, it was something that was decided in the service of public relations. Having seen Secretary Rumsfeld in action, I can certainly imagine him saying, in the wake of Abu Ghraib, *If our soldiers do anything that could be interpreted as detainee abuse, we'll take measures to court-martial them out of the army.* As opposed to, say, running a fair investigation and determining whether disciplinary action should be taken. I have to admit: on the scale of bad things that had recently happened—Eric being killed, the Iraqi contractor who had died on Christmas Day, the three American soldiers killed on Christmas Eve, the death and destruction in Balad—pushing two guys into a river didn't rate very high for me. It never has. There were a vast number of things going on that seemed far worse, and far more lethal, than this particular action.

After the meeting with Fred, I went back to Matt. "Don't say anything about the water," I instructed.

Despite Colonel Rudesheim's threat, I doubted that anything would come of the incident. After all, I had tried to initiate a formal investigation into the deaths of five elderly men returning from a prayer meeting and gotten absolutely nowhere. This incident seemed to pale in comparison. I had hoped that it would fall off Colonel Rudesheim's radar and that later I would be able to discipline the soldiers involved. I acknowledge that this was a pathetic strategy, mainly because, as it turned out, I was woefully uninformed about what was really going on.

I just couldn't shake the notion that my soldiers had done nothing to merit a career-ending punishment, let alone jail time. The guidelines regarding the handling and processing of detainees were hopelessly flawed, and never were those flaws more apparent than on January 3. Another of the ironies of the war in Iraq (and this is not uncommon in guerrilla warfare) is that the rules of engagement allowed for greater leeway in the killing of insurgents than in the handling of detainees. If my soldiers had killed both detainees and reported the incident as a combat action north of Samarra, no one would have questioned it. The two men had been detained in an area typically infested with weapons and insurgent activity. They had broken curfew. It was logical for any American soldier to conclude that these guys were not Boy Scouts. Lethal force, necessary or not, would have gone virtually unchallenged.

They did not use lethal force, instead, they committed what amounted, in my mind, to a high school prank. Was it a tactical mistake? Yes. Was it a criminal mistake? No. They made a poor decision, but the bottom line was, I couldn't march my soldiers up to the brigade commander and turn them in to be court-martialed simply because they had pushed two guys into a river. The whole thing seemed . . . ludicrous. Certainly I do not condone detainee abuse, but the army in Iraq did a terrible job of separating detainees from the soldiers who captured them. We never had a good system of capturing alleged targets or legitimate targets, and moving them through the detainee process. I knew this from the very beginning, when we started the war off with Operation Peninsula Strike, which resulted in four hundred potential detainees being lined up on a tarmac and whittled down, over the course of several days, to a mere sixteen legitimate detainees.

Intelligence had improved dramatically by the night of January 3, 2004. We were far more selective in the targets that were chosen. Every Iraqi citizen understood the risk and danger associated with being out after curfew. I can't emphasize strongly enough the extent to which Samarra felt like a ghost town late at night. So it's hard for me to imagine that these two young men didn't understand the implications of breaking curfew, or that their activities were benign. That being said, my soldiers made a bad mistake, and I compounded that mistake by instructing the company commander to say nothing about the water. I would never have said that if Fred hadn't indicated that a court-martial awaited anyone involved in forcing detainees into the Tigris River.

This was my exact thought that night (and I articulated it later, to General Odierno, in my Article 15 proceeding): *I'll be damned if I'm going to let two Iraqi insurgents bring down all the good work we've done in Samarra in the course of the last three weeks.* Even Colonel Gonsalves had acknowledged our effectiveness ("You guys have done in three weeks what my battalion failed to do in seven months"). It was just a matter of being the American army and taking charge—and not taking any of the crap they're throwing at you. Call it prideful or arrogant or stubborn or whatever. I was operating with a take-no-prisoners attitude by then—I was not going to let two insurgents take us down through some misinformation campaign.

It's hard to say if I'd do anything differently if I had a chance to do it all over again. I suppose if the circumstances were the same and Fred was still intent on court-martialing my guys, there's a good chance I'd respond just as I did the first time. What do I wish could have happened? I wish I could have laid it all out for Colonel Rudesheim, but we simply didn't have that type of relationship. Perhaps I should have picked up the phone on January 7, when I first found out about the incident, and called General Odierno, and said, "Sir, which way do you think I should go on this, because I'm really against these guys being court-martialed."

The whole thing smacked of undue command pressure; I

should never have been told there would be a court-martial—that decision isn't made until an Article 32 investigation is complete anyway, and that hadn't been done yet. I was in way over my head. We were fighting a war, and I had no legal adviser at the battalion guiding me through how things were going to work, so I instinctively tried to protect my soldiers, but I never had a chance. The deck was stacked so far against me that I was foolish for even thinking I could somehow have even the slightest amount of control.

General Odierno would later accuse me of failing to be a proper leader: "You just had to be one of the boys." That wasn't true. I thought I was being exactly the right kind of leader: one who sticks up for his men, regardless of the consequences. These guys had just come off forty-eight hours of nonstop operations. They were exhausted, and they had just seen a company commander killed. In Iraq we asked our soldiers and young officers to do more than the average American citizen can even fathom. It's a shame that the army demands so much, under the most difficult circumstances, and then allows its senior leaders to sit back in their sterile, austere environment, with their four meals a day, and their eight hours of rest, and exercise some Monday-morning quarterbacking on decisions made in the heat of combat.

They were going to court-martial my men for making a poor decision?

Over my dead body.

CHAPTER 13

We're near the Fallujah Cut, traveling from Samarra to Balad, when the IED erupts. There are four vehicles in our patrol, two Humvees and a couple of Bradleys, and at the sound of the blast—a deafening, heart-stopping roar—we all come to a halt. I turn around and see a large mush-room cloud billowing at the side of the highway, not far from one of our Humvees. As the cloud lifts, it becomes apparent that none of our vehicles have been hit. Instead, the bomb went off right next to a bus that had at-tempted to pass our caravan, and in so doing had made the fatal mistake of slipping onto the shoulder.

Obviously, the IED was supposed to be detonated on the Humvee right behind my Bradley, but the bus absorbed the entire blast. The left side of the bus is now peeled back, much as a can of tuna might look when pried open using an old-fashioned can opener, exposing the last dozen rows of seats. The unfortunate passengers in those seats—Iranian Shias on their way back from a religious pilgrimage to the Golden Dome Mosque in Samarra—have been sprayed with shrapnel. The most seriously wounded are a half dozen elderly women with massive cuts to the upper torso and face. The rest of the passengers, naturally, are in a state of complete panic. I board the bus with several of my soldiers and a medic, and we quickly try to care for the wounded, and all around me I can hear people screaming in Arabic, crying, wailing in pain. An Iraqi translator who was on leave in Baghdad stops at the scene of the accident and offers assistance, which is a good thing, because none of us speak fluent Arabic. There is chaos, and we do the best we can to deal with it—patching up the wounded, dispatching a vehicle to take the old women to a hospital. The bus driver approaches. He is shouting at me, flailing about, tearfully and plaintively asking . . . something.

"What is it?" I say to the interpreter.

"He wants to know why the Americans attacked his bus."

In the two weeks that followed Eric's death, the 1-8 Infantry experienced some of its greatest success, militarily speaking. Working out of Balad, with three companies at our disposal, we captured three Iraqi Intelligence Service general officers—two- and three-star generals who had been high on our hit list for months. Capturing any one of these men would have represented a significant coup, and we landed all three. It was a performance that did not go unnoticed. On January 14, General Odierno flew in for a congratulatory visit.

"What do they have in the water down here?" he said. "You guys are on fire!"

And we were. Stoked in part by anger over Eric's death, and a subsequent commitment to patrol aggressively and violently, we took down targets with stunning efficiency and soon restored a sense of order to the region. Two days after General Odierno's pat on the back, we received a far more formal visit. This time it was one of the Army's highest-ranking officers, General Larry Ellis, a four-star general, who was coming to Balad, ostensibly to offer encouragement and appreciation to one of the Army's highest-achieving battalions in all of Iraq.

So it's fair to say that we were on a roll. At the same time, however, the incident at the Tigris River hung over my head. Using some of my own intelligence contacts, I sought information regarding the two detainees. They were cousins, I had learned, and their names were Marwan Fadhil and Zaydoon Fadhil. Marwan had emerged from the dunking unscathed; Zaydoon, allegedly, had drowned in the river. Much of the intelligence we utilized in Iraq came not from U.S. sources, but from our own contacts within various tribal factions. I turned to one such group in early January and asked for information regarding Zaydoon Fadhil. Specifically, I wanted to know just one thing: was he alive or dead? The answer came quickly: alive and well. I shared this information in a classified report that I presented to General Odierno's aide on the day that General Ellis visited our base.

I also asked Major Gwinner to visit the site of the incident. "Humor me, Rob. Have them show you where the guys jumped in, and tell me about the depth of the water. Is it two feet or is it eight feet? I just want to know."

Rob is a bulldog. I should have known that he'd take that request and run with it. Which he did, in the form of a full-blown reenactment. He took the platoon out to the dam, asked people to jump in the water, and reported back with his findings: the water was two to three feet deep, the current barely perceptible. More like a pond than a river, he said. Summation: there was no way anyone could have drowned that night, especially since the flex cuffs had been removed before the detainees were forced into the water. It is true that a body would eventually turn up, but never was there any proof that the corpse was that of Zaydoon Fadhil.

(No autopsy was ever performed, at least not by an American medical examiner; I've often wondered if an autopsy was performed by the Iraqis, and perhaps revealed conclusively that the body was not that of Zaydoon.) Yet, the family was paid and our soldiers were charged with crimes. The Iraqis by this time knew that the U.S. Army was quick to write a check to compensate for the death of anyone, regardless of whether the person might have supported insurgent activities. So it wasn't unheard of for deaths to be faked in an attempt to squeeze the Americans. All one had to do was find a corpse—the circumstances surrounding the death were irrelevant—and claim negligence on the part of American forces.

There were other motivations as well. It was, in fact, common practice for top blacklisted Iraqi insurgents to fake their deaths in an attempt to divert interest from a particular terrorist cell. They'd leak word that someone had been killed, and then someone would show up with a mangled corpse as "evidence." Sometimes they would go to extraordinary lengths—such as smashing in the face of a dead man, to the point that he was completely unrecognizable, and then staging an elaborate funeral for some top insurgent leader. Meanwhile, the insurgent was perfectly healthy and carrying out his work in some other area.

I believe that it's likely this is what happened in the case of Zaydoon Fadhil. Certainly the outcome of the various criminal investigations that evolved over the coming months and years, which caused severe mental anguish for the soldiers involved, but limited punitive action considering the supposed seriousness of the infraction, would seem to support skepticism all the way around. The word "scapegoat" comes to mind again.

I was largely uninformed and naive throughout the early part of January, clinging to the hope that the whole thing would just go away; at worst, I figured someone would come down and ask a few questions, get his answers, and eventually the matter would be put in my hands for proper adjudicating. Then the case would be closed. Two Iraqi insurgents were forced into the water. They were last seen walking down the road, soaking wet, as our soldiers left the scene. Bad call, sloppy soldiering, but no criminal intent. Then I could deal with my guys differently.

It didn't turn out that way. A couple days after General Ellis's visit, I had another meeting with Colonel Rudesheim, during which he reiterated his belief that something more nefarious had transpired. Regardless of whether anyone had actually drowned in the Tigris, he said, "If water was involved, soldiers are going to be court-martialed."

He said it twice, then, and in so doing confirmed my belief that the subject of water was best omitted from any future conversations. It wasn't until I received a phone call from Colonel Rudesheim, informing me that several soldiers from the 1-8 Infantry were already sequestered in Tikrit, undergoing intensive questioning about the incident, that I began to understand what was happening.

"Sir, are you launching a criminal investigation?" I asked.

There was a pause, and in the response, it was obvious that Fred was surprised by my lack of awareness.

"Nate, we launched a criminal investigation back on January fourth."

So there it was. I was the battalion commander, and apparently the last man to find out that my soldiers were facing serious criminal charges. Now, you can chalk that up to exhaustion, naïveté, focus on the mission in Balad . . . or just plain ignorance. I don't know, but the news came as a shock to me. For the next few hours I paced back and forth at the front of my base. Finally, I picked up the phone and called General Odierno (bypassing my boss, Colonel Rudesheim, and speaking directly with the only senior commander I trusted in the division). Tearfully, and as candidly as possible—with Darron Wright and Rob Gwinner sitting by my side—I came clean with everything. I explained to General Odierno that I had told the company commander (Matt Cunningham) to make sure that we didn't tell anyone about the water involved that night. Then I asked for something along the lines of grace.

"Sir," I said. "I take full responsibility. This was my decision. Basically, you hold in your hands my entire career and everything I've done in the army. I will respect whatever decision that comes down from headquarters."

There was another moment of silence.

"Nate, there are two separate issues here," General Odierno said. "One, the action at the bridge; two, your decision to tell the men not to talk about the water."

"Yes, sir. I understand."

I am not unwilling to accept the possibility that there may have been a leadership failure on my part—and I'm not referring merely to a supposed "cover-up." I'm talking about a more fundamental mistake, one related to the delicate balance of personalities that must be taken into consideration by any battalion commander. There is, for example, a symbiotic training process that exists between a sergeant first class and a platoon leader. The platoon leader probably does not run physical training as well as the sergeant, does not understand all small-unit tactics as well as the sergeant, and certainly can't run a health and welfare inspection as well as the sergeant. The platoon leader—frequently a West Point graduate, and certainly a college graduate—has had four years of what I'd call values-based decision-making training. So when it does come time to make a hard ethical or moral decision, he's capable of making it; when the staff sergeant says, "Take this guy around back and beat the living daylights out of him," that's when the platoon leader has to have the moral fiber to stand up and say, "No, that's wrong, and I'm making the call."

Tracy Perkins was a very aggressive young platoon sergeant. Young in terms of having been promoted ahead of his years; aggressive in that he was a true warrior who did not turn away from the uglier aspects of combat. Only five foot seven but rock solid and fearless, Tracy had grown up in the Midwest. His father had served in Vietnam, and Tracy had known from a young age that he wanted to follow in his father's footsteps. He loved the army and was tailor-made for it. He enlisted right after high school graduation and quickly ascended through the ranks.

I've talked about the uninspiring leadership actions of Colonel Rudesheim and Lieutenant Colonel Gonsalves in the theater of combat—they were rarely in the fight, and they appeared cowardly in the way they appeased and paid off Iraqis. Well, there are sergeants on the ground who are cowards, too. It's hard for me to say this, because I am a soldier, too, and on some level I have respect for anyone who wears the uniform. It's different in combat than it is in peacetime, however, and it should be noted that there were some actions in Iraq in which staff sergeants, paralyzed by fear, cowered behind their vehicles and failed to do their jobs. There were times when young sergeants and specialists took up the mantle of leadership, moved the squads on to the target, and accomplished the mission.

I saw it happen to one of my staff sergeants, in one of my platoons, and he instantly lost the respect and loyalty of his men. Everything was gone in a moment. It never came back for the duration of his deployment. I think crippling fear is common in all wars, but there were certain things unique to Iraq because of the nature of the insurgency . . . the fact that we were fighting a guerrilla war, rather than a traditional enemy. These factors combined to bring out the best in some soldiers, and the worst in others.

Generally speaking, I think they brought out the best in Tracy Perkins. He was a top sergeant in every way, but he was paired with a young lieutenant, Jack Saville, who was similarly aggressive and confident in nature. Jack was a type A personality; Tracy was double-A, maybe triple-A. Both were hell-bent on winning the war, not unlike their battalion commander, and I respected and admired their devotion to duty and their commitment to the cause. Their union, however, was unusual. Typically, the army prefers to pair a stronger platoon sergeant with a weaker platoon leader, or vice versa. Jack and Tracy did not balance each other out. In retrospect, I can see that. During the fight, it never occurred to me that their aggressive tendencies might result in anything other than military success. I knew I had some initial leadership problems with noncommissioned officers in Bravo Company, but not with Alpha Company. These guys were just strong and committed, and I was happy to let them do their job.

Looking back, I realize that I had my most aggressive platoon sergeant, who was young, sharp, and very persuasive, linked up with an aggressive, bright, young, fit lieutenant, in a company led by my most aggressive company commander, in a battalion that was clearly the most aggressive battalion in the entire division.

Someone is going to get wet tonight.

That, supposedly, is what Sergeant Perkins said on January 3, when the two Iraqi cousins were detained. I didn't realize until much later that on at least one previous occasion, this same platoon had been responsible for forcing detainees to jump into the

Tigris River, near the Ad Duluwiyah Peninsula Bridge, back in December. I do not believe Sergeant Perkins intended any harm to the detainees; I also know he regrets his decision. I know that Jack Saville regrets not standing up to Sergeant Perkins, at that very moment, and telling him, *That's not the right thing to do.* Instead, they fed off each other, one thing led to another, and two detainees wound up in the river.

I can also tell you this: after seven or eight months of combat, and doing some of the things we've asked these soldiers to do, I totally understand how these guys felt. I sympathize with them and I forgive them for trying to take some action against insurgents who were continually shooting at and sometimes killing their comrades.

Civilians tend to have a romantic and idealistic notion of American soldiers as being able to throw the switch in a heartbeat and not let their emotions take over. That's totally unrealistic. As a peacetime commander, I expected my soldiers during the week to be trained killers in unbelievable physical condition: they could rappel down the face of a cliff, road march twenty-five miles, shoot their weapons with pinpoint precision, put a Claymore in blindfolded, and be a ruthless hand-to-hand killer. On the weekends I expected something different. I wanted them to wake up on Sunday morning and take their wives and little ones to church. I expected them to be choirboys and not have one ounce of trouble. Then, when they came back on Monday morning, I expected them to run to hell and back with me, and fire their weapons with lethal intent. You know what? It doesn't work that way. You can't just turn it on and off. That's why some soldiers get in trouble on the weekend. They go to a bar and some fat guy makes a comment about their girlfriend, and they want to beat the guy to death. We instill in these men the desire (and the capability) to kill the enemy, and then we expect them to use it judiciously, thoughtfully, and never recklessly. We expect them to be machines, but they aren't: They are human beings.

The basic premise of an insurgency, a guerrilla warfare force, is to break down the good order and discipline of the more traditional force that it is fighting. In so doing, it sometimes shatters the moral compass of that traditional force. Abu Ghraib, the raping of an Iraqi girl and the murder of her family, the killing of five elderly men on their way back from prayer service—when you see data points like that . . . incidents suggesting the erosion of order and discipline in the most professional armed force in the world . . . well, frankly, it's time to get the hell out, because the insurgency is achieving success. The terms of winning and losing are over once those things start happening; it's nearly impossible for a unit to recover once it has crossed that line. This happened on a grand scale in Vietnam, and it had begun to happen on a limited scale in Iraq by the time I left. U.S. soldiers in Vietnam routinely referred to the Vietnamese (civilians included) as "gooks." In Iraq the blanket term was "Hadji." Guerrilla warfare does this to a soldier—it provokes feelings of anger and helplessness, and it leads one to dehumanize the opponent and its citizens; then there is a devaluing of human life.

I saw more than my share of combat actions, and by the end I had become steeled to them. You're talking about a man with a good education and a strong Christian background. I knew right from wrong. If I could experience some of those darker feelings, imagine what it was like for the typical U.S. soldier on the ground, fighting for his life, day in and day out. I can recall one incident in which we were searching through a series of chicken farms north of Ishaki, in an area where weapons had been found in the past. The search proved fruitless, so we got back on the highway and headed south, feeling a little frustrated and agitated.

It was a small group—just me and Darron Wright in our Bradleys, with scout vehicles and two Humvees. As we neared the turn onto Highway 1, a beat-up Chrysler sedan approached from behind. We began to turn south, and as we pulled away, I looked back at the driver and he waved to me. This was strange, I thought, because Americans typically were not embraced in this area. A public display of support or camaraderie, such as waving to American soldiers, was highly unusual.

"Stop that car!" I yelled to one of the scout vehicles. "Nobody waves to me up here. Nobody! Find out what's going on."

Perhaps thirty seconds later I looked back and was stunned to see the sedan on the side of the road, its two occupants having been removed. Half a dozen American soldiers—my troops—were beating the living daylights out of these guys, just whaling on them with their fists and weapons.

"Turn back!" I shouted. I figured we had about a minute to intervene or we'd be dealing with two dead Iraqis.

I stopped the Bradley, jumped out, and ran back to the scene. "What is going on!?"

One of my men led me to the back of the car. In the trunk were two howitzer rounds—fully prepped with fuses and detonation devices. By now we'd all witnessed firsthand the devastation of IED attacks, so it wasn't surprising that our soldiers were enraged by this discovery. According to the rules of engagement, we could have killed both men on the spot. We had caught them red-handed with explosives obviously designed to kill Americans. They were insurgents in the process of doing harm, but the rules of engagement do not permit the beating to death of insurgents.

It was all so murky and morally ambiguous. I can recall seeing videotape, taken from an attack helicopter, of an incident in which two Iraqi insurgents were discovered burying weapons in a field. The men hiding the weapons were just getting ready to pile into a truck when the chopper's Hellfire missiles destroyed them. Now, did these men actually have weapons on them? No, the weapons were in the ground. Were they shooting at the helicopter? No, they were climbing into a truck, getting ready to leave, but the Apache caught them in its sights, clearly hiding a weapons cache at night. The rules of engagement fully supported the obliteration of the enemy in that situation. Similarly, it allowed for the killing of anyone caught with IEDs. My guys would never kill anyone in cold blood—they would never simply deliver a bullet to the head; but for some reason, I guess, in this particular situation, it seemed more civil to beat these men to death. Or maybe the discovery of IEDs brought out the hatred, the emotion . . . the dark side. Whatever you want to call it.

I jumped in and stopped the beating, although, by that time, enough blood had been spilled, enough bones broken, to satisfy everyone involved.

On January 27, 2004, at LSA Anaconda, an investigator from the United States Army Criminal Investigation Command took my formal statement regarding the events of January 3. Here, reprinted verbatim (with only some explanatory material related to abbreviations and/or acronyms included in brackets) is the text of that handwritten statement:

> Here is what I know to be true.
> I returned back to Samarra [Brassfield-Mora] on the day of CPT Paliwoda's memorial service (7 Jan 04). As most know, Eric's death deeply affected me. In the days afterward, I was definitely not myself—basically having one of my company commanders die in my presence—had left me pretty

much grief stricken and very upset. It also bothered me a great deal that Eric died on Paliwoda FOB [formerly Eagle] while 1-8 IN was still in Samarra. Anyway, I was still pretty upset when CPT Cunningham and LT Saville approached me with a report of the incident in Samarra.

I needed to meet the Bde Cdr [brigade commander] and the 1-66 AR Cdr for a transition meeting since I was returning back to Balad the next day to relieve 2-3 Infantry. So, in a 10 minute meeting or so, CPT Cunningham relayed to me the events that on the night of 3 Jan 04, 1st Platoon, A Company had detained 2 individuals breaking curfew up near the SDI Complex in Samarra; however, instead of moving them to the CMOC [Civil Military Operations Center] or police station across from the CMOC, they moved the two detainees to a location just past checkpoint K2 and had them get out of the Bradley, they uncuffed the detainees, and motioned to have the two individuals jump into the nearby water—the 2 Iraqis did just that and then soldiers watched as the Iraqis got out of the water and walked away. The soldiers then remounted their Bradleys and continued their movement back to Brassfield-Mora.

As a result of this information, I made a poor, hasty decision to have everyone involved just talk about dropping the Iraqis off on the road. First, I was clearly not myself—still focused on the mortar attacks in Balad, Eric, and finding his killers. Second, I thought the water was inconsequential since the soldiers had watched them get out. I was very upset with the platoon's leadership, their poor judgment/ actions, and wanted to handle this at my level.

CPT Cunningham is my best company commander and A Company is my best infantry company. Well-trained, organized, effective, and aggressive, A Company has done a *phenomenal job in both phases of engagement. Eliminating attackers while also engaging in a highly successful civil affairs campaign in Balad. So, I told the company Cdr and platoon leader to not mention anything about the water. And then I left the next day for Balad and basically took my "eye off the ball" in Samarra since we launched into several consecutive operations to capture/detain CPT Paliwoda's killers— and by the time I came out of those operations—CID was involved, the investigation was on-going, and everything was clearly out of my hands. And so, though I am quite sure Zaydoon is alive and well—it has come to this.*

I have made hundreds of decisions out here in combat— many split-second under fire, many that fall into the "life or death" category, and many on the future of detainees (release or hold). In all cases, I know I have made the right call—but in this instance, I did not.

I do not excuse the behavior of those involved in having the Iraqis jump into the water—it was an act of stupidity, but no one drowned—and hopefully in two weeks or so I will be able to detain Zaydoon and prove that.

I also do not excuse my decision—of the hundreds of right calls I have made, this one was wrong—no matter that I was still suffering from Eric's death, I should have conducted a formal commander's inquiry and presented the facts to the Bde Cdr. I wish I could have a "re-do" on this part.

So I take full responsibility for what has happened since the incident.

—LTC NATHAN M. SASSAMAN

The response of the CID agent who took my statement was sympathetic, but not optimistic. "Sir, you're going to want to make sure you get yourself a good lawyer, because based on my experience, I'm not sure you'll be in command much longer, and you're probably going to be court-martialed for directly disobeying an order and for being involved in this." He paused. "It's too bad. . . . You've got such a great reputation as a commander."

Not long after that, Tracy Perkins and Jack Saville were removed from my command, and Alpha Company had to start over with a new platoon sergeant and a new platoon leader, which was somewhat remarkable (and not a little dangerous) considering that we were still in the thick of the fight. Indeed, I had to pull that platoon out of some of our actions because its new platoon leadership was not sufficiently trained. That was only part of the weirdness—the strangest thing of all was that I remained in charge of the 1-8 Infantry, despite having been fingerprinted and charged with impeding an investigation. I was assigned legal counsel, a Judge Advocate General (JAG) lawyer who would supposedly look after my interests, and whose youth and enthusiasm were tempered by an almost comically bleak outlook.

"We're going to fight this thing," he said, pumping his fist.

"Okay . . ."

"How long have you been in the army, sir?"

"Almost nineteen years."

He nodded. "All right, the main thing we want to do here is protect your retirement—make sure you get your twenty years in."

"That's it? That's how we're going to fight?" I was shocked. At the time, I was still confident that I would beat whatever charges were thrown my way, and that my combat record would supersede all other considerations. The lawyer clearly didn't see it that way.

"Colonel Sassaman, you are never going to command a brigade, and your military career is over. You're going to be relieved of command, and in all likelihood you're going to go through a court-martial. But if we can protect your retirement, all is not lost."

To me, this actually sounded a lot like losing. I held nothing against the lawyer. His job was to give me a pep talk and make sure that I was prepared for the worst-case scenario. Clearly, though, we were from different worlds. He was a short, rumpled captain, not too far removed from law school, who obviously had no idea what it was like to carry a weapon, let alone fire it in the heat of battle. It seemed completely implausible that he had any notion of how to handle a case that centered on alleged detainee abuse.

In fairness, though, I was as much a fish out of water as he was. I was good outside the wire—don't get me wrong—but I wasn't as good inside the wire, where politics and policy ruled the day. When I was cast into the legal arena, I was totally out of my element. After a year in Iraq I had become a fighter in every sense of the word, but here, in a fight that hinged on paper and posturing, I wasn't the least bit savvy.

Typically, these types of legal investigations will tear a unit to pieces, but we really tried to focus on the task at hand. My XO, Rob Gwinner, was aware of what was happening, as was Matt Cunningham, but just about everyone else in the unit was uninformed. We continued to patrol aggressively, and to fight at every opportunity. If I'm entirely honest with myself, I will acknowledge a desire to seek revenge for Eric's death, and for all of the bad and violent actions that had happened in the previous month and a half. I sought . . . compensation—but it never came. At the end of this extraordinarily violent period, I discovered that Eric was still gone; my heart ached no less than it had before, and no matter how many Iraqis we killed, or how violent we became in our actions, Eric was never coming back. The sickening feeling that I, as a commander, had failed both Eric and Staff Sergeant Panchot was never going away. So I can say from firsthand experience that revenge is not the answer; you can, in fact, become a very old and bitter person, despite exacting whatever amount of retribution you think is appropriate for the hurt.

In mid-February, during a meeting with Colonel Rudesheim, I was informed that I would be facing an Article 15 nonjudicial proceeding. While not as grim and potentially life-altering a fate as a formal court-martial, this still represented seriously bad news, and it had the unique effect of making the hair rise on the back of my neck. An Article 15 out of the Uniform Code of Military Justice allows for the internal handling of an offense or violation. I'd adjudicated many of them in my career—enough to know that they were extremely rare at the level of lieutenant colonel. I also knew that while the Article 15 would preclude criminal prosecution, it would likely result in the end of my military career. It turned out that I had been way too optimistic. I kept hoping that somewhere along the line, someone would stand up and say, *This is a guy we really do want to keep in the army.* But apparently because I did not side with the brass, and I didn't just step aside and bring my soldiers forward, it sent the message that I'd gone over to the other side. If I hadn't intentionally impeded the investigation, the Article 15 implied, neither had I been appropriately cooperative.

Responsibility for the southern portion of the Salah Ah Din Province was transferred from the 1-8 Infantry to the 1-77 Armor on March 13, 2004, during a short, formal ceremony in Balad. Immediately afterward, Captain Cunningham and I jumped on a Black Hawk helicopter bound for Tikrit. There, in one of Saddam's Water Palaces that served as our division headquarters, the two of us would face and learn the outcome of the Article 15 proceeding.

Matt was summoned first. I wished him luck and watched him walk away. Perhaps fifteen minutes later he returned. Our eyes locked as he went by.

"Letter of reprimand," he whispered. "Local fiche."

"Fiche" meant "microfiche." His letter of reprimand would be placed in a local file that General Odierno could destroy or discard at any time. In other words, it was not to be on Matt's permanent record. It was, for Matt, the best possible outcome under the circumstances. The letter of reprimand would remain hidden in his file, and therefore have minimal impact on his career, at least in the short term. In the long term, however, it was a bit more complicated than that. Eventually, if you rise high enough, all files become subject to review. Still, at this moment, it seemed a fairly positive result for Matt, and I was happy and relieved for him. General Odierno could have crushed Matt if he had elected to do so, but he didn't. I think the primary rationale for leniency was that Matt had simply followed my orders. I later found out that they had asked him why he didn't disobey the order and "do what the army would have wanted you to do—the right thing."

"Because what Colonel Sassaman did *was* the right thing," Matt had answered.

As I walked through the palace's vast anteroom, and came upon General Odierno, Colonel Rudesheim, and Lieutenant Colonel Tracy Barnes, Fourth Infantry Division's judge advocate, who had been named legal adviser to the commanding general (and who clearly viewed this case as the career-making opportunity that it was), I wasn't so sure. I wavered between wanting to grab Fred and smack him around in front of everyone, and just being a humble servant and taking my lumps.

"Lieutenant Colonel Sassaman reporting as ordered," I said.

The room was fairly small, with one rectangular table and six chairs. General Odierno sat at one end of the table, while Colonel Rudesheim and Lieutenant Colonel Barnes both sat on one side of the table. General Odierno motioned for me to sit on the other side of the table, directly across from Fred. I could barely breathe. My mind raced, and the temperature in the room felt as if it had soared to a thousand degrees. Most Article 15s are routinely scripted and follow a normal progression of events (including offering me the option of rejecting the Article 15 hearing in favor of a court-martial, which, as you might expect, is rarely a good idea). General Odierno next read me my rights, reiterating the charges against me (impeding an investigation). He then launched into a determined lecture, which, again, seemed scripted, but really reminded me of a father scolding his son. Most of it actually seemed to be for the benefit of Fred and Tracy, rather than for me, but as his big voice boomed off the walls in that small room, I remember a couple of phrases that will stay with me forever.

"You just wanted to be one of the boys," he said. Then he said, "You did not trust your leadership; you didn't trust us."

General Odierno was dead wrong on the first call, but right on the money with the second comment. I did not trust my commanding officers. I didn't trust my brigade commander at all. And General Odierno? He lived in the palace in Tikrit. He was in the same room Saddam used to be in. I was in the streets. I was in the orchards. I was sweating my ass off in firefights in the middle of the day and the middle of the night. General Odierno had no clue. Nevertheless, General Odierno as a division commander probably had more of a clue than my brigade commander. His assertion that I was trying to be one of the boys, however, was baseless and ill-informed. I had court-martialed two of my own soldiers earlier in the year because of desertion. I had done Article 15s, and I had punished my own soldiers on countless occasions. I'd thrown one of my own men out of the army because he'd stolen $20 of goods out of an Iraqi storefront, when he knew full well that the rules of warfare expressly forbid soldiers from stealing or looting. I punished one of my team leaders to the point where he couldn't recover, because I knew he was unfit to lead men into combat. So General Odierno was wrong when he said I wanted to be one of the boys. I never wanted that, but I'll tell you what: the boys don't get many people standing up for them. The dogfaces are fighting, day in and day out. They get crucified when they make a bad call. You can't make the right call, a great call, every time. There is crazy and twisted logic in a combat zone, and sometimes people will make mistakes. In Vietnam, they used to say, "You have to destroy the village to save the village." Sounds crazy—until you've been on the ground in Iraq. Then it makes sense.

"Do you have anything to say?" General Odierno asked.

"Sir, I know in your eyes I messed up," I began, "but I really can't say too much with my brigade commander and this legal officer in the room." At that point General Odierno excused Colonel Rudesheim and Lieutenant Colonel Barnes, which was probably not in strict accordance with protocol, but General Odierno and I went way back. Not only were we both West Point grads, but we had both played football at the academy. I knew, deep in my heart, that while General Odierno was not happy with the current situation, he understood what it took to win the war in Iraq, and he admired and appreciated the work of the 1-8 Infantry.

"All right, Nate," he said after we were alone. "What's the deal here?"

I relayed my sentiments about the Samarra insurgents, the recent deaths of my soldiers, and the lack of proof that anyone had died that night at the Tigris. Further, there had been no reason for me to believe there had been an ongoing criminal investigation when I had asked the company commander and platoon leader to not say anything to anyone about the water. Because "I was going to be damned before I let a couple of Iraqi insurgents breaking curfew, openly defying American authority, and executing operations against us to set back all the hard work we had accomplished in bringing peace to a city the 1-66 Armor had completely abandoned."

I didn't get too terribly far into my statement before electing to take the high road. "Sir, I take full responsibility for all my actions. I take full responsibility for the decision."

At the end, General Odierno settled back in his chair and said, "Nate, what would you have me do?"

Usually, by this point, the decision has been made, so it was a rhetorical question (and one I had used myself when presiding over these types of affairs). I didn't bite at all.

"Sir, my career is in your hands."

"Okay," General Odierno said. Then, more formally, he added, "You're receiving a letter of reprimand under an Article 15 proceeding; I will put this in your restricted personnel microfiche file."

What this meant, really, was that I would have the opportunity to be promoted to full colonel. Command boards at successive levels, however, always review an officer's restricted microfiche; any negative action effectively disqualifies the officer from further command opportunities. So, basically, what General Odierno said to me was this: *You will never command a brigade, but if you want to be promoted to colonel and serve the army for thirty years, I'm going to allow you to do that.* A ceiling was placed on my career at the rank of colonel, with the promise that no one would ever know what punitive action arose from our time in the room.

(That, unfortunately, would prove to be untrue. By this time I had already received three e-mail messages from a reporter at the *Washington Post* who was working on a story about an incident involving the drowning of a detainee at the hands of soldiers from the 1–8 Infantry. In April the story appeared, with names and supposedly confidential information aplenty, as well as quotes from Colonel Rudesheim. By that point, discretion was not an option, and my career was as good as dead.)

The Article 15 proceeding ended with General Odierno handing me the formal letter of reprimand, which stated, among other things, that my conduct had been "wrongful, criminal," and that it "will not be tolerated."

Before those words even had a chance to sink in, however, General Odierno softened. "Nate, if there's anything you ever need, just let me know."

I stood and saluted. "Thank you, sir."

Then I left the room.

That night I called my wife and shared with her, for the very first time, the full extent of what had transpired. Until that night I had tried to spare her many of the ugly details; in fact, I'd mentioned the investigation only once, and even then just in passing: "You may hear some things about a controversial decision I made over here. Don't worry—it should all be over now."

Well, in actuality the storm had only increased in strength and severity, and there was no longer any point in withholding information from my wife, who also happened to be my best friend. Marilyn was understandably distressed, in part because the Article 15 effectively signaled the end of my career, but also because I had kept her in the dark for so long. It was a relatively short conversation, the gist of which was this: *I'm coming home. I'll finish out my twenty years, and then we'll move on in life and do something different.*

Marilyn was incredibly supportive; the idea of leaving the army and not being told where to live anymore, and packing up the house every two years . . . well, that sounded all right to her. The conversation was startling in its simplicity and earnestness. This was the very first time in Iraq that I called my wife and engaged her in a heart-to-heart talk. Our discussions typically had been rare and brief, covering only the most mundane and superficial of topics. They were safe, clean, unemotional conversations, deliberate in their refusal to acknowledge the pain of separation or the danger associated with my work. It was mostly just me asking them how they were doing. Sometimes Marilyn would be involved in trying to help the family of another soldier, and she'd enlist my support in that regard (I'd do whatever I could from such a great distance), but it was rare for us to share intimate feelings over the phone. This was different. This was the first time in nine months that we talked like husbands and wives should talk when they're sharing something important: their hearts, their fears, their dreams, and their aspirations. It was a difficult call, but one that needed to be made. I was hurting pretty badly that night, and I probably had hurt my wife more than once over the nearly two decades of my military career—there were so many times when I had put the army first and her a distant last. So this was a turning point for me. It was almost as if I had both a wife and a mistress (with the army being the latter), and now the mistress had turned on me.

We fought until the very end, even as we were driving south, heading for Kuwait, with no particular mission and nothing more urgent to achieve than simply staying alive. Outside Baghdad my men responded to an errant RPG attack with lethal and merciless force. The response obliterated a farm building in the proximity of the RPG attack, and even then my soldiers were intent on tracking down the insurgents and emptying their magazines into their bodies. They were in a fighting mood until the moment we crossed the border into Kuwait, on March 27, 2004, and suddenly the war, for us, came to an end.

It was an astonishing and disorienting process, really, as complete and sudden in its immersion as the act of entering the country and beginning the fight. There was a camp right at the border—an army rest stop—where we emptied our weapons, turned in all ammunition, removed our Kevlar helmets and flak vests. Just like that, it was as if we had traded Iraq for New Jersey. No sense of elation or even relief accompanied these actions. I just felt . . . empty. Life at the base in Kuwait did nothing to alleviate that emptiness. The mess hall was the largest I'd ever seen, and it served four terrific meals a day. This little camp, which had barely existed when I arrived in the late spring of 2003, had been transformed into a veritable shopping mall, with the world's biggest food court, mountains of recreation equipment, and endless opportunities to throw away money and get fat and lazy.

Within a few days, our unit was cleared to leave the country. We boarded a United Airlines flight—a commercial 747 filled entirely with 1-8 Infantry personnel—bound for Colorado Springs, with a short layover in Prague. I was fortunate to get a seat in first class, where I could really stretch out; I can't say much about the flight, because I was asleep before we left the ground. As we descended toward Prague, I woke to the voice of a flight attendant strolling down the aisle.

"How are you?"

"Fine, thanks."

She'd been working these types of flights for months now—flights carrying hundreds of soldiers, all deliriously happy to be going home. She was accustomed to the routine—the soldiers high-fiving each other as the plane climbed, yelling at the tops of their lungs, bidding farewell to the Middle East, sometimes with tears in their eyes. This flight, she said, had been different. "There wasn't even a whimper," she noted. "I've never seen it so quiet. Everyone was asleep."

I wanted to tell her about what we'd been through—the endless patrols, the combat actions, the reconstruction projects that almost no one seemed to notice or have any interest in discussing. I wanted to tell her about Dale Panchot and Eric Paliwoda, but I couldn't. So I just nodded.

"Yeah, I'm not surprised."

CHAPTER 14

Sir,

First of all, thank you for taking the time to write me and keeping me in your thoughts and prayers. There is not a day that goes by that I don't think of you and our other comrades. . . . I am sorry for what has happened to you for my actions on that night. I think many others would have left me on the side of the road, abandoned, but you have not. I will forever be in your debt, sir. Thank you . . .

STAFF SERGEANT TRACY PERKINS
ARMY REGIONAL CORRECTIONAL FACILITY,
FORT KNOX, KENTUCKY,
MARCH 8, 2005

We arrived at the airport in Colorado Springs to virtually no fanfare. This was by design; the army had arranged a rather large and formal reception at nearby Fort Carson. Disoriented and groggy from a day of travel, we stumbled off the plane and were ushered to a waiting bus. Someone shoved a bag of traditional American sustenance (McDonald's burgers and Gatorade) into my hand, and I ate it without taking a breath.

Within a few minutes we were at Fort Carson, standing outside a gymnasium that had been transformed into a makeshift welcome center. We milled about for a while; then someone had us form up, and as music erupted through loudspeakers (Lee Greenwood's patriotic anthem, "God Bless the USA"), the doors of the gym blew open and we marched inside. The bleachers in the gymnasium were filled to capacity with friends and family members, all standing and applauding and screaming at the top of their lungs. It was an unbelievable scene, with so much emotion that it's hard to convey, soldiers craning their necks, straining to find their loved ones, to make eye contact with their wives or girlfriends or children, with their parents, and with their brothers and sisters. Astutely the speaker's introductions were kept to a minimum, just a few brief words—"Welcome home!" basically— before the soldiers were cut loose and allowed to reunite with their families.

For a few seconds, pandemonium reigned as the gym became a massive, swirling scrum of humanity—three hundred uniformed soldiers pushing through a crowd of more than one thousand civilians, crying and shouting as they reached out to their families. As I scanned the gym, searching for Marilyn and the kids, I had a moment of revelation: those video clips I used to see when I was a boy, the scenes of POWs coming home from Vietnam and collapsing into the arms of their wives and children? This is what it must have felt like.

"Daddy!"

Nicole, my daughter, spotted me first. I heard her yell and saw her running toward me. I'd spent no more than a few weeks with my family in the previous two years, so it shouldn't have come as a shock that Nicole had changed rather dramatically—but it was a shock nonetheless. She had grown—taller and more beautiful—and my eyes filled with tears the moment I saw her. Nathan was right behind her, bigger and stronger than I remembered, a boy on the cusp of adolescence. And Marilyn, smiling, crying, looking so pretty that my heart ached. It's so hard to describe this sensation—the joy at being home, alive, and touching the people you love; the pride of having fought for your country; and the profound appreciation for all that you once took for granted.

For a while, everything seemed new and worthy of wonder. Marilyn had lined the front lawn of our home with little American flags, the sight of which left me breathless and sucked nearly all the bitterness from my bones. There had been honor in our work; there had been dignity. In some circles, at least, there was gratitude, and that realization was comforting. Unfortunately, it was short-lived. The dreamlike quality of those first few days at home—sleeping on a firm mattress with crisp, clean sheets, my arms around my wife; playing with the kids; eating at Pizza Hut!—dissolved the following week, with the publication of a story in the *Washington Post*, by a reporter named Tom Ricks.

I hadn't seen the story, wasn't aware of its content (although the reporter had made several calls to my home in an attempt to interview me for the story) until I received a phone call one morning from General Odierno. He wanted to know if I was all right.

"Yeah, I'm fine, sir."

"Then you obviously haven't seen the *Washington Post*."

The article, published on April 5, 2004, carried the following headline:

Commander Punished as Army
Probes Detainee Treatment

The opening paragraphs read as follows:

The army is investigating an allegation that U.S. troops killed an Iraqi detainee when they forced him and another man to jump from a bridge into the Tigris River, and a battalion commander has been disciplined for impeding the probe, officers familiar with the investigation said.

Lt. Col. Nate Sassaman, well-known in the army since he was a star West Point quarterback two decades ago, received a reprimand for helping subordinates mislead army investigators as they began their inquiry, an officer familiar with the situation said. Several other soldiers received similar punishment.

The story presented a reasonably accurate and prosaic overview of the incident at the Tigris and its aftermath—Ricks did, for example, note that there was some question as to whether anyone had died or even been injured as a result of the incident. I took no real issue with the substance of the article; rather, what I found disturbing was the fact that it had been written at all—that could not have happened without some assistance on the part of the army—and that my boss had been heavily quoted.

"There are elements of what happened in Samarra . . . that still are under investigation and in dispute," said Col. Frederick Rudesheim, commander of the brigade that includes Sassaman's battalion. "What we don't know is what really happened that evening. What I know is that we did something wrong."

If something went wrong, the battalion commander was responsible.

> Sassaman's "lapse in judgment," Rudesheim said, was
> in not telling investigators that it was true the Iraqis had
> been forced into the river. "What was being said initially was
> that they were dropped off, and the flex cuffs cut off them,
> and that was all there was to it. . . . They left that piece out,
> that they had actually been in the water."
>   He added: "It came as a complete shock to me that there
> was any cover-up—it just floored me."

Fred threw a bone my way toward the bottom of the story,
acknowledging the fine work done by the 1-8 Infantry during its
ten months in Iraq, and "mitigating circumstances" (the death of
Captain Paliwoda) around the time of the alleged detainee abuse.
Not that it mattered. With the publication of this story, the incident of January 3 took on a life of its own, and my role in that incident became a very public matter.

Fred tried to exercise damage control right away, calling me
on the phone and insisting that he had been misquoted, or that his
statements had been taken out of context. I'd been around the
media long enough to know that most people are not misquoted;
they're just careless in choosing their words. To the very end, Fred
tried to bury the hatchet with me, largely, I think, out of concern
that I would run off and tell the world that he was not the great
combat commander that he envisioned himself to be. Unfortunately, it's so typical of the army to honor and reward men who
take no risks and merely protect the status quo. Iraq forced me to
take a good long look in the mirror and decide what type of
man—what type of leader—I wanted to be. Had my career not
involved combat duty—had I merely been another peacetime

officer—I might well have been able to play the game the way it's meant to be played. I could have been the politician, kissed the right rings, and ultimately advanced to the rank of general officer. Iraq taught me something: I am not made that way. I am a soldier, not a politician. It's one thing to blindly follow ignorant orders in a time of peace; it's quite another when you're at war.

I made mistakes—I don't deny that. I take responsibility for everything that happened on my watch, but I tried to do the right thing. I tried to be a warrior. I tried to protect my men and serve my country to the best of my ability. Fred, like some other senior officers, from what I witnessed, rarely put forth the effort. In my view, he failed his battalion commanders and soldiers by not approaching the fight with the will to win. I have come to view the army in a different light now, and I understand the way it works at a certain level—a level occupied by men too scared to make a decision that might have negative consequences. They reach the rank of full colonel, so close to the brass ring they can taste it, and they become paralyzed by fear. Or, worse, slaves to their own egos. Our annual brigade ball was held in late April. It's common at this event for a guest speaker to be invited, someone with no formal connection to the brigade, but someone capable of entertaining and inspiring the audience. On this occasion, the guest speaker was . . . the brigade commander! That's right—Colonel Rudesheim chose himself.

It was, to my knowledge, an unprecedented act of vanity. Fortunately, I missed the brigade ball that year. Marilyn had arranged a weeklong vacation in Maui, so while Fred was boring his audience to tears, I was on the beach with my wife. It was like a second honeymoon; in fact, it was better than our honeymoon. My toughest decision of the day was to try to figure out where to eat dinner that night. We went parasailing and snorkeling; we sat on the beach and read mindless novels; and we traveled all over the island. This trip was all about connecting, though, and just getting to know one another again.

I find it difficult to not do anything top-drawer. So it was that on June 4, 2004, I might have been fairly accused of overzealousness in the orchestration of a ceremony at Fort Carson honoring the soldiers of the 1-8 Infantry. More than 150 Purple Hearts and Bronze Stars were distributed during a rousing celebration that included an Army band, bagpipes, a blinding light show, and a tireless smoke machine. The auditorium was packed to capacity (with a crowd of perhaps 1,500 people), and the local media turned out in droves. I had attended other ceremonies in the past, and while the effort had usually been earnest, the results were typically less than overwhelming. It was all kind of rote: come to attention, read the names, pin a medal on the uniform, send them on their way. I wanted to make sure that we did it right . . . that we honored these guys in a manner commensurate with their sacrifice, and that we gave them something to remember.

To that end (in addition to the atmospheric elements), we invited the regimental sergeant major and the regimental colonel— a couple of old-timers who had fought in Vietnam. We invited all the 1-8 Infantry veterans in the entire state of Colorado, and about thirty of them showed up. The point was to honor the men who had fought in Iraq by reminding everyone that our unit was part of a proud tradition. The soldiers of 1-8 Infantry had fought at the battle of Antietam in the Civil War; they'd been among the first to land at Normandy on D-day in World War II; they'd fought off the Tet offensive in Vietnam.

They'd done a commendable, sometimes heroic job during Operation Iraqi Freedom, against almost insurmountable odds. Some of that work was displayed to the audience in the form of a Victory Tape (as I liked to call it), which was basically a synopsis of our time in Iraq. Befitting a ceremony to honor a group of soldiers who were mostly in their late teens and early twenties, the tape was fast-paced and loud, with lots of jump cuts and musical accompaniment. When it came time for Colonel Rudesheim to take the microphone, his introduction was accompanied by a clip, and music, from *Star Wars*, with the focus on Darth Vader.

This came courtesy of Rob Gwinner—there had been no love lost between Rob and Fred, and I suppose this was Rob's way of getting even. Fred didn't have much of a sense of humor, particularly when he was the butt of the joke, and it was obvious as he approached the podium that he was not amused.

"I'm sorry, sir," I said, trying not to laugh. "What can you do?"

Among the honorees, of course, was Staff Sergeant Dale Panchot, who posthumously received a Purple Heart and a Bronze Star for valor. These medals, along with his combat infantryman's badge, were presented to Dale's parents, Arland and Karen Panchot. At once brokenhearted and filled with pride, the Panchots accepted the awards graciously. Marilyn had met them some months earlier, at a previous ceremony for the families of the 1-8 Infantry, but this was my introduction, and I was instantly taken by their strength and quiet dignity. The Panchots were salt-of-the-earth folks from Northome, Minnesota. No pretense, no guile. Just like their son. Dale had been a quiet leader, the kind who rarely raised his voice, but let his actions speak for him. His weapon was always the cleanest, and he had the highest of standards for everything that he did. He was an avid basketball player and outdoorsman—typically, my best riflemen were hunters, and certainly this was true of Dale. He had been the third soldier from the state of Minnesota to be killed during OIF, and the governor spoke at a memorial service in his honor. The service was held at the high school gym because it was the only place in

Northome large enough to accommodate everyone who wanted to attend.

Meeting his parents, it wasn't hard to understand how he had come to be so popular.

"I'm sorry," I told the Panchots as I presented them with their son's medals. "I'm so sorry that we couldn't bring him back."

Arland reached out, wrapped me in a bear hug, and gave me a pat on the back. That's the kind of people they were—in a moment of enormous pain, having suffered an unspeakable loss, they were capable of comforting someone else. Someone ostensibly responsible for protecting their son while he served his country half a world away. Their generosity was overwhelming.

Eric Paliwoda was recognized, as well; his fiancée, Wendy Rosen, accepted the honor on his behalf. Eric's parents, unfortunately, did not attend the ceremony. I would later come to realize that while only two men in my unit had been killed, their backgrounds and families could not have been more dissimilar. While the Panchots were working-class people from the heartland who quietly supported the war effort and their son's involvement in Iraq, the Paliwodas were opposed to the war, and indeed were bitter about Eric's career choice. For them, at this time anyway, the wounds apparently were still too raw, the pain too severe. So they stayed home.

In July a separate, vastly more subdued ceremony was conducted to honor the officers of the 1-8 Infantry Battalion. It was held in the parking lot of the brigade headquarters, with only a handful of people in attendance. There were no soldiers, aside from the half dozen officers receiving awards. There were no reporters or television cameras. There was no music, no videotape. The entire affair, presided over by Colonel Rudesheim, lasted perhaps ten minutes. I received a Bronze Star for valor on that day, an award specifically linked to the combat action of August

2003—my first of the war. As he pinned the medal to my uniform, Fred said something interesting . . . something that actually startled me a bit.

"Nate, of everyone in this brigade, no one deserves this more than you."

Fred knew the deal. Somewhere in the deepest recesses of his soul, he understood that the 1-8 Infantry had fought courageously, and that we had been committed to winning the war. Politics and bureaucracy aside, ours was one of the most effective fighting units in Iraq, and he knew it. This was the only time he acknowledged it. Why? I don't know. Perhaps because we're all soldiers at heart. Or, if you want to be a bit more skeptical about things, maybe it had something to do with the fact that Fred's tenure as brigade commander was coming to an end, and he wanted to do everything he could to patch things up, so that we'd part on good terms. In my opinion, Fred's primary motivation was the knowledge that there was an officer in Iraq who fought the fight . . . and who knew that Fred did not fight. Americans tend to see all returning soldiers as warriors . . . heroes. We all fought to win and we all served our country proudly—but it really wasn't that way. Some people fought; most did not. That's just the way it worked. Fred was doing damage control in an attempt to regain my trust, but it was way too late. In reality, I'm sure he would have loved it if I'd gotten run over by a bus.

"Thank you, sir," I said.

We turned and faced the American flag, and together we saluted.

Comrades . . . brothers in arms.

For much of the next year I rode an emotional roller coaster, bouncing between days filled with hope and happiness, and days of abject despair. I wasn't alone—indeed, I find it hard to believe that anyone who saw combat duty in Iraq can possibly escape the effects of post-traumatic stress disorder. We all deal with it differently, but no one comes home unscathed. As the investigation continued, and it became apparent that the legal battle would be fought primarily around the actions of Lieutenant Saville and Sergeant Perkins, my mood darkened considerably. There were endless interviews, depositions to be taken and sworn statements repeated ad nauseam. If court-martials were to be held, I would be expected to testify. Having already been punished under the Article 15 proceeding, I would receive immunity, but that did little to quell my anger and anxiety. Given the opportunity, I would testify on behalf of the defense.

All of this unfolded slowly and painfully, and I can't say that I handled it particularly well. Many nights I lay awake, staring at the ceiling, replaying events in my head. When I did sleep, invariably, I fought the war all over again. I'd wake up bathed in sweat, Marilyn holding me tight.

"You're back in Iraq, huh?"

"Yeah . . ."

Part of it was the memory of the war—the battles and the blood and the horror of it all—but another part of it was a restless doubt about my own performance. *Did I make the wrong decisions? Am I a failure?* I'd been a winner my entire life—how could everything have turned out so badly over there?

Then there were the good days—days when one of my soldiers would call and say, "Sir, thanks. Without you, a lot of people would have died. I'd go to hell and back for you." But those days were too few. Overall, I was an emotional wreck, and my marriage and my children paid the price. I couldn't relax . . . couldn't sit still and just enjoy spending time with my family. To a degree, that continues to this day. I've always been a bit on the energetic side, but prior to serving in Iraq, I could find a place for relaxation; I could sit in a movie theater for a couple hours. Now? No way.

The irritability and anxiousness were unmanageable in the year after I returned from Iraq. I was ridiculously quick to anger, yelling at Marilyn and the kids over the slightest of things. Dirty dishes in the sink? I'd snap. If we were two minutes late dropping the kids off for some school activity? I'd go ballistic. It was ridiculous. Eventually Marilyn (and a couple of my closest friends) suggested that I needed professional help. In my heart, I knew that I had a problem, particularly because I had seen similarly self-destructive behavior among other officers who had served in Iraq.

You can fight the war only so many times in your head, but I couldn't turn off the noise. I tried not to read the newspapers or watch the news on television, but still the information filtered through, and each time it would send me into a funk. I got a call at home one evening from Major Darron Wright.

"Sir, I'm listening to some talk show on the radio, and they are taking you to the cleaners."

"Darron, thanks . . . but I don't want to know about any of this stuff."

The charges leveled against my men were serious, the consequences potentially devastating. Sergeant Perkins and Lieutenant Saville, along with Sergeant Reggie Martinez, were initially charged with a variety of offenses, involuntary manslaughter being the most serious, following an Article 32 hearing (basically the equivalent of a civilian grand jury hearing) in the summer of 2004. Specialist Terry Bowman was accused of assault and making false statements. By October, however, criminal charges against Martinez and Bowman had been dropped (both men received administrative punishments), leaving Saville and Perkins at the center of the storm.

Sergeant Perkins's trial came first, in January 2005, at Fort Hood, Texas. Prior to the start of the trial, I was informed by my new brigade commander that I had come under scrutiny for allegedly attempting to influence the testimony of both Sergeant Perkins and Lieutenant Saville. My personal and military phone records had been investigated, and the result, of course, was that I hadn't made any calls to either Perkins or Saville; the claims were completely bogus. Nevertheless, even as mere background chatter, they made me nervous, for I knew that the lead investigator, Lieutenant Colonel Tracy Barnes, was trying to get at me in any way possible. On another occasion, in the months leading up to the trial, my new brigade commander, Brian Jones, called me in and asked, cryptically, whether there might be any grounds on which the army could relieve me of my command.

"I don't know, sir. Are there any?"

Colonel Jones is a decent man, and I suspect he was trying to give me some sort of an exit strategy, if that is what I wanted. He went on to list four areas in which the army evaluated its senior officers: leading, training, caring, and maintaining.

"As far as the first three, I'd say you're the top battalion commander in the brigade," he said. "The only area where you might need some work is in maintaining."

"Maintaining" refers to maintenance, as in taking proper care of equipment in the motor pool and that sort of thing. I would have disagreed with him, but when your brigade commander tells you that you're the best in the brigade in three of four categories (the three most important categories, in my opinion), you consider it a victory and walk away. When the subject of relief was revisited a few weeks later, and Colonel Jones again pointed out my supposed weakness in regard to the motor pool, I lost my temper.

"No offense, sir, but why don't you just go ahead and relieve me if that's what you want to do? Nobody has any guts in this division!"

None of these guys had a clue as to what they were about to get themselves into. I knew Tracy Barnes and the way he was approaching the investigation. I knew he was out of control, but I intended to go down swinging, and to challenge every accusation and assumption. It wore on me—a lot. I was trying to prepare my unit to fight, trying to keep my family together. I was trying to maintain a tenuous grip on my own sanity. All the while I was receiving notes about my performance, insinuations that I would be relieved of command. The overarching theme was one of mistrust—and it stretched in both directions. The bottom line was this: to senior army staff, I had become a pariah.

A jury of six—three enlisted men and three battalion commanders—heard testimony in the Perkins trial. I personally knew two of those battalion commanders (Steve Russell of the 1-22 Infantry, whose unit had fought well in Iraq, and Daryl Gore, a forward support commander), and their presence on the jury gave me cause to be optimistic. The trial, however, was something of a joke, presided over shoddily by a milquetoast judge who appeared to have difficulty making even the simplest of decisions. I'd been through probably two dozen court-martials by this point in my career, and this was easily the most poorly run. There were constant recesses to make decisions on procedures. It was amateur hour from the beginning.

Matt, Rob, and I all testified. The thing I recall most vividly is being asked several complicated questions, and having my answers interrupted by the prosecutor, who repeatedly asked the judge to instruct me to limit my responses to two sentences.

"The United States government has waited a year to put this case together, and now you're going to restrict my comments to two sentences?"

The judge cleared his throat, straightened his back. "Colonel Sassaman, just follow my instructions."

So I did. For the most part, anyway. The prosecutor at one point asked me to explain the background and environment of the fight—I'm going to do that in two sentences? I just found it sad—the whole ongoing process.

So I finished my testimony; at one point toward the end, the prosecution asked me a question about Colonel Rudesheim.

"Make sure you're ready to go down this path," I responded, "because there's a whole lot to talk about there."

The prosecutor withdrew the question, but what came out in subsequent trials was that by informing me that there would be a court-martial if anyone had been pushed into the water, there existed sufficient grounds to investigate the brigade commander for undue command influence upon the battalion commander. The other interesting thing from the CID report was that I had been accused of withholding information from the investigators—which is actually kind of humorous when you consider that everyone above me in the chain of command knew more about what was happening than I did. Yet I was supposedly impeding the investigation by not being forthcoming with my knowledge.

In the end, Sergeant Perkins was convicted on lesser charges of assault and obstruction of justice, and sentenced to six months in jail. I was given an opportunity to speak during the sentencing phase of the trial, and I told the jury, in no uncertain terms, that I was disappointed with its decision. That was putting it mildly; I was disgusted. Steve Russell should have known better—his battalion had fought a similar fight in Tikrit. Lieutenant Colonel Russell should have understood the murky nature of the rules of engagement. It was not a fair or clean fight in Iraq; in fact, it was a very dirty and morally ambiguous fight. I know from personal experience that the 1-22 Infantry was involved in some seriously unpleasant incidents. It seems like when we get back in the States, and we all put on our Class As, our fancy green uniforms, and walk around with our medals, however, the war becomes very cut-and-dried. You either followed the laws of land warfare to the T . . . or you didn't. It's just not that simple; that's not reality.

In the sentencing phase of the trial I was asked if I regretted my actions regarding the night of January 3, and the subsequent investigation. I said, "No." But that wasn't entirely true. I did regret what had happened, and there were things I should have done differently, but I was exhausted by this point, beaten down by the incessant fighting and the never-ending assaults on my integrity. If I had it to do over again, I would have called General Odierno the moment I first learned of the incident, and I would have expressed my concern about the way things were being handled; I would have sought his advice.

I was chastised by the prosecutor for not understanding "army values," a laughable assertion considering that the Eagle Vision cards carried by every member of my battalion were based on army values. We knew army values—inside and out—and, in fact, strictly followed them.

Sergeant Perkins was taken directly from the courtroom to jail, with only a brief moment to say good-bye to his family. That evening I had dinner with Sergeant Perkins's brother and parents, along with Matt Cunningham and Rob Gwinner. Tracy's father was an army veteran, and I know the trial was extraordinarily difficult for him and the entire family. I felt sympathy for them, and not a small amount of responsibility for what had happened to their son, who was, I hasten to point out, a crack soldier, fighter, and small-unit leader, this incident notwithstanding.

When I think of Tracy, I try not to think of a single lapse in judgment in Iraq, but rather the commitment he showed to the mission and to his fellow soldiers.

The trials came in succession over the next few months. In March, Jack Saville pleaded guilty to a lesser charge of assault and received a sentence of forty-five days in jail. This represented a mere slap on the wrist compared to the punishment originally sought by the prosecution, whose case had unraveled spectacularly in the absence of physical evidence that anyone had drowned or been seriously injured on the night in question. Jack's trial was far different from Tracy's, primarily because the presiding judge was an astute and commanding presence who tolerated little posturing in his courtroom, and who clearly viewed as frivolous the prosecution's attempts to pin a long jail sentence on Jack. Indeed, if not for the fact that Sergeant Perkins, an enlisted man, was already serving time at Fort Knox, I believe the judge might have tossed the case out; barring that, he might well have spared Jack any time in jail. But a precedent had been established; as it was, I know that some people viewed Jack's lighter sentence as an example of favoritism: *Oh, sure . . . the enlisted man gets six months, while the officer gets forty-five days.* Really, though, it was nothing more than a case of Jack getting a better draw when it came to the presiding judge.

Regardless, both trials represented substantial losses for Lieutenant Colonel Tracy Barnes, who had hoped to hang multiyear sentences on both Sergeant Perkins and Lieutenant Saville. Although both trials received significant media attention, neither resulted in the career-making outcome that Lieutenant Colonel Barnes had pursued. The fact is, the army threw a lot against the wall in this case, and not much stuck. (Similarly, in May, another soldier from Fourth Infantry Division, Staff Sergeant Shane Werst, was acquitted of murdering an unarmed Iraqi; the jury decided, appropriately, that Sergeant Werst had feared for his life and acted in self-defense. I was the only officer to testify on his behalf at the trial.)

For me, though, there was little sense of peace, or any satisfaction at all. It hurt too much to watch my guys endure such pain and mudslinging. I've come to view the Uniform Code of Military Justice legal system as inherently unfair. Then again, life is unfair, and I think the UCMJ system models a lot of the failures of the human race. As in the civilian system, much is left to chance: Will your fate be decided by a judge or a jury? What evidence will be allowed or disallowed? In the military world, as I've said, you are guilty until proven innocent, and that makes all the difference.

When a commander such as General Odierno says it's a serious enough offense to merit the consideration of criminal charges, and needs to pass it off to the legal people, then it's completely out of his control, and it goes into another realm that baffles and bewilders most participants. That's why I feel there was a leadership failure within my division—certainly at Colonel Rudesheim's level, probably at my level, and maybe even at General Odierno's level. The lines of communication had become so badly broken that the three of us could not get in a room together and discuss, candidly and openly, what happened on the night of January 3. I should have called General Odierno sooner, but it never occurred to me that a criminal investigation would be launched, and maybe part of that stemmed from the fact that when I tried to initiate an investigation into the deaths of those five elderly men who had been killed in November 2003, nothing had happened. This seemed so tame by comparison. There are gradations of bad behavior in war, and while I do not excuse the actions of my men, I did not then, and never will, believe they rose to the level of criminal activity. I believe the *little guy*—the soldier on the ground—got needlessly hammered in this case. The truth is, Iraq is the war of the little guy. It was, and remains to this day, a small-unit fight. A fight best served by tough and courageous platoons marching through the cities and restoring order and taking control through sheer strength of will. Brigade commanders and generals, of course, do not want to hear any of that. They think technology, strategy, and overwhelming military might will win the war; and they're just flat-out wrong.

In the midst of the legal wrangling, command of the First Battalion, Eighth Infantry Regiment was transferred to Lieutenant Colonel Jeffrey Martindale. The official change-of-command ceremony took place on February 14, 2005, at Fort Carson's Manhart Field. I used the occasion to pay tribute to the men from the 1-8 Infantry who had served so courageously in Iraq, and to put into words my feelings about all that had transpired, with a heavy emphasis on accomplishment, and little regard for my own personal circumstances and frustrations. Following is the text of my change-of-command speech:

> *Major General Thurman, Command Sergeant Major Riling, Brigadier General Roe, Colonel Jones, Command Sergeant Major List, friends, families, and soldiers of the First Battalion, Eighth Infantry Fighting Eagles, thanks so much for attending today's change-of-command ceremony. Let me be the first to say "Happy Valentine's Day" and give fair warning to probably over half the men here to pick something nice up for their special Valentine before the day ends. Good luck and might I recommend the Passion Truffles at the Post Exchange. . . .*

They shall not grow old
As we that are left grow old
Age shall not weary them
Nor the hourglass condemn
At the going down of the sun

And at the rising of the sun
We shall greet them in our hearts
Undimmed, forever young, and at play
In the fields of the Lord.

I stated those words at Captain Eric Paliwoda's memorial service in Balad, Iraq, and not a day goes by that my thoughts don't drift back to both Staff Sergeant Dale Panchot, killed on 17 November 2003, and Captain Paliwoda, killed on 2 January 2004. There is no greater honor than leading American soldiers in combat on a foreign battlefield in defense of the United States of America, and there is no greater sense of failure for a commander than to lose men in combat. Command is all about focusing down, and the greatest leaders that I have served with are those that possess an unwavering commitment to quality service to the soldiers they lead. Every single day of my command was devoted to the men and women I led, whether in combat in Iraq or here at Fort Carson.

I am struck by the dichotomy between my assumption of command at Samarra East Airfield, Iraq, twenty months ago, and today's change of command. The ceremony in Iraq was brief, held in a broken-down hangar, without a parade; it was well over one hundred degrees, and instead of a reception, we moved quickly to my command post to brief Major General Odierno on the status of Operation Peninsula Strike.

Today is much colder, it's on a nice parade field, there will be a pass in review, and the battalion prepares for their semiannual gunnery density in a few weeks. The lesson here is that change is really the only constant in the army. We are an army at war, an army in transformation, and as such we must be prepared to fight against all threats and train in all conditions.

French essayist Michel de Montaigne wrote in the 1500s, "No profession or occupation is more pleasing than the military; a profession or exercise both noble in execution and noble in its cause. For the toughest, most generous and proudest of all virtues is true valor." And true valor exists among the Fighting Eagles! From the incredibly steady hand, superb medical expertise, and commonsense maturity of fifty-six-year-old Idaho native Major Wayne Slicton, fighting in his third war for our country, to eighteen-year-old Private Ricky Brown, from Center, Alabama . . . and everyone in between . . . the courage, bravery, and compassion exhibited by 1-8 soldiers in Iraq exceeded my wildest expectations. From the orchards of Balad to the streets of Samarra, to the dense vegetation of Albu Hishma along the Tigris River, I was taught a real-life lesson that soldiers in combat will courageously fight for their buddies, compassionately care for noncombatants, and form the tightest bonds known to man.

Now, instead of citing all the normal data points used to measure a battalion's success, here are some of the truest forms of this unit's success. The city of Balad, with over one hundred thousand men, women, and children, voted for the first time in over forty years on 17 October 2003, for their first ever city council. It was the happiest day for thousands of Iraqis in the Sunni Triangle. Over several concerns from the Coalition Provisional Authority officials, 1-8 Infantry pulled off the first major election in the Sunni Triangle, if not the entire country . . . and the Iraqis loved it! And at the following city council meeting, the members voted on something. It was akin to a junior high student council, but we knew it was a start and we knew we had something special going when Iraq government officials and clerics from Baghdad started showing up and taking notes at our meetings. Likewise, we organized and trained police forces in Ishaki, Balad, and Baldah using an SOP from a Nashua, New Hampshire, police station, and soon Iraqi police were patrolling the streets and securing their own cities. And, finally, we formed a five-hundred-man ICDC battalion, commanded by Muquadem Shaker Faris, that was featured in Time *magazine with Lieutenant General Petraeus as a model Iraqi outfit that was taking the fight to the insurgents. Our success is measured by those we trained to fight, police, and govern in our area of operation who are continuing to take steps toward Iraq's democracy. General Richard Myers, chairman of the Joint Chiefs of Staff, stated that Balad, with its council, police force, and ICDC, was the model for success in Iraq. His visit to our TOC and comments to the world press represented a historic moment in this battalion's lineage.*

Gone are the combat veterans like Brown, Cunningham, Ryan, Sinden, Saville, Joyce, Garcia, Trotter, Perkins, Kapheim, Ironeyes, Watson, Foster, Williams, Puthoff, Edwards, and Contat, only to be replaced by the likes of Beattie, Knoth, Landsberger, Kavanaugh, Ullrich, Zimcosky, Carnes, Schaeffer, Clark, Ayala, and Krause. And they are joined by a select few that have already fought once and will fight again. Warriors like Dailey, Dean, Forlano, Balcom, Dykstra, Bolyard, Tymensky, Hays, Bagley, Price, and Pease. All these men and women represent the finest this nation has to offer as we fight the war on terrorism. This battalion wants to win, and is never, and will never be, interested in just the status quo. We are winners and we always fight to win. And this outfit not only discovered the formula to success on the battlefield in Iraq, but we also have so enjoyed keeping the Seventh Infantry Division Fort Carson Commander's Cup, courtesy of the commanding general, in our battalion trophy case this past year. Whether on the ball field or on the battlefield, this battalion is loaded with winners!

Two memorials remain today at Thermopylae. Upon the modern one, called the Leonidas Monument, in honor of the Spartan king who fell there, is engraved his response to the Persian king Xerxes' demand that the Spartans lay down their arms. Leonidas's reply was two words: Molon Labe. "Come and get them."

That memorial reminds me of this battalion: tough, aggressive, unrelenting, and always focused on winning the fight! I would like to thank my field grades in combat, Major Robert Gwinner III and Major Darron "Hook 'Em Horns" Wright. You both were at the right place at the right time, and your unwavering loyalty to our soldiers will never be forgotten. And at home station, Majors Johnny Digiambattista, Connor Cusick, and Lance Kohler, absolutely professional in all aspects, and you all will do great in Iraq. To my fine sergeant majors, Command Sergeant Major Dailey and Sergeant Major Stokes, thanks so much for your leadership, professionalism, and high standards. To all the commanders and first sergeants, thanks so much for what you did and for the job you do every day. And to those special commanders who fought with me in Iraq—Cunningham, Brown, Pfuetze, Ryan, and Shirley—we really did live the dream!

Marilyn, thanks for your awesome job of picking up the

Battalion Family Readiness Group midstream while the battalion and I were deployed eight thousand miles away. Your organization, support, and kindness were so refreshing and reassuring. And to all the special ladies who helped—Catherine Gwinner, Amy Topasna, Holly Dailey, Amy Cunningham, Dana Watson, Kristan Brown, Kelli Dean, Marilyn Cunningham, Lorraine Grisez, and Dawnette Waters—thanks for all the hours of fund-raising, sending packages, and supporting all the wives and parents involved in your readiness groups. You all were so awesome in support of your soldiers deployed overseas.

Fighting Eagles—you not only look great today, you are great! You represent the finest our nation has to offer as we fight the war on terrorism. You have met the challenge before, and you will meet it again . . . through your blood, sweat, and tears. Thanks for what you have done and what you will do. You are the absolute best!

General MacArthur stated, "Yours is the profession of arms, the will to win, the sure knowledge that in war there is no substitute for victory; that if you lose, the nation will be destroyed; that the very obsession of your public service must always be: Duty, Honor, Country."

I cannot think of a better command team to take over the Fighting Eagle Battalion than Lieutenant Colonel Jeff Martindale and his wife, Mary. I have known Jeff since Command and General Staff College and he is an outstanding infantryman with a superb reputation. Mary is a dedicated army wife, and both Marilyn and I know they will take the 1-8 Infantry to all new highs. Jeff and Mary, have a great time. We know you are going to do fantastic!

And finally some parting shots. Bob Stack, Bob Murphy, and Mike Camp want to win. I really appreciated Major

General Wilson's kind and supportive comments; he did not have to say anything to me, but he did. I will always respect Lieutenant General Ray Odierno. He had a tremendously difficult job in Iraq. Brigadier General Leszczinski and Brigadier General Keen are the epitome of professional warrior-leaders, and I really appreciated their notes of advice while I was in Iraq and back here training the force. Both Colonels Hickey and Hoag brought it in Iraq. Colonel and Mrs. Weininger—thanks for what you have done for this post. Colonel Jones, Command Sergeant Major List, Lieutenant Colonel Rice—you have created a superb professional command climate in this brigade. You have no idea how refreshing that has been. Laura, Bill, Aubrey, Joe, and Jeff—it has been the best working with you guys. To Joe—your support in Iraq was awesome. And to Aubrey and Laura—only you know the special kind of hell we fought in; you two are true heroes! Command Sergeant Major Kinloch—you are a special soldier; great job in Iraq! Command Sergeant Major Dennis Johnson—I would fight with you anywhere, anytime, anyplace. Irma—thanks for the great BLTs. Mihwa—you are the best barber on post. And Staff Sergeant Elwin—thanks for your tremendous selflessness in reenlisting great soldiers in this battalion. To the soldiers of 1-8 Infantry—if I ever run into you down the road at your local VFW chapter . . . just know the beverage will always be on me!

The second monument at Thermopylae, the ancient one, is an unadorned stone engraved with the words of the poet Simonides. Its verses comprise perhaps the most famous of all warrior epitaphs: "Go tell the Spartans, stranger passing by, that here obedient to their laws we lie."

I want to publicly apologize to the families of Dale Panchot and Eric Paliwoda. I really thought I could accomplish

*the mission and bring everyone back home. Unfortunately, it
was not to be, and I am truly sorry that your loved ones were
killed in Iraq. Their sacrifice will not go for naught, because,
as President Bush so aptly stated on 11 September 2001 . . .*

*"We will not tire, we will not falter, we will not fail. Free-
dom itself was attacked this morning by a faceless coward,
and freedom will be defended. Make no mistake, the United
States will hunt down and punish those responsible for this
act. We will do whatever is necessary to protect America."*

God bless First Battalion, Eighth Infantry.

*Use common sense, take care of soldiers, and always do
the right thing!*

Fighting Eagles

Strikers

Ironhorse

A few months earlier, a more somber ceremony had been
conducted at Fort Carson's Memorial Park, including the unveil-
ing of a monument dedicated to the soldiers from Fort Carson
who had lost their lives in Iraq. Around three o'clock on the afternoon of the ceremony, I received a phone call. Alfred and
Mary Paliwoda, Eric's parents, were in town, and they wanted to
meet their son's battalion commander.

It was not a warm encounter, at least not at the beginning.
Mr. Paliwoda was openly hostile toward me, questioning not so
much the circumstances surrounding Eric's death, but the delay in
communicating the sad news to his family. He was angry that
he'd never spoken to me personally, and I don't fault him for that;
I tried to explain that Eric's death had hit me hard as well, and
that I simply couldn't bring myself to call his parents right away.
The army had assigned a casualty assistance officer whose job was
to ensure that the family was cared for through the burial and

memorial services, and that all payments and reimbursements warranted on behalf of the dead soldier were properly authorized. That may sound somewhat feeble, but it's the truth. Eric's death knocked me off my feet, and maybe I didn't handle some aspects of it as well as I might have. I tried to explain that to Mr. and Mrs. Paliwoda, but they weren't particularly understanding. The father was angry, and the mother . . . well, she was clearly distraught. She'd lost her son, and though nearly a year and a half had passed, the wounds remained fresh. For me, as well.

"You know, this isn't easy on any of us," I said to Mr. Paliwoda. "Eric was my friend."

He softened a bit as the meeting wore on. I told him of Eric's talents and accomplishments . . . and how much I valued his friendship. Mr. Paliwoda nodded. I offered him a commemorative coin and a DVD copy of the Victory Tape that had been played at the awards ceremony one year earlier. Mr. Paliwoda seemed uninterested.

"Eric is a big part of the DVD," I explained.

Mr. Paliwoda shook his head. "I don't think I can watch it."

There was one other thing: I'd given Arland and Karen Panchot a handful of 25-millimeter shells that had been fired back at the insurgents on the day that Staff Sergeant Dale Panchot was killed; the shells were packed with dirt scooped from the spot where Dale had fallen. I'd done the same for Eric (using shells packed with dirt from FOB Paliwoda), and now, after holding them in my possession for the better part of eighteen months, it was time to let them go. I presented the shells to Mr. and Mrs. Paliwoda.

"These represent Eric's spirit . . . his sacrifice," I said, holding them in my hand.

They politely declined. I have the shells to this day. I suspect I always will.

EPILOGUE

And when our work is done . . . may it be said, "Well done."
—FROM THE "WEST POINT ALMA MATER" BY P. S. REINECKE,
CLASS OF 1911

JANUARY 31, 2007

It was a clear, crisp afternoon on the campus of the United States
Military Academy, with the sun hanging low and reflecting bril-
liantly, almost blindingly, off the Hudson River. It was a fine day
for a redoubt run, so that's what we did—I and about a dozen
cadets jogged for miles across the historic grounds of West Point,
up and down the hills, stopping periodically to recount the lessons of battles fought long ago, on this very site, during the Rev-
olutionary War.

How strange it was to be back there, in that place where time
seems to stand still, technological advances and capital improvements notwithstanding. The cadets were still baby-faced and

wide-eyed with wonder, fiercely driven and ambitious men and women eager to join the Long Gray Line, and to embrace the myriad challenges that awaited them. Ghosts whispered in the hallways of West Point, their voices seeping into the hearts and minds of impressionable young soldiers . . . warriors in waiting. I can hear them still.

MacArthur . . . Patton . . . Grant . . . Lee . . .

And countless others.

My hands were wet on the wheel a day earlier, on the drive up the Palisades Parkway. After all these years, I thought, how strange and yet somehow reassuring that West Point still made me nervous. It's an intimidating place, to be sure, but at least I didn't get sick to my stomach; I'd made some progress, anyway. The purpose of my visit, in theory, was simple enough: to speak with third-year cadets who had enrolled in a class on leadership. In reality, though, this was a far more complicated trip, one that carried a lifetime of emotional baggage.

I had retired from the army in the summer of 2005. Made it to twenty years and called it a career. By that time my story had become a rather public matter, culminating with a long and detailed article that appeared in the *New York Times Magazine* in October 2005. I cooperated with the story, in large part because I trusted and respected the author, Dexter Filkins, one of the rare Western journalists who had been willing to roll up his sleeves and get a real taste for the fight in Iraq. It was dangerous work, covering the war, and few reporters had the guts to do it well. The *Times* story became required reading in a West Point course that focused on the challenge of making ethical decisions in a time of war. To some people in the military—senior officers, mainly—I had become an outcast; I'd broken ranks, and that was unforgivable. To others, I suppose, I was something of a curiosity.

But to the cadets at West Point I represented something far more practical: experience.

For weeks prior to the visit I'd wrestled with the outline for my presentation. There was so much to say, so much information I hoped to share. Some of these young men and women would be deploying to the Middle East in a matter of months. They were scared, anxious, and excited. What was I to tell them? I couldn't just stand up there and throw out a "hoo-ah" and encourage them to kick butt. The conflict they were about to enter was so much more complicated than that, and so far beyond mere chest thumping. Could I tell them what I really felt? Could I look them in the eye and say what I think our next president (whoever he or she might be) ought to do?

Bring the soldiers home—now. Start today.

That is not an unpatriotic sentiment, and it's not worthy of shame. It's the right thing to do. I don't care how many generals, colonels, captains—whatever—think they can win the war. You know why? Because I thought I could win the war, too. But there is no war right now. It's law enforcement, and we're losing ten, fifteen soldiers a week to law enforcement. We had a chance to win the war in the first year, and we didn't. Now we're sending over tired troops on old, worn-down equipment, with an American public that is not as fired up about this as it was in 2003, and I just don't see the Iraqis shouldering the load as much as they should. Let them fall into civil war and fight through this on their own. They'll still be better off than they were when it comes to having a voice in how their government should run.

I do think that's worth dying for. If there's one thing I've learned in traveling to Asia and Central America and the Middle East, it's this: people want to have a voice in what is happening to them and to their familes and their communities. That's what it's about. So many places don't have a chance for that voice. Iraqis haven't had a voice for more than thirty-five years. Now they do. But it's their fight at this point, and we should leave it to them. I believe we did a lot of good work in Iraq; sadly, we failed to communicate that work to the rest of the world. There isn't much more that can be done now. So why not tout the highlights of the campaign . . . and leave?

It's odd that I would feel this way, since I've always taken a fairly aggressive approach to leadership. The leaders I have admired were not afraid to make difficult decisions, particularly in combat—men like William Wallace, the great Scottish warrior. They are all gone now, and even if they were here, there would be no place for them in Iraq. Sometimes I think I was born into the wrong era—I was born about seven hundred years too late.

The right warrior for the wrong war . . .

Maybe so. The conflict in Iraq is not a "war" in the traditional sense of the word, as just about everyone knows by now. In my tour of duty, however, I did not think of myself as being much different from warriors of the past—men who studied the enemy, adapted to changing tactics and strategies, and fought with the intention of winning. Now, as I watch soldiers—some of them friends of mine, some of them men and women who served under my command—going back to the Middle East for their third and even fourth tours, I can't help but think that we've reached the point of diminishing returns. There's even kind of a sick sense, for the military, that it's almost *good for business.* Money is being spent, contracts are being negotiated, and soldiers are being trained. I used to say that one month in Iraq was like three months of peacetime duty. Every day we were working on our equipment and going out in the field. But now the force is getting beaten down—physically, spiritually, and emotionally. There has been no brilliant campaign plan to win the war, just more of the same grind—year after year after year. Here's what I believe: unless a presidential candidate comes forward, personal courage in hand, and displays the fortitude to bring this thing to a close, nothing will change. The United States will continue to maintain a large occupational presence—a police force, in other words—in the Middle East for years, perhaps even decades, to come. I'm convinced of that.

The dilemma, for me, was in choosing how much of this to share with the cadets at West Point. In the end I chose to focus on the work that we had done, the accomplishments we had achieved, and the obstacles that would likely be placed in their way as they assumed the mantle of leadership in the United States Army. I met with six different classes over two days; in each presentation, I showed the cadets specific photos that emphasized a critical leadership trait, discussed my philosophy of leadership, particularly in a time of war, and then let them ask whatever questions happened to be on their minds. There were many, of course. Mostly they were the questions that soldiers have always asked—questions about fighting and surviving. Questions about leadership.

"I'm one of you," I said. "So fire away. There's no such thing as a bad question."

The cadets were warm and welcoming, and seemingly unfazed by the controversy surrounding my departure from the army, but it was an unusual and sometimes awkward visit. Some officers hugged me; others refused to make eye contact. While I admire West Point for having the courage to extend the invitation, there were some moments of puzzlement. Initially, for example, I'd been invited to stay at the commandant's house, but that offer was later rescinded—the commandant's schedule, apparently, had been changed, and he'd no longer be on campus during my visit. Similarly, I'd been scheduled to speak with the staff and faculty in the Behavioral Sciences Department, but that opportunity was withdrawn as well. In fact, there were absolutely no senior officers seeking me out at all. A few colonels, people I would consider to be friends—yes—but they were the exception. Indeed, there was a clear line of demarcation between the levels of lieutenant colonel and colonel. To everyone at or below the level of lieutenant colonel, I was part of the brotherhood . . . a comrade. To those at the level of colonel or higher, I was something else entirely. Something far less noble. Actions speak louder than words, I guess, and my actions spoke volumes. I had left the army. I had chosen to do something else with my life.

We talk about selfless service ad nauseam in the army, but in reality, there is a lot of selfishness. That's not true of the entire force, but there are a great number of officers in the military for whom this hypocrisy holds true. We need more folks to be self-less. I had a general tell me a while back, "You have a social and moral obligation to write a book that reveals how senior officers behaved in combat; it's unacceptable for our generals and colonels to behave in a cowardly manner and not be held accountable."

So here I am.

I did not return to West Point expecting applause or a fatherly embrace. I sought neither forgiveness nor approval. My intent was simply to offer whatever advice I could in the hope that it might enable other young officers to survive their first contact. That's it, really. It was that simple. Nervousness notwithstanding, I think I delivered a strong message to the cadets; I had a chance to touch them and share my experiences, and in that sense, at least, the trip was worthwhile.

This was among the highlights, jogging around the grounds of West Point, touring the various redoubts. It's a smoker of a run, really, with undulating terrain that challenges heart and lungs. Many of the cadets had never visited some of the redoubts, so at each stop we covered the basic history of the site and then I tried to attach some relevance to my own personal history, whether in peacetime service or in Iraq. This was physical training, and I'm all about that. I was forty-three years old, roughly twice the age of the cadets, but I put it to them a little bit, trying to show them not only that there were lessons to be passed on from one generation to the next, but that old warriors die hard.

Death is part of the contract, though, and I wanted them to understand that. So our last stop was at the grave site of Eric Paliwoda. We stood silently, heads bowed. I said a few words about Eric—what a fine young leader he was . . . what a good friend and soldier. We said a short prayer and then jogged back to the barracks. I looked around the pristine, sparkling campus—at the football stadium, the chapel, the plain—and I was struck by how West Point seemed at once ever changing and timeless. Thirty, forty years from now, long after I'm dead and gone, this place will continue to educate and produce great leaders—male and female army officers who will fight in foreign lands for this country or for this country's leader. They will go off in support of whatever effort the president deems worthy. They will do it without complaint. Indeed, many will go just as I did, with an eagerness that defies all rationality.

They will say to themselves, "I have been trained to fight and to lead. I have the tools. I can win. . . ."

CPSIA information can be obtained
at www.ICGtesting.com
Printed in the USA
LVHW09s1846120918
589925LV00001B/152/P

9 780312 563967